Ray Barker wastes no time in getting his readers involved and from the first page the action holds the interest of wartime years seen through the eyes of one man, whose pride in his ship, *HMS Victorious*, shines through every page. The hazards of taking off and landing on the precarious runway of an aircraft carrier are brought home vividly, the sense of loss when friends were killed in these accidents even more bitter than when they were killed by the enemy; the sense of camaraderie, the concert-party fun as even in appalling conditions they kept their spirits high. From the icy conditions of the Arctic convoys, through the heat and humidity of the Indian Ocean, to the Pacific where *Victorious* joined the fleet that was to hammer the Japanese during the last months of the war, culminating in the surrender after Hiroshima and Nagasaki.

Truly, **VICTORIOUS THE WORLD OVER . . .**

VICTORIOUS THE WORLD OVER

Victorious escorted by battleship Rodney and closely guarded by the destroyer Opportune.
Painting by Stanley Rogers

VICTORIOUS
THE WORLD OVER

Ray Barker

A Square One Publication

First published in 1991 by
Square One Publications
The Tudor House
Church Street
Upton upon Severn, Worcs WR8 0NU

This edition published 1998

British Library Cataloguing in Publication Data
Barker, Ray
  Victorious the world over
  I. Title
  359.1092
  ISBN 1 872017 37 1

This edition: 1 899955 32 1

Typeset by Wyvern Typesetting, Worcester, in 10/12 Palacio
Printed by Antony Rowe Ltd, Chippenham, Wiltshire, England

This book is dedicated by the ship's company and squadrons of
HMS*Victorious* (1941 — 1945) to their comrades who gave their lives
to defend the freedoms we have since enjoyed.

Their selflessness will be remembered always, their laughter never lost.

We do not gaze at the sea and cry
They are not there, they did not die.

Acknowledgements

I am indebted to many who have supplied material for this book. I must single out the following, their anecdotes, remembrances and encouragement greatly appreciated.

James Carbines, Ernest Crimp, Phil Davis, 'Charlie' Frise, Roy Harris, Charles Minett, Richard C.V. Ross and Frank Short.

Special thanks are due to Ray Kennedy for editorial assistance and some technical aviation input, to James Jobling, whose letters to me evoked memories of surrealistically comic behaviour under trying, nay atrocious, conditions.

Offical sources of material are Admiralty Documents 0217/8270, S 7766 and S 6152.

Finally, my unbounded gratitude to Leslie Vancura whose diary, crammed with the trivial, the mundane, the extraordinary, the amusing, the tragic, furnished a huge one-way mirror through which I could see so clearly again the myriad events of those remarkable years.

INTRODUCTION

I had long harboured ambitions to write about my five years on HMS *Victorious* but a busy business life allowed no time for such self-indulgence.

Shortly after retiring to Herefordshire, in 1989, my wife died, and the many plans we had made for an active leisure-orientated life had to be abandoned. I sought initial consolation from my grief in writing a book about Carol and found the experience soothing and therapeutic.

What better time to start on my *Victorious* narrative? How to begin was the initial problem. I needed to talk to some old ship-mates, but where were they? One Sunday evening, driving back from Worcester after putting my daughter on the London train, I heard the Charlie Chester programme on Radio 2. He was putting war-time friends in touch with one another. I wrote him a note.

Two weeks later I had letters from Les Vancura and Charlie Frise, and quickly met them both. Les I had known very well, Charlie less so. The remarkable by-product of the meeting was the discovery that Les had maintained a daily diary, all through the war, including his four and a half years onboard *Victorious*. It was an offence to keep a diary but Les had filled several tiny notebooks with his daily jottings. These have been the basis of this book, as each entry stimulated, indeed occasionally jolted, my memory and brought back vivid recollections. Incidents which had faded into half-remembered images became totally alive; it was as if I was reading notes I had written myself.

Shortly afterwards, in June, 1990, I heard of the HMS *Victorious* 1941—1945 REUNION ASSOCIATION and found 200 plus more old shipmates, including my second Commander—now aged 90—and President of the Association.

The window was now wide open for me to gaze at my old comrades and seek their most precious memories and anecdotes of those fascinating days. Many of these are incorporated in this story; indeed it is the men who made the ship, and it is their story as much as hers.

CHAPTER ONE

From ''Civvie'' to Sailor
From Shore to Ship

We had been under training for 20 weeks; the final examinations had not proved too difficult, and we were now poised for drafting to our respective depots.

Mid June 1941 had witnessed our assembly at Chatham: 22 young men in their late teens, eager to learn the appropriate skills which would allow us to join a ship and the war.

A disparate group, with every type of background and from homes as far apart as Inverness, Strabane and Helston, we were welded into a cohesive unit by a fierce disciplinarian. Stocky, hard, with a weather-beaten, much-lined face, Leading Seaman Hughes drilled us to exhaustion on the barrack square at Chatham. Every one of the early days held forth the prospect of humiliation from physical collapse or enduring the indignity of scrubbing toilets, peeling vegetables, polishing articles already worn thin by constant cleaning.

It was only natural that we should seek solace and comfort from one another. After all Mum was over 200 miles away and couldn't have borne the grim details of her son's new circumstances. Sleeping in a hammock, interrupted by guard duty in the middle of the night, treatment by dentists bordering on the sadistic, half drowned in the swimming bath by being clad in a soaking wet canvas suit and thrown in the deep end. Was it any wonder we sought and found friendship from sources totally unbelievable a short time previously?

I became the chum of Don Tregenza, a mild-mannered Cornishman who had hoped to train in Devonport but perversely was sent as far from home as possible. Quiet, reflective, Don seemed ill-suited for service life. He spoke constantly of home; I suppose most of us did. Those who didn't no doubt thought of lost comforts and care. We were all volunteers and this fact was not lost on Leading Seaman Hughes.

'Thinking of your mothers, then?' he would shout. 'I'm your mother now. Don't forget you wanted me as your mother and I'm the best you've got.'

We couldn't even imagine him as anyone's father: to us he appeared to be a marginal member of the human race.

There was another Cornishman, Bill Webb, constantly smiling as if our training was a welcome change from home in Helston. He and Don helped me to maintain some semblance of normality.

On reflection it was probably no better or worse than the rigorous introduction endured by millions, but the culture shock was very profound. The language for a start. There were those seasoned battle-scarred salts who could utter an entire sentence of swear words. It hardly squared with my Sunday School upbringing. Don and Bill, conversing in their burring West Country drawl seemed foreign enough but their clean chat was a welcome relief.

Tommy Drean, a Catholic from Strabane, was also disturbed by the cursing, much of which was blasphemous to him. Mind you there were those of us who could scarcely understand what he said in normal conversation. Tall, handsome, reddish-haired, Drean was very intelligent and I often sought his company for mental stimulation. We argued the merits of Catholicism and Non-Conformist beliefs without rancour for hours on end.

Part of our training was undertaken in Borstal. Chatham Barracks having been bombed was short of accommodation. Our class was sent to Borstal in Kent, and there we were housed in Winder Block, two to a cell, whilst across the square the normal Borstal inmates enjoyed the privacy of single cells. The paths of our class and the Borstal boys crossed occasionally, always at Church parade. They would try and prevail upon us to post letters, give them cigarettes, chocolates and other creature comforts. We also found rude messages secreted in the hymn books. Oh what a change from my hometown, decorous Lytham St. Anne's!

Now it was all over. The class was sectioned into three parts. One for Chatham, one for Portsmouth and the remaining unit for Devonport. I was seconded to Devonport, 'Guzz' in naval terms, along with Webb, Tregenza, Roy Castle (who hailed from Torquay and excelled in reciting dubious poetry) and one other whose name escapes me.

Plymouth and Devonport had been heavily bombed. Vast parts of the city and the naval town were laid waste. In consequence there was no accommodation available within the Barrack complex and after some hesitation by the depot authorities we were despatched to a school at Stoke Damerel. It was warm, crowded, but clearly only a transit stop. We slept on the floor of the Gym and ate in a make-shift dining room converted from the school hall.

After a few days I was called to the drafting office, so was Bill Webb. We were handed our orders, took them outside and excitedly looked to see what Fate, or the Drafting Officer, had decreed.

I was earmarked for Alexandria, for an administrative post on a submarine depot ship. Bill had been drafted to HMS *Victorious*, an aircraft carrier, launched earlier in 1941, and instrumental in the chase and ultimate sinking of the *Bismarck*. My journey for the Middle East was scheduled for sometime in January, Bill had to leave Devonport within days. He was clearly unhappy.

'What's the problem?' I asked.

'I was hoping to get married soon. This draft will prevent that, I just won't have time to call the banns and complete all the preparations.'

My heart leapt at his words. To be honest the last posting I had wanted was to be sent to a depot ship, swinging at anchor for week after week after week. Whilst at Chatham I had managed to visit HMS *Cumberland*, a County class cruiser. I was beguiled; I wanted to go to sea.

'What if I took your draft and you had mine; would that help? I honestly don't mind.'

He looked at me, his eyes suddenly moist.

'Would you do that for me?' he said. 'What a friend! You are serious aren't you?'

'Of course I'm serious. There's no reason for me not to go tomorrow if necessary. I have no ties, no commitments. If I can do you a favour it will help repay for all the pleasure and support you gave me in our days in Chatham and Borstal.'

'Do you think the Drafting Office will wear it? After all, the documentation has been drawn up and we know what a bureaucratic machine the Navy can be.'

I could see that the possibility of HMS *Victorious* was more than just a slim chance; I dearly wanted to join her and Bill Webb did not.

'Come on back to the Drafting Office. Do you want to do the talking or shall I?'

'You do it, you will be better at it than me.'

'OK, let's go.'

I went to the partially opened window and waited whilst the Petty Officer, head down over a mound of draft chits, slowly raised his bored gaze and curtly asked, 'Yes?'

'A few minutes ago a colleague and I received draft notices. We would much appreciate being able to switch.'

'You do realise that very careful assessment of all the factors was made before these orders were issued?' he said pompously.

'Yes indeed, but there is a compassionate element of which the drafting authorities could not have been aware when they reached their conclusion. My colleague Webb has planned to marry soon in Helston, and the draft to Alexandria will allow him to do so, whereas the virtual immediate move to *Victorious* will deny him and his bride-to-be the joy of early matrimony. I have no such commitments and can go to Scapa Flow tomorrow.' I sounded rather pompous too.

He smiled bleakly. 'You are a real Sir Galahad, aren't you?'

I didn't reply. The fact that his face had shown some emotion merited caution.

'Where is Webb?'

'Waiting not far away.'

'Hang on a minute.' He pushed his chair back, got up and went to the rear of the office. He spoke to a Warrant Officer, showed him the two Draft Orders and waited.

I was shifting from one foot to another, my stomach churning as I waited for a decision which would affect the rest of my life.

The discussion at the back of the office was quite animated but seemed good-humoured. I could see pieces of paper being exchanged and finally the Petty Officer returned to his desk. He didn't look at me as he sat down, shifted a few certificates around, opened a drawer and took out a rubber stamp. This he applied heavily to the papers held in his left hand. At this point he looked up.

'You've never been to Alex, have you?'

'No,' I replied.

'You don't know what you are missing. It's a classy place and Pension No. 17 has some of the classiest bints in Egypt.'

I didn't know what a bint was—even less a Pension.

'Here you are. You are off to the joys of Scapa Flow, your friend to the sunshine and security of Alex. Don't let me see you back here for years. Alright?'

I couldn't get my hands on the orders quickly enough. When I was clutching them safely I said, 'Thank you Chief,' (he wasn't a Chief) 'both Webb and I will be eternally grateful.'

'He may be; you could find this has been the worst day of your life.' He slammed down the window, his head dropped down and he resumed his paper shuffling. I turned my back and walked towards Bill.

I tried not to smile. He was anxiously endeavouring to interpret the look on my face. As I drew nearer to him he felt obliged to call out, 'Well, what happened?'

Thoughts of shaking my head, grimacing, thumbs down, all flashed through my mind, but I couldn't contain myself.

'Make sure your tropical gear is clean,' I shouted with a huge grin on my face.

He ran forward, put his arms around me, then, as if embarrassed, stood back and shook my hand.

'Well done, I am so grateful. Was it difficult?'

'Not really. I told him the truth, he went to see the WO and prepared new Draft Orders. I believe we are all just bodies to them and so long as they fit one in an empty slot then that's fine.'

'When are you going then?' he asked.

'Nothing was said, Bill, but I saw a notice on the Draft Office wall about a special train leaving for Scapa Flow in three days' time.'

The following day I was informed that I would be travelling up to Thurso and then from the small port of Scrabster to Scapa Flow and HMS *Victorious*.

My excitement was intense. To go to sea at last, and in a virtually brand new capital ship. I had never seen an aircraft carrier and knew little of what their role was. The loss of the *Courageous* and *Glorious* was well publicised as were the recent exploits of *Ark Royal*, but what were these ships doing when not in the news? I would soon find out.

Unhappily I didn't see Bill Webb again. It was some three months before I received a letter from him, safely ensconced on board his depot ship in Alexandria. Life was seemingly all that the Drafting Petty Officer had foretold. Swimming, sun-bathing, trips to Cairo, marvellous food, all amidst an uneasy, unreal peacefulness as Rommel was driving remorselessly eastwards towards his longed-for prize, Egypt. I wrote back, giving as much news as censorship allowed, but never heard from Bill again.

The station was fairly crowded on the Wednesday evening. Sailors, baggage, hammocks, suitcases, spread the entire length of the platform. The train pulled in. There were no announcements: everyone knew where it was going and the stops were irrelevant; no one would be getting off. Naval police were there in force, barking instructions and ensuring no one slipped away. It was a long train and there were seats for everyone, but hardly any to spare. There would be no stretching out for a sleep, we would have to be content with snoozing until discomfort brought back consciousness.

There was a Buffet Bar but no staff. I tried to fathom out the reason. No one seemed to know, few seemed to care. Everyone smoked; there was the odd non-smoking compartment but these were regarded as the result of aberrations by the railway staff. Surely they must be aware that all sailors smoked, drank and had women in every port. My own experience at that time was that there were few non-smokers, abstinence was looked upon as 'cissy', and whilst there was continuous talk about conquests, most of the stories were thought to be 'spinning a yarn'.

We all carried a small, folded identity card, on which was written name, rank, service number, religion, ship and most importantly 'G', 'T' or 'UA'.

The initials signified 'GROG', 'TEMPERANCE' or 'UNDER AGE'. They governed your right to the Rum Ration—Grog. Those unfortunates not yet 18 were 'UA', those who elected to be tee-totallers received 3d daily in lieu of rum. Those non-drinkers who were wise claimed their daily tot and, if practicable, sold it to the long-serving sailors whose rum-soaked stare bore witness to their addiction. It could yield the equivalent of thirty duty free cigatettes a day, and who knew about smoking related diseases in 1941? It was manly to smoke. The UA's just longed for the day when their Pay Book and Identity Card were amended and they became, officially, men.

I looked around the compartment. My companions were all older. A couple of them sported beards, wore ribbons from the First World War and had long service stripes sewn on the left arm of their uniforms. They had that slightly bored 'this is routine' look on their faces in contrast to the nervous excitement of their young colleagues. Of course they had been in the Navy for more years than I had lived, and as the train pulled stutteringly away the tales of the China Station, West Indies and South African fleets began to be related.

Sitting in the dimmed-out compartment, almost smoke-filled, I listened intently to the stories. Truth to tell I could barely understand half of what was said. Naval slang, laced with Egyptian and Indian words, even more liberally sprinkled with oaths and curses, sounded like a kind of pidgeon English. Roistering laughter punctuated the tales. I said nothing, feeling inferior and inadequate. What did I have to contribute? A few stories from my junior reporter days, two months in the Home Guard as I waited to join the Navy, a certificate in aircraft identification from the Observer Corps. Small beer compared with Jutland, Dardanelles, Dunkirk, Norwegian fjords, Atlantic submarines.

The chat subsided as we rattled eastwards to Bristol, then north. Despite eight bodies in the compartment it became very cold since there was no heating on the train. I dozed fitfully until dawn broke by which time we were well on the way to Crewe. This nondescript railway town was the most important junction in Britain and, in common with most trains, we were held outside the station until there was room for us at one of the long platforms. There was no public address system on the train so a Regulating Petty Officer, bristling with authority, pushed his way down the corridors shouting 'No one allowed off the train. Stay on board the train.' When we finally drew to a halt the carriage doors were locked, just to reinforce his instructions.

We lowered windows, stumbled along corridors littered with kit bags and hammocks, trying to exercise our legs and lungs. The air in the station, an eye-smarting smog of engine smoke, was no improvement on the nicotine-laden atmosphere of the train.

It was obvious from the bumping and shuddering of the carriage that our engine was being exchanged. I was hoping that a more fundamental change was happening: staff for the Buffet Bar. I was ravenous, and longing for a drink.

A miracle. As we left Crewe a Salvation Army worker slid back the door of our compartment. Bright-eyed, scrubbed pink face, soft Lancastrian voice. 'There's tea, cocoa, sandwiches in the Buffet Bar. Free, but if you could spare a few pence the "Army" would appreciate it.'

I would have given a week's pay. Well, a day's.

'Don't rush,' she warned us, 'there is plenty for everyone and we can deal with you all more easily if there's a steady flow.' With that she pushed the door closed and moved to the next compartment where her announcement was greeted by a cheer.

The atmosphere on the train was transformed; the drear, dark dullness of early morning had been replaced by animated conversation, laughter and the general buzz of activity.

Tea was sweet and strong, the sandwiches cheese, thick with only a smear of margarine. But food and drink had never tasted so good.

As we trundled from Cheshire into Lancashire the chat resumed in our compartment. There was all round praise for the Salvation Army. At last I could contribute. My aunt Frances who had run away from home to join the 'Army' as a 'Miriam' was now a Brigadier, renowned preacher and evangelist. I gained a new respect—nephew of a senior officer—some of her credibility and fame (she once stopped a Royal and shook a collection box in front of him) rubbed off on me.

The train stopped in Preston. I looked nostalgically out of the window. I could see the waiting room where Ron Gregory (later Chief Constable, West

Yorkshire) and I used to play shove-halfpenny as we awaited our train home to St. Anne's after a day at college in Preston. If we tired of shove-halfpenny we would write down the names of some of the marvellous locomotives passing through—Queen Maud of Norway, Morning Star, Private Sykes VC. I wondered which engine might be hauling us northwards to a new life.

The journey seemed to last forever. Delays, extra locomotives to push us up Shap, slowly into Scotland as night fell once more.

Stories and anecdotes had dried up, as had the Buffet Car. Unwashed, unshaven and untidy, we lapsed into a silence disturbed only grunts, groans, heavy breathing, the odd flare of a match lighting yet another cigarette.

Perth. Fresh Salvation Army staff. Scots accents and faces, bright and cheery. I wondered if we would be offered porridge. No such luck, but there were egg sandwiches and lashings of sweet tea, plus a few scones and cakes.

It was nearly mid-day on Friday when we finally pulled into Thurso. We had travelled almost the length of Britain and as the cramped leg muscles were exercised on the platform there was relief that we were almost at journey's end.

Almost, but not quite. There was a naval bus ride to Scrabster and then across the Pentland Firth to the Orkney Islands. Would it never end?

Megaphone-shouted instructions advised us that it would be some time before we would need to board the buses, so I walked out of the station to the nearby Royal Hotel, ordered myself a cooked meal and managed to find a washroom in which to shave and generally freshen up. By the time I had to go on to Scrabster I felt half civilised.

The tiny fishing port of Scrabster had a number of Drifters awaiting their human cargo. They scraped noisily and uncomfortably against each other, straining at the strong lines which secured them. There was no shelter and as I looked out to sea I could discern the white-capped water surging eastwards directly across the route to the Orkneys. Experienced sailors were muttering darkly about the Pentland Firth, a mill race of Atlantic Ocean and North Sea meeting in tempestuous union.

I had to board the outer Drifter, necessitating climbing across three others, all heaving and rolling gently, but disconcertingly for someone carrying the standard green suitcase and other impedimenta. Making myself as comfortable as practicable, I reflected on my previous nautical experience. It didn't take long; an hour and a half of outright misery on the *Mona's Isle* plying between Fleetwood and the Isle of Man. Maybe that, and the fact that most of my friends were joining the RAF prompted me to seek airborne fame as well, but the queasy stomach which plagued me on the Irish Sea also let me down when, after being spun round in a chair and asked to walk a straight line, I drunkenly staggered into the MO's desk and so into medical rejection for air-crew.

What was I doing here then? I knew. Waiting for that debilitating nausea of sea-sickness to remind me I should have joined the Army.

Whistles, shouted commands, ropes writhing around, a soulful blast on a hooter and we were away, butting northwards out of Thurso Bay. Still in the lee

16

of Dunnet Head, the Drifter was coping well with the regular chop of the sea but once clear into the open I earnestly prayed for survival. Bucking and writhing, twisting like a corkscrew, shipping spray, spume and water, the Drifter pugnaciously thudded on. The mast seemed to sway through 180 degrees, my Royal Hotel meal joined others in the swirling, angry peaks and troughs of the sea. In the fading light I gazed with desperation at the islands of Hoy and Ronaldsay which seemed to be drifting northwards as we pursued them. Putting my head in my hands, looking down at the sodden planks of the deck, I bemoaned my ever having rejected Alexandria for the tossing torment of this late afternoon in December.

It was not quite dark as we moved into calmer waters, and through the anti-submarine boom defences which had failed to prevent Gunter Prien and his U-boat crew from sinking the battleship *Royal Oak*. I offered a silent prayer that the powers that be had tightened up the system and that as we slipped through the parted boom we were not being followed by another U-boat. Was I really mentally equipped to be a sailor? Nineteen years of living at the seaside now seemed a dubious qualification.

The Isle of Flotta to the left of us; soon I was to know almost every square inch of that barren, inhospitable wind-swept rock. Scapa Flow at last. Not totally calm, but like a gently undulating waterway, it revealed ships of all types, shapes and sizes, riding at anchor, some nodding regularly and rhythmically into the low swell.

I could now identify *Victorious* and as we drew near, her vast bulk blotted out the fast-fading daylight. The Drifter manoeuvered alongside and tied up. Looking to the left, right and upwards, I could see little else but dark grey steel and armour plating. The ship seemed enormous; surely it would never roll, pitch or toss, I thought.

'Look lively!' someone cried out. 'Watch how you get on that gangway, move when the Drifter rises to the same level.'

At last, stood on the base of the gangway, my wordly naval possessions around my feet, I was on board *Victorious*. Little did I know it was to be my home for five years, or what lay in store before I would be hauling my case and baggage off that ship forever.

CHAPTER TWO

Settling at Scapa

At the top of the gangway I was met by a Junior Officer and Regulating Petty Officer Tucker.

'Welcome on board. Follow me to the Regulating Office where we will check you in, arrange your accommodation, allocate your watch and generally sort you out.'

We stepped through an open water-tight doorway into the Hanger. It was empty. Brightly lit, shiny steel deck, it was cavernous. Almost 250 yards long and 25 yards wide, it was the largest covered space I had ever seen. Up in the roof I could see aircraft wings and other stores, and at each end the hydraulic lifts to raise the planes to the Flight Deck or lower them back for parking or service.

The most noticeable feature was the smell. It seemed to be a blend of oil, petrol and hot chocolate with a slight trace of polish. Then there was the faint creaking as the ship moved very slowly, almost imperceptibly in the swell. First impressions were flooding into my mind, excitement rising as we arrived at the Regulating Office. The door was slipped back to reveal a couple of desks, some chairs, charts, a clock, mugs and mail.

A tall, thick-set man rose, looked at me and asked in a soft Irish brogue, 'What's your name and service number, lad?'

'Barker Sir,' I replied, 'number DSMX 623.'

'You don't call me Sir. I am the Master at Arms; you call me Master, understood?'

'Yes, Master.'

'Right. You are to work in the Captain's Office. You will report there at 0800 tomorrow morning. I know it's Saturday, but everyday is the same at sea. The Germans don't believe in weekends off. Give me your identity card and I will have a new one ready for you tomorrow. RPO Tucker will take you down below to settle you in, organise some grub, introduce you to your colleagues. Everything clear?'

'Yes Master,' deferentially. He smiled briefly.

'This is a fine ship. You're lucky to be aboard. Make the best of it.' With that he sat down and resumed his paperwork. I was to get to know him well, enjoy his company and admire his efficiency, loyalty, sense of duty, pride in the Navy and thorough understanding of sailors and all their foibles.

Accommodation was in a Mess which housed accountancy, secretarial and supply staff. The administration of the ship was their task, pay, service records, correspondence, ship's stores, aircraft stores, victuals, clothing; these duties were their brief. There was a mix of regular personnel, serving their twelve year term, and 'HO's', hostilities only—at this juncture of the war all volunteers.

Long, well-scrubbed mess tables were the main feature, with leather covered benches on steel supports. All were anchored securely to the deck which was covered in a dull red 'corticene'—a rubber compound, hard-wearing and well polished.

Clothes and personal belongings were stowed away in lockers: shiny steel, outward opening doors revealing two deep, capacious drawers with smaller ones for toilet gear and other items.

I was tired, hungry, excited, confused, and somewhat shy among these strangers, all of whom had recently chased the *Bismarck* and engaged in other acts of derring-do.

Someone went to the Galley and brought me egg, bacon, bread and tea. I ate in silence then unpacked and went to discover more of the ship. Lost within minutes—I had been trying to find the Captain's Office—I was obliged to ask someone to take me back to 'where all the accountancy staff are.'

It was a fitful night's sleep, with unfamiliar sounds and an unknown environment. I lay awake from 6 o'clock, keeping my eyes closed to blot out the lights which were never switched off but were dimmed to a glow allowing sufficient light to move around safely. At 6.30 the stentorious voices of the regulating staff began to call the sleeping to consciousness. Some of the greetings were sung to the tune of 'Beautiful Dreamer', such as:

'Beautiful Dreamer, lash up and stow (put hammock away)
Cooks to the Galley has gone long ago (Breakfast is ready).'

The age-old 'show a leg' and 'wakey wakey' and other exhortations echoed through the mess-decks and gangways. By a quarter to seven the ship was fully awake and cooking smells began to drift out from the Galleys. Bacon, rubbery eggs cooked hours earlier and set like yellow pimpled white plastic into sheets of 20 or so. 'Where do they find such small eggs?' I mused; the yolks were about the size of a half penny. Loaves of bread and slabs of margarine with tinned jam and tea completed the menu.

The mess was a mess. Bodies on the benches refusing to acknowledge the new day, hammocks and bedding littering the place. Some were still slung from the deck head and from the heavy depression in the hammock shape, rendering it into a banana-like curve, it was clear that some had ignored the blandishments of the regulating staff.

Most of those awake were already inhaling their first cigarette of the day, wheezing asthmatically and coughing in sharp spasms. The air was like a fug of feet, bodies, smoke and food. I was already washed, shaved and fully

19

dressed at seven. As soon as I had eaten I found my way up to the flight deck. It was vast, fringed by clusters of pom-pom guns and batteries of 4.5 inch guns. On the starboard side, amidships, the superstructure rose dramatically, housing the command positions for the Captain, the Commander (Flying) and the Gunnery Officer. It was called the Island; on its front, just above the Bridge windows, was the ship's crest of a flying angel, arms aloft, wings outspread, the whole surmounted by a crown atop the name, *Victorious*. I stood and gazed at it. I was impressed by its design, size and slightly religious connotation. No doubt these emblems replaced the figure-heads jutting proudly from the old men-of-war and sailing ships. I found it strangely comforting, like a talisman, a rabbit's foot, a good luck charm.

At the Captain's Office I was greeted by a marine who was the messenger and general factotum. One member of the staff was already at his desk. His eyes had a slightly manic look; he stared without blinking.

'Good morning,' I said. 'My name is Barker, Ray Barker. I have just joined the office staff.' I held out my hand. He stood, shook my hand limply, sat down, and said in a flat, disinterested voice: 'Pleased to meet you. I am Mac, that's what I'm called by everyone, I don't like the ship, the Navy or most people on board.'

I could scarcely believe my ears. Where was his enthusiasm, patriotism, spirit of adventure, sense of comradeship?

'Is life that bad?' I asked him.

'No, it's not bad. I just don't like it, I wish I had never joined, but here I am and I suppose I'd better make the best of it.'

At that moment a Petty Officer entered the office, his peaked cap straight and flat on his head. A gaunt face, prominent cheek-bones, dark eyes flickering glances around the place. He removed his hat, revealing thinning hair and a high forehead.

'Petty Officer Hall. You must be Barker. Glad you are aboard—we have a lot to do in this office. By the way, you call me "Nobby" in the Andrew (Royal Navy): all Halls and Clarkes are called Nobby, as all Millers and Rhodes are Dusty. How long have you been in the service?'

'Six months.'

He was a regular, and had long service chevrons on his left arm, with both peace and war-time service behind him.

'That's all.' He looked with a simulated stern face. 'I've wrung more sea water out of my socks than you will ever sail on. So when I give you advice, you take it. Listen to Nobby and you won't go far wrong.'

Mac raised his eyes heavenwards. He had clearly been subjected to the same homily.

'Thank you Nobby. Obviously I don't know anyone on board, or even my way around. I will be grateful for your advice and help.' Our marine suddenly sprang to attention.

'Morning Sir.'

'Morning.' The Captain's Secretary moved swiftly to his desk at the end of the office, put his hat on a chair and turned to me, although he spoke to Nobby.

'Who is this Hall?'

'Our new member, Sir; just been giving him a few words of advice.'

'Good. What's your name?'

'Barker, Sir.'

'Which Division?'

'Devonport, Sir. Arrived on board last night.'

'You type, write shorthand?'

'Yes Sir; although I haven't written any shorthand for some months now.'

'We will soon put that right. Is that Underwood at the typing desk all right for you?' He hadn't even told me his name. As if he knew what I was thinking, he continued: 'I am Lt. Berrey, Esmond Arthur Berrey RN.'

The 'RN' was to remind me that he was not RNVR or RNR, but the real thing, regular Navy, as opposed to the Volunteer Reserve or Naval Reserve. Clear distinction was emphasised by the gold stripes on the sleeve: straight, RN; wavy, RNVR; interwoven, RNR.

'Yes, the Underwood is fine thankyou.'

'Good. I have a lot of mail to deal with. It has mounted up pending your arrival.'

With that he took out a pipe and clouds of heavily aromatic Balkan Sobranie smoke drifted around the office.

The work was interesting. Lots of letters to the Admiralty, various bases, the other ships, Naval air stations; some over Berrey's signature, most for the Captain to read and sign. The office was inordinately peaceful though busy. Nobby, as right-hand-man to EAB, had a quiet, thorough efficiency about him. He seemed to have encountered every problem, every set of circumstances; answers were freely and cheerfully given.

That first lunch time he took me up to the Flight Deck to indicate points of interest and especially other ships.

'There's the *King George V*, battleship, sister of the *Prince Of Wales*, *Howe* and *Anson*. That peculiar capital ship with the enormous forecastle and truncated stern is the *Rodney*, 16 inch guns, oddly shaped because of Naval Treaty restrictions agreed whilst she was building. The cruisers are the *Kenya*, *Nigeria*, *Sheffield* and *London*. Then there are a dozen or so destroyers.'

'What are we all doing here instead of being at sea, sinking submarines, escorting convoys and the like?'

He laughed. 'Hold on a minute! We have only been here a few days. Ships need to return to port; to store, fuel up, victual, repair minor defects, allow some of the crew to go on leave. We have a number on shore at the moment. The lucky ones will be at home for Christmas; I'll be aboard as will you. Might be fun unless we have a panic.'

I looked at the islands. Hoy, Mainland with Kirkwall the capital, Flotta and several very small ones. Nobby guessed my thoughts.

'We are allowed to go to Flotta. There is one road which leads to a gigantic canteen, housing hundreds, and often almost awash with beer. It's a good job the road is straight otherwise dozens would never make it back to their Drifter.'

'Is that all there is?'

'Yes, that's it. A few sheep and a lot of chat about frustrated randy sailors chasing them across the rocky fields, but I've never seen anything myself.' He lit a cigarette and inhaled deeply. Almost immediately he started coughing and continued until his eyes watered. Regaining his breath he said, 'Had TB a couple of years ago. Lots of ship-borne men contract it. The lack of fresh air below decks I suppose.' Then, with a sudden subject switch as if he didn't wish to elaborate on his illness, 'By the way, it will be Church Parade on Deck tomorrow and Divisions. Maybe the Captain will do the inspection. Make sure you are neat and well shaved.'

He must have caught me glancing at him. Baggy, crumpled trousers, jacket wearing thin at the cuffs and elbows, shirt collar points bent.

'This is my working suit. Don't go polishing the seat of my best pants on the Captain's Office chairs.' Changing the subject again, he asked, 'What watch are you?'

The ship's watches were divided into two: Starboard and Port. The day divided into seven periods, or watches, five of four hours and two of two hours. This uneven number ensured a daily change of duty period. In effect half the ship's company were on duty whilst the other half rested. At ACTION STATIONS everyone on board was on duty, many in unusual jobs. There was no call for administrative staff to work in the office when the ship was under attack, so we were allocated tasks that were related to action circumstances.

'I'm Starboard watch.'

'Good, so am I. That means we will be able to go ashore together. I will show you all the many attractions of Flotta.'

There was little else to do but work. I spent Saturday afternoon alone in the office. There was plenty to do. By now I had been given my Action Station duty. In the open air on top of the Bridge with the Gunnery Officer. Because of my brief experience with the Observer Corps I was regarded as a useful visual aid to 'Guns'. I was given a pair of binoculars, Barr and Stroud, which weighed a ton, as well as a Duffel Coat—the camel-coloured loose garment, secured with wooden pegs threaded into thin rope loops. It wasn't heavy but it was fairly warm. The hood was useful to protect the neck and ears. I thought it would be handy if we encountered any really cold weather—I didn't know the half of it!

Sunday morning was bright and clear but cold. A Church Service and Divisions to be held on the Flight Deck: everyone to be neatly turned out, ready for inspection. The service was Church of England; Roman Catholics were excused.

On joining the Navy I was asked my religion. Baptist, I informed the questioner.

'Don't hold with any of those funny faiths lad. Are you C of E, Catholic, or Jewish?'

'Better put me down as C of E then.'

22

'That's better. If you are ever in the "oggin" (sea) praying to be rescued, the Almighty will want a clear shout for help. He won't have time to sort out Baptists, Methodists and the like.'

We had formed up on deck in our various groups. Seamen, Stokers, Accountancy and Administration, Fleet Air Arm, etc. The Royal Marine band played. I wondered what was the purpose of bandsmen on a warship; what did they do when not beating drums or playing trumpets?

The Captain was not carrying out inspection. Each group or division was to be inspected by its own senior officer or his deputy. Lt. Commander Holland was to cast his eye over us. He was known as 'Dutchie' for obvious reasons, and was renowned for sharp, pithy observations as well as outright sarcasm. Not popular, and aware of it, he seemed to enjoy his reputation for cutting comment.

He walked slowly down the line of which I was a member. He stopped in front of the man on my right. He looked him up and down and then said,

'You a fighter pilot today then, Plant?'

'Not today, Sir, no.'

'There are three buttons on your jacket. The top one is undone. It may go down well in the RAF but not here, understood?'

'Sorry Sir, I must have failed to fasten this button properly.'

He moved on to stand in front of me. My shoes were highly polished, suit well brushed, shirt clean, peaked cap held neatly at my side in my right hand. I stared straight ahead.

'You're new.' It was neither a question nor an assertion.

'Yes Sir.'

'Where do you work?'

'Captain's Office Sir.'

'They are inclined to feel superior in the Captain's Office, do you know. I hope you will keep your feet on the deck. I don't care for prima donnas.'

He waited for any response. I said nothing. It seemed he stood for minutes and I felt myself blushing with total embarrassment. He walked away and completed the inspection without speaking to anyone else.

The Vicar was a fat man with rheumy gin-washed eyes. He was in charge of a small church on board, St. Christophers, which could accommodate about fifty. He spoke in a thin reedy voice, most of what he said being carried away on the fresh breeze. We only knew what hymns to sing when the Marine band commenced playing. We sang with gusto if not conviction, mumbled the prayers and shuffled listlessly as we heard only snatches of the sermon.

I found the Vicar to be a strange man to be ministering to our 2000 souls. He was aloof, almost snobbish and rarely acknowledged let alone spoke to any lower deck personnel. On occasion I would meet him, dressed in surplice and resembling a galleon under full sail, on his way to the church near to our office. Standing aside to let him pass, an obligatory action because of his size, I would wait for some recognition. None ever came. I began to wonder if he was really a sailor's parson or just playing the role. Either way he did the Church no favours; how could one approach the unapproachable?

The days seemed to flash by. The work was fascinating, much of it confidential, and each day I was eager to take dictation, type letters, enter up service records and generally become more familiar with how such a mighty ship was administered.

It was like a small town with policemen, shop (NAAFI), church, power station, transport, cooks, cleaners, plumbers, electricians, carpenters, band etc. It operated well because of discipline and a warm sense of comradeship. We were all interdependent, needing each other to the benefit of all.

One day Nobby took me ashore. We disembarked from the Drifter at a wooden pier, walked to the end and then turned on to the road. There were hordes of sailors wearing cap-ribbons of the various ships in Scapa Flow. They were oddly tribal, many shouting the name of their ship in ritual chorus. Some were en route to the Canteen, others, palpably drunk, were slowly making Z lines back to the pier. I found it understandable yet disturbing. Boredom, deprivation, separation, all harsh factors, but what of self-respect, pride in the uniform?

The Canteen was like a small aircraft hangar with a huge bar counter along one side. There were tables and chairs, and an empty platform at the far end. The atmosphere was like the fringe of hell. Incessant noise, a thick blue haze, clinking and clatter of heavy pint glass tankards, bawdy songs, shouts of abuse, laughter, stamping of boots and gum-boots—I had never witnessed anything like it. Not far from the entrance was a totally naked sailor having pints of beer poured over him, others were in various stages of undress and drunkenness. It was like a scene from Hieronymous Bosch.

'My God Nobby, how do they allow this?'

'These matelots are letting their hair down, some of them for the last time. There are those who have just returned from a Russian convoy, some who have already lost one ship and think they might lose another. I honestly don't blame them.'

'Doesn't anyone care what they are doing?' I asked.

'There are plenty of regulating staff about. If they see anything ugly, fights starting and the like, they will step in and sort it out. Want a drink?'

I really didn't want to stay but it would have been churlish to refuse. Drinking had never been of great interest to me and was now even less so.

'OK thanks. Do we have any choice, Nobby?'

'No, so I'll get you some beer. See if you can find space to sit; not to far away, so I can find you.'

Looking around I saw two empty chairs at a table for eight. The other six occupants seemed fairly merry; there was scarcely room to put any more glasses on the table. I felt self-conscious. They all looked seasoned sailors; here was I in my virtually brand new navy blue belted raincoat, obviously having done nothing more daring than sail the Pentland Firth. Looking up, one of them said:

'What ship?'

'*Victorious*,' I replied.

'Ugly flat-topped bastard,' he answered. They all broke into loud, beery laughter. What a descriptive witticism, it appealed to them in their maudlin state.

'What's your ship?' I ventured.

'*Punjabi*, tribal class destroyer, a sodding good ship.'

At this point Nobby turned up with two pints of beer, the foam running down the sides of the heavy glasses. Our companions fell silent momentarily, then started chatting among themselves about 'boats'—as destroyers were known—looking after battleships and carriers. 'The hound dogs of the fleet,' one of them kept saying.

We drank our beer slowly, looking around at the extraordinary behaviour of many of the sailors.

'What do you think?' asked Nobby. I found he was forever asking questions.

'Amazing. I find it hard to express my thoughts. It's difficult to believe that these men would behave like this anywhere but here, desolate and depressing place that it is.'

We drank up and walked back to the pier. One Drifter was already heavily loaded. It belonged to the cruiser *London* and its occupants kept breaking ito song. To the tune of 'Ask The Saviour To Help You' they chorused mightily and with great conviction:

> Ask the *London* to help you
> She's the ship that will help you
> Ask the *London* to help you
> The *London* will carry you through.

A mighty cheer burst forth at the end of each rendition, thrown down like a challenge to any other Drifter.

There were no other takers—at least not choral—but plenty of vocal responses. I wondered what their mothers might think if they could hear. Then again anything was permissible against the background of their precarious future. Ships crews jelled into prickly defensiveness as if this would safeguard them. They drew strength from each other and shouted this to any listener. The *London* would carry you through because, despite anything, she was going to survive—this was the significance of their boastful hymn.

As we nudged past the *KGV* Drifter and headed for *Victorious*, I suddenly found I wanted to shout about the '*Vic*', all 753 feet and 35,000 tons of her; massive, strong, indestructible with a guardian angel bolted to the bridge. Yes, I was proud of her, believing that this pride would add to her strength.

Of course I didn't shout or sing, but stood with Nobby, listening to the fading cries and songs drifting in wind-borne surges from Flotta Pier.

CHAPTER THREE

Action!

It was Christmas Eve, great excitement on board. With about 400 men on leave, there was no possibility of our going on operations.

As *Victorious* had only been at sea since April, this would be her first sea-borne Christmas. Old salts regaled us with tales of the 25th Decembers spent among dusky maidens in the West Indies, white Russian beauties in Shanghai, busty blondes in Durban and Capetown. To them, Christmas seemed to be a celebration of the female body. Of course we listened with awe, spiked with a little scepticism, to each story laced with anglo-saxon descriptive terms and remembered with fevered exaggeration. I found that many of these yarns were not original but had been handed down, like fairy tales and folk songs, from one generation of sailors to the next. A little extra was given in each re-telling. The living lore of the Navy.

There was a ritual on Christmas Day. It was decreed that for part of the morning the youngest member of the crew would be the Captain, the second youngest the Commander and so on until a party of about eight was formed to inspect the ship. There was a 16-year-old Boy Seaman selected as Captain. He was dressed in full Captain's uniform; his companions also wore the dress appropriate to their assumed rank. Preceded by a Marine Bugler, they commenced 'Captain's Rounds' at 10.30.

We were required to stand to attention whilst ourselves, office or mess were subjected to the 'Captain's Inspection'. It was hilarious. Our 'Captain', the real one, was not too big, but his uniform baggily clothed his usurper. The 'Captain' ran his finger along desk tops and sternly demanded to know, 'Why is there no dust?' He criticised shiny shoes, ordering a member of his retinue to 'dirty them a little', drew his palm along your chin and criticised, 'You have shaved this morning: shore leave denied for seven days.'

His procession was followed by rowdy sailors demanding that he order 'Splice the Mainbrace'—an extra rum ration to be given—and indeed, his last command before relinquishing his captaincy was just that. Loud cheers and banging of spoons on plates.

It was fun yet, even though I was only 19, I questioned the wisdom of having 16-year-old boys on a fighting ship; surely there were no 16-year-old aircrew or members of battle regiments? Pushing all these moral reflections aside, I joined in the festivities. The galley staff had done everyone proud. Roast turkey, roast pork, brussels, roast potatoes, giblet gravy.

'Taff', our messman, a great character, non-stop worker, came in with the Christmas Pudding. Not quite Mrs. Beaton, but fruity and black, along with a large steel can of thick, dark yellow custard.

Those who had been able to scrounge successfully at the NAAFI canteen were lighting up small cigars and sipping their rum contentedly. Tables were cleared and the cribbage boards appeared. Gambling was prohibited, but once a week or when conditions permitted, Tombola was played (Bingo). It would be supervised by an Officer and a member of the Accountancy Staff. They would take the cash, issue the cards, work out the 'line' and 'house' prizes and then pay out. A small percentage of the take would be retained for the Ship's Welfare Fund. Crib was usually played for matchsticks, though I have known occasions when each match represented a penny and gambling debts were settled later in cash or rum.

On Boxing Day I went ashore alone to walk on Flotta. It was a clear, crisp day, pale sun offering minimum warmth but mercifully there was little wind. I needed exercise to combat the excesses of Christmas Day.

After walking around for about an hour I made my way back to the pier, passing a man in a brown trilby hat, sports jacket and trousers walking the other way. Only a few yards on I heard him call, 'You there; a word.' I turned and retraced my steps to where he stood.

'Do you know who I am?' he asked crisply.

'No, I am afraid I don't,' I replied. I was beginning to wonder what a civilian was doing on the island. He had the look of a naval officer, a middle-aged one; reddish cheeks, slightly veined, clear eyes, flat accentless voice.

'What is your ship?' He spoke sharply and with some irritation.

'*Victorious*, Sir.' I felt the time was appropriate to call him 'Sir'.

'And your name?'

'Barker Sir, on the Captain's secretarial staff.'

'Carry on, Barker,' he said, and turned briskly away, walking stick tapping rhythmically on the concrete road.

I told Nobby of my encounter when I returned on board.

'Was he tall, with a little bit of facial hair on his cheeks?'

'That seems to fit him, yes.'

'My God, it was Admiral Tovey. There will probably be a rocket on its way from the *KGV* any minute now.'

He was right. There was a signal to the effect that the proper mark of respect, a salute, had not been paid to the Admiral and that the miscreant should be chastised.

Lt. Berrey took me on one side, officially rebuked me, and advised that if I ever saw anyone on Flotta in civilian clothes I should salute. 'It may even be a junior member of an ENSA concert party but raise your right arm and throw a crisp, emphatic signal of respect and recognition.'

Did it matter, I wondered? Was the conduct of the war at sea affected by my misdeed? Yours not to reason why, Barker, just do the right thing.

New Year's Day came and went then, on 2nd January 1942, *Victorious* put to sea—though not for long. In the months and years to come, I would get used to the 'Pipes' (loudspeaker announcements) of 'Sea dutymen fall in' and the sundry other orders necessary to unshackle the ship from her Buoy, raise anchors and proceed slowly through the Boom Defences into open water.

We were to fly off one of our Squadrons of aircraft, 832, Albacore, torpedo bombers. I was given time off to watch our departure and the flying operation. I went up to my Action Station on top of the Bridge, an incredible view some 60 feet above the water and with the whole flight deck in sight.

The Albacore was a refined Swordfish, obsolescent as opposed to obsolete. A bi-plane, slow, poorly armed, yet sturdy and durable. It was a stop-gap until a better aircraft was built, by us or the Americans—who were now in the War and suffering grievously. To fly off or land aircraft, the ship had to be steaming straight and into the wind. A steam valve at the forward end of the flight deck emitted a white plume of steam which, when streaming back down the deck, indicated we were directly into the wind. Commander (Flying) stood on a projecting waist-high platform, giving him an unfettered view of the flight deck. From here he gave instructions to the Flight Deck Officer (FDO). Engines started up, revved noisily, aircraft handlers lay on the deck waiting to pull the chocks away, a Take Off flag was waved round and round above the FDO's head and then dramatically dropped. At this the chocks were pulled away, the engine gunned to full power and slowly the Albacore rolled forwards.

I was quite certain that neither the first one, nor even any of them, would gain sufficient speed to lift themselves airborne. Sounding like heavy motorcycles they stuttered then rasped along the deck, streaking to at least around 40 miles an hour when they were caught in the up-draught created by the ship's momentum. Occasionally one would disappear over the bow to be seen seconds later frantically struggling along, 20 feet above the waves. Eventually all were off, they formed into three flights of three and headed for a Scottish Naval Air Station. Each Squadron had a home base ashore.

We turned out of the wind and steered course for Scapa Flow. The ship seemed remarkably manoeuvrable, slewing sharply to Port or Starboard at the Captain's command.

The Captain was Henry Cecil Bovell, known as 'Hard-over' Cecil. It would seem nothing pleased him more than to give the instruction: 'Hard a Port/Starboard' whereupon the vast ship would heel and turn to left or right. There were side effects. Typewriters and documents would slide along the desk tops, ledgers would move just as an important entry was being made, pans would skid off stove tops in the Galleys, open lockers shed their drawers and contents over the mess-deck. Anything loose rolled into a corner and sailors rolled into each other. Back at Scapa nothing seemed to have changed.

Suddenly there was great excitement on the mess-decks. The Notice Boards had boldly scrawled announcements that, in two days time, there would be a Tea Dance on board. Music by the Marine Band, females courtesy of the WRENS and other women staff being ferried from Kirkwall. The Lotharios were at the NAAFI shop for Brylcreem, the bath and shower rooms were filled with steam-enveloped sailors scrubbing industriously at bodies and clothes. Jaunty walks and whistles characterised movements down gangways and passages; Jack the Lad was clearly about his business.

The day dawned, wet and windy. As the hours went by the waves that slapped the side of the ship began to thump and then thud heavily. Anxious eyes scanned the sea, old 'Stripeys' who knew the moods of the oceans from years of sea-going shook their heads. They were no longer of a mind to wonder about the length of WRENS' black-out drawers, so their predictions on the weather conditions were regarded as impartial. They were gloomy and with good reason, for not long after mid-day the dreaded call: 'Do you hear there. Do you hear there. Due to adverse weather conditions, the visit of on-shore personnel to partake in a Tea Dance has been cancelled, repeat cancelled. That is all.'

Dick, the womanising champion of the Stores Staff raised his eyes to heaven: 'Why have you denied the men-starved women of this bleak and lonely place the pleasure of my morale-boosting company?' Envied, but admired by his compatriots, Dick seemed uniquely endowed with a special homing device which not only detected available women from a quarter of a mile distant but which also appeared to have magnetic qualities, drawing them to him. Suave, good-looking, dark haired, Dick was obsessed by the opposite sex. The denial of their company, even for two hours in very open surroundings—the gigantic hangar—depressed him.

'I don't believe they can't get a Drifter alongside,' he complained.

'Maybe they could, but if the weather continues to deteriorate they might not be able to get them off,' replied Van, one of his friends.

'Now you're talking!' Eyes briefly agleam at the thought, then 'Maybe they will just postpone it.' Dick looked hopefully at Van.

'Depends on our movements; I have a feeling we've been here long enough. All the leave parties are back on board. The Squadrons seem to be worked up, all spares replaced.'

Van was virtually in charge of aircraft stores. Shortish, about 5'6", born of a Czech father and a Welsh mother, he was the complete action man. From dawn to 'Pipe down' he worked, clambering in the Hangar Deck-Head, moving aircraft wings, tail planes, fins, engines. His life was centred on *Victorious* and Beth, his fiancée, working in Dursley, Gloucestershire. He wrote to her every day and she to him. We used to ask him what he put in his letters bearing in mind it was forbidden to mention the ship, other ships, the weather, where we were, where we had been. Writing to Beth gave him strength; temporarily united with her by pen and paper he seemed to recharge his batteries and set about his work with renewed heart. The Navy needed thousands of 'Vans' if it was to survive the Germans and the Japanese.

The following day we heard that the *Empire Audacity*, a merchant ship converted into an aircraft carrier, had been sunk. We knew that the age of the battleship was over; conventional sea battles fought gun to gun would never reach the scale of the First World War. Seaborne aircraft would dominate the remainder of the War; carriers would either sink other ships, destroy aircraft, or be sunk themselves.

Already the Royal Navy had lost the *Courageous*, the *Glorious* and *Ark Royal*, and whilst waiting for the commissioning of the new class of carriers, *Victorious*, *Formidable*, *Indomitable*, *Implacable* and *Indefatigable*, only *Illustrious* was a truly custom-built vessel. Thus emergency measures were taken to place flight decks on merchant men hulls, carry a dozen aircraft, and help to defend convoys. *Empire Audacity* was such a ship.

The *Ark Royal* had been sunk in the Mediterranean on November 14th 1941. Hit by a single torpedo, she survived the initial impact, but just 23 miles south-east of Gibraltar she had begun to list heavily then shortly after the crew had abandoned ship she sank. There was speculation as to whether the *Ark* had been prematurely abandoned; was the list (tilt) of the ship tolerable and could she have been towed those few miles to safety, even listing heavily?

Captain Bovell, mindful of the possibility of handling *Victorious* in a similar situation, decided we should have a 'Tilt Test' and so, whilst most of the ships crew were asleep, he arranged for fuel to be transferred from the port to the starboard tanks. By 0600 the ship had assumed a 15 degree list. It was organised chaos for a while; everyone found it difficult to maintain balance. Walking through the Hangar meant sliding across the shiny steel deck and finishing in an undignified heap on the starboard side. Items not properly secured had fallen or tumbled. The lighting was also dimmed to emergency levels to simulate *Ark Royal* conditions.

Just near the Captain's Office was a large brass 'Inclinometer', an arrow pointing straight downwards on a dial which was measured from 45 degrees starboard to 45 degrees port. The arrow moved as the ship rolled. It was now steady at just over 15 degrees starboard.

Everyone carried out their normal duties. I found the typewriter carriage refused to move and the keys struck the same spot all the time. After four hours the ship gradually assumed a level and stable attitude. The Captain announced himself pleased with the exercise, assuring us that the ship could list up to 58 degrees without sinking! It was difficult to understand how anyone could orientate safely in those conditions; we would not be walking on the decks, could watertight doors be opened easily. 'Stripeys' expressed doubt, but then again one elderly Able Seaman, aged 50 plus, confided in me that he didn't really believe in airplanes. He described them as 'those things sculling around a hell of a depth up' and was not convinced they were anything but a passing fad.

Yet 'Stripeys' were the fount of all knowledge. Young sailors could be found sitting in the Cable Locker telling their problems to one of these old sages, wise in the ways of the sea and the 'Andrew'. Advice was not always freely given;

occasionally a tot of rum had to be sacrificed—crossing the palm with spirit—and partially consumed before, 'When I was in Simonstown,' presaged the homily which might deal with affairs of the heart or how to cope with a difficult Petty Officer. They performed a useful service and I came to believe that was their function, in the full knowledge of the authorities, as some were clearly unfit for anything else.

At this time the ship was alive with speculation that the *Tirpitz* was about to break out of her lair on Foetten Fjord near Trondheim in Norway.

This mighty ship, pride of the German Navy, could decimate a Russian Convoy in a couple of hours if she was allowed to sidle up the Norwegian coast to ambush the shipping lane to Murmansk in Northern Russia. Her very presence, even in hiding, was such that a major part of the Home Fleet was preoccupied with her movements. Also moving up to the area were the pocket battleship *Admiral Scheer* and heavy cruiser *Prinz Eugen*. The latter had escaped some seven months earlier when the *Bismarck*, whom she was escorting, was sunk en route to Brest in France after sinking the *Hood*, only three surviving the massive explosion that caused the ship to disintegrate in seconds.

The German Naval authorities knew that *Tirpitz* was a massive asset, like an aggressive queen on the chess board, always threatening the opposition but rarely risking being taken.

They had no wish to operate her in the open Atlantic, where she would be exposed to air and sea attacks, but leap-frog her from one safe fjord anchorage to another. In this role she alarmed convoys, kept our naval forces indecisive and, in ensuring that destroyers remained in Scapa with carriers, denied their support to merchant shipping by giving freedom to U Boats.

There was also a 'buzz' (gossip, rumour) that the RAF would bomb the daylights out of *Tirpitz*, in the same way that the Japanese had spectacularly sunk the *Prince of Wales* and *Repulse*—but they were out in the open, not lodged alongside a towering cliff of a narrow, twisting fjord.

Finally the Admiralty could wait no longer. Possibly they had in mind springing a trap. It was on 17th January that *Victorious* in company with battleships *King George V, Rodney,* cruisers *Kenya, Nigeria* and *Sheffield,* plus 12 destroyers left Scapa Flow for northern waters.

The seas were calm, the weather cold. Standing in my Action Stations position I watched the fleet form up as the Orkneys fell below the horizon to our stern. The destroyers formed in a V shaped screen within which the heavier ships were protected from submarine attack. At 20 knots (about 23 miles an hour) we zig-zagged in unison, an added precaution devised to prevent a U Boat enjoying too long an opportunity to predict a position at which to fire a torpedo.

There was the odd mine bobbing in the sea, most likely having broken loose from its mooring in a minefield and now drifting with the wind and tide. Occasionally a Marine sharp-shooter was summoned to the flight deck to loose off a few rounds in an effort to explode the mine. It seemed a singularly unsuccessful enterprise, misses being greeted with jeers by the seamen on watch or the anti-aircraft crews at their pom-poms.

That night, my first at sea, I listened to the steady throbbing vibration of the turbine engines, driving the three propellors located below the enormous 45 ton rudder. As *Victorious* steamed on she creaked and groaned, alarmingly, it seemed to me. Were her riveted plates to be pulled apart by the strains and forces of the ocean? 'Stripeys' smiled indulgently at this thought. 'When she doesn't creak, when the plates remain absolutely rigid, that's the time to get your Carley float!'

Then I was seized with panic. It was dark, pitch black. Who was looking out for mines and how could they see them anyway? Was that metallic clink the sound of a mine nudging against the port side? I sat up in my camp bed which was tucked away neatly and almost free from sleep-denying light, in a space near an ammunition hoist. Perspiration, the dampness of genuine fear on my forehead. Where was my life-belt—under my camp-bed; and my Abandon Ship Station? A Carley float hanging from the bridge structure. Slowly I relaxed. No one else seemed worried, no animated chatter, signs of alarm, reluctance to get into hammock or bed. I lay down again and woke only to the 'Wakey Wakey' of RPO Tucker.

The 19th January saw us approaching Iceland, whose snow-capped mountains and volcanoes were clearly visible. Two destroyers suddenly left the escort line, signalling with an urgent 'whoop, whoop, whoop' that they had probably located a submarine. Depth charges went cartwheeling into the air, plopping into the ocean soon to raise massive fountains of foaming sea displaced by the explosive force of the charges. The destroyers raced around like terriers shaking a bone, the dull rumble of their attacks slowly died away as the rest of the force pressed on. We arrived in Hvalfjord at noon. This spectacular natural anchorage not only sheltered units of the fleet, but was an assembly point for convoys to Russia and a base for US warships, now about six weeks into WW2. All in all there were 29 naval vessels in the fjord and the mess-decks were buzzing with gossip about 'taking on the *Tirpitz*. The sinking of the *Hood* and the humiliation of the *Prince Of Wales* still rankled and although *Bismarck* had paid the price, the ordinary sailor wanted to sink the *Tirpitz*. Pride was at stake and the prospect of failure was never considered.

It came as no surprise when we heard on the radio that questions had been asked in the Houses of Parliament about the sinking, by the Japanese Air Force, of the *Repulse* and *Prince Of Wales*. 'Why was there no carrier protection as these ships sailed into waters known to be dominated aerially by the Japanese?' The facts were obvious: the Navy did not have sufficient carrier strength to cover South East Asia as well as the Atlantic and Mediterranean theatres of war. But it made carrier crews feel that they were now the front line fighting ships, with all others (battleships, cruisers, destroyers) playing vital support roles of protection from air and sea attack.

Thus, when rumours abounded about the *Tirpitz*, the carrier crews throbbed with excitement at the prospect of proving their new-found importance in naval warfare. Hadn't Japanese carriers decimated the US fleet at Pearl

Harbour?

I remember that the second night in Hvalfjord was cloudless and there was an amazing display of the Aurora Borealis. The clear, smoke-free sky shone and shimmered with a myriad stars and constellations. Huge glowing galaxies, milky white, reached into infinity. Comets and shooting stars careered across the blue-black backcloth of endless space. I felt so small and insignificant as I wondered about the wretchedness of man, so busily engaged in trying to destroy a miniscule segment of all that stretched about us.

With no news of when we might be leaving our anchorage, there was the opportunity to go ashore. Iceland was not at war with Germany; the Americans and the British were not exactly welcome guests and the Icelanders were very reserved, some downright sullen. This was easy to understand; their island was the staging point for aircraft and convoys as well as providing anchorages at Hvalfjord and Seydisfjord. Their traditional industry of fishing was being dislocated by warships and submarines fighting with each other just off their coast-line. True, in Reykjavik, where some Americans were able to reach, they provided a boost to the local shops and interest for the girls.

In company with George Plant I clambered into the ship's whaler and chopped through an uncomfortable quarter mile of water to the tiny pier. There was a canteen and a store. Anywhere to eat, other than the ship, was a pleasure—not necessarily gastronomic—but social, with a change of both surroundings and people. Other sailors, and especially US personnel provided a distraction. Of course the Americans were paid more than us, had better quality uniforms, smoked cigars and generally appeared like Fred Astaire in 'Follow The Fleet'—all singing and dancing. We liked to talk to them, and those of us who had pursued the *Bismarck* were quick to remind them of such battle experience.

Food in the canteen was usually tea or coffee, cake, tinned fruit (American) and soft drinks. The shop sold postcards, which we were not allowed to send, and, among other things, silk stockings. Those who wistfully recalled running their hands, however fleetingly, over their girl friend's silk-clad legs were to be found buying up to six pairs. The presents, to be given when the sweethearts next met, would provide a clue as to what the naval lad had been thinking during those lonely night watches in the engine room or gun turrets.

It was an unsuitable day for walking far, and clad in polo necks and sea boots we just tramped around the vicinity of the pier. We resolved that if we came again, in better weather, a sharp climb up one of the low mountains would be relaxing.

The fjord was now filling up with shipping of every type. Something in the order of a quarter of a million tons of naval strength was anchored as well as countless merchant men, tankers and supply ships.

Still no news of movement. The weather deteriorated and an American naval cutter capsized on returning to its ship. Four sailors were lost. What a way to go, I thought, drowned in freezing water in an inhospitable foreign fjord, without ever firing a shot in anger. 'Killed on Active Service' when possibly the cutter should never have gone ashore at all. The following day our own whaler was caught in a sudden squall and blown on to some rocks; she eventually worked her way back to the ship and safety.

An interesting interlude was the presence of the former supply ship to the *Bismarck*. She had been captured, boarded, re-named *Empire Garden* and brought to Iceland. Her stores were then unloaded and distributed to Royal Naval vessels. We received soap and cleaning materials. 'Very inferior' was the verdict of our own stores staff—I could never have imagined them saying anything else!

Boredom set in, we had been in Hvalfjord for three weeks. The crew was listless and the lack of news as to our objectives was debilitating. I found the failure to keep the crew fully informed a strange policy; it was not based on a 'need to know' theory but more that whatever was known was to be kept from the men. Thank God for the BBC, we said, even though all the news was gloomy if not disastrous. The battleship *Barham* was hit by four torpedoes in the Mediterranean, over 1000 lives lost when she sank in a few minutes. The *Matabele*, a tribal class destroyer, was mined off Murmansk: only two survivors.

Worse was to come. The *Gneisau*, *Scharnhorst*, German battle cruisers, sailed up the English channel with virtual impunity and reached Kiel. The entire German fleet was now in North Sea ports—German and Norwegian. There was sadness on board *Victorious*; Lt. Commander Esmond, who had led the attack on the *Bismarck* from *Victorious* had been killed in the abortive strikes against the German ships. He was remembered as a quiet, studious man, much admired and respected by his squadron, air and ground crews. The news of these ships escaping up the Channel was heard with disbelief and shame. Where were our torpedo boats, the Royal Air Force? Would the Japanese have allowed such an indignity to occur?

Then on 15th February we heard that Singapore had surrendered to the Japanese. Impregnable citadel of British military might, defended by over 100,000 men, had given in to a quarter that number of Japanese troops, some riding bicycles. Would it ever end? As we strained at our buoy there was a frustrated impatience; Britain was losing out and we were virtually on the sidelines.

To relieve the tedium of life in the lonely northern outpost, we played deck hockey. This was similar to field hockey, except there were no rules. Instead of a ball we used a puck, a five inch circumference of rope, dipped in aircraft 'dope' to harden. This took on the form of a semi-lethal weapon. Sticks were an inch thick with a flat striking part instead of the curved hockey stick. Goal posts were usually aircraft chocks. Seven players including the goal-minder made up the team. A reasonable supply of pucks or grommets was necessary as they often flew over the side.

The Accounts Division, which comprised the administrative and stores staff, had a strong team. We wore blue and white quartered shirts, black shorts and plimsolls; I actually played in Indian-type moccasins. The game was rough but fair. There were times when its use as a recreation had to be balanced against its incapacitation of ships crew; for instance, one 'very good' match ended with one cerebral concussion, two sent to the Hospital Ship and one in the Sick Bay with a broken wrist. But the Captain looked benignly on these activities, especially as they distracted players and spectators—vociferous and numerous—from loss of morale through boredom.

On the 18th February, 30 days after arrival, we moved into open waters for flying practice. We ranged and flew off 832 Squadron, 12 aircraft, in just seven and a half minutes, beating the record held by *Formidable*. Something to cheer about. The weather was still very cold; only a few days earlier our deck had been snow-covered and the water in the Fire Buckets in various parts of the ship froze solid. At 0500 on the 19th we finally left Iceland. The coastline was beautiful, fjord after fjord stabbing into the mountains all snow-covered in the crisp winter air. We were to accompany a convoy, or at least protect its southern flank, our own escort being the *KGV*, HMS *Berwick* (cruiser) and seven destroyers. As a further measure to cover the convoy and harrass the enemy, the *Victorious* was to attack shipping in the area of Tromso. Intelligence was poor and it was more or less assumed that there would be suitable targets. In the event, a change was hurriedly made to the plan. It seemed that the German ships *Admiral Scheer* and *Prinz Eugen*, which had been lurking off Jutland or in one of the more southerly Norwegian fjords, were now sailing northwards. They were hugging the coastline but were clearly intent on creeping nearer to the convoy routes. The Tromso operation aborted, we steamed quickly south to position ourselves between the German ships and their likely merchantmen prey.

The report on the movement of the German warships had been sent by a patrolling aircraft of the RAF, but, unknown to us, this had been sighted by *Admiral Scheer* and *Prinz Eugen*. At least we were bound to assume this as they steamed as far as Bergen then sought refuge and safety in a nearby fjord.

Temporarily we turned northwards again, with Tromso in mind, only to receive a signal from the Admiralty that it was believed the German ships were on the move again, fjord-hopping up the Norwegian coast.

The force about-turned, the weather was deteriorating, but it was believed there was a genuine opportunity to find and attack these potential convoy raiders.

We raced southwards escorted by the *Berwick* and four destroyers, leaving the *KGV* and three destroyers following more slowly. Our speed built up to about 25 knots, say 33 miles an hour, as we headed to a fly-off point from which a strike could be launched. Excitement was intense, rumours spread around the mess decks like wild-fire. Our torpedo bombers were about to avenge the death of Lt. Cdr. Esmond and the brave officers and men of his flight, so recently our colleagues and so selflessly sacrificed in the English Channel only weeks earlier. Was it the big one—*Tirpitz*—we hoped so, but pocket battleships and heavy cruisers would be acceptable.

The plan was for our aircraft to go into the search and destroy operation whilst we headed back to a rendezvous near the Shetlands and meet up again with *KGV* and her destroyers.

Meteorological forecasting was a primitive and fairly unreliable science in those days. We carried a couple of simple wind speed indicators and rainfall measurement instruments. The primary aid was a helium balloon, released by the Met. Officer from the flight deck, its progress by height and direction being tracked by high-powered binoculars. The height and direction of the balloon was recorded until it disappeared from sight. When the cloudbase was low, this could be a very early event. From these almost high-school type experiments a value judgement was made as to the likely weather in the next 24 hours. Oddly enough our Met. Officer was also the Ship's Schoolmaster (Education Officer) charged with the continued schooling of the boys, under 18 years of age, we carried as part of our crew. His forecast was optimistic: poor weather would improve.

As we neared the ranging and fly-off point, the weather seemed to get worse. The wind became stronger, there was heavy rain, turning to sleet and then snow. The sea roughened and long, heavy swells were creating a wave pattern that made the ship pitch and toss slowly but deeply. The flight deck was rising and falling through 30 feet or more and visibility was hardly the length of the flight deck. It became difficult to communicate by signal to our companion ships. Messages were normally passed by semaphore flag or flashing Aldis lamps flickering morse code instructions in plain language. We could not see *Berwick* and time slipped by until finally all ships knew our intentions and we turned into wind and hoped the snow would cease falling.

It was now after midnight, pitch black and wickedly cold. Stood in the open, above the bridge, I speculated on the possibility of success. Unless visibility improved and conditions moderated, it would be a miracle to achieve the objective. Beneath my duffel coat were two polo-necked thick sweaters, my feet encased in a pair of fur-lined flying boots illegally obtained from a colleague in stores. Yet I was half frozen, teeth chattering, body trembling and continually stamping my feet and wrapping my arms around myself to maintain some semblance of warmth. Looking down on the flight deck at the Albacores ranged for take-off, I pondered on the bravery of the crews. Pilot, Observer and Rear-Gunner in each aircraft, about to fly from a heavily pitching surface into total darkness, in search of well-hidden, strongly protected ships.

The Squadron, 832, which had achieved the record deck landing time now faced an exceptional new challenge. Of the 10 aircraft, only one had any equipment that was likely to prove useful in the search for the targets.

Slowly the Albacores, Bristol Pegasus engines straining at full power, lumbered down the deck. I waved to each one, not that they could see me, but these men deserved some recognition and gesture to give them heart and wish them luck. For some this was to be their last sight of *Victorious*. Conditions were so atrocious that the final aircraft in the Squadron took off into a blanket snow-storm and immediately became detached from his companion Albacores. He never made contact with them again and flew a lonely, hazardous and ineffective mission before landing in the Shetlands several hours later.

Meanwhile 817 Squadron, seven aircraft, had also been lined up, awaiting the signal from the FDO to leave *Victorious* and follow their fellow squadron into the black, wintry Norwegian night. Flight crews were almost petrified with cold, the chock handlers of the rear aircraft having to endure the vicious slipstream of icy air from the aircraft in front. Finally the full 17 Albacores had disappeared into the darkness and silence fell on board.

Those of us now standing down from Action Stations returned to the comparative warmth of the mess decks below. My thoughts were with the aircrews. Even though I had been on board just over two months, several of the Pilots and Observers were well known to me. They frequently came into the office on some pretext or other and wanted to chat. Usually they were anxious to learn if their names had arisen in correspondence: for promotion, transfer or whether some lacking documentation relating to them had arrived on board. There were some remarkable characters, and I grew to admire, respect and like them.

The Squadron Commanders had seen a good deal of service, some in the pre-war RAF. They were regular career officers, usually thoughtful reflective men, very conscious of the responsibilities of leading up to a dozen aircraft. One such man was Lt. Commander Plugge whose Albacore disappeared, presumed crashed into the sea, on this operation.

During that black night, the two squadrons searched the Norwegian coast for their prey. The weather had now worsened to a degree that visibility was virtually zero. After a fruitless search in impossible conditions, the Albacores turned and headed west to the Shetlands and safety.

Flying into a westerly wind of almost gale force, these obsolescent machines faced possible disaster. Some dropped their torpedoes into the sea to lose weight and so conserve their rapidly dwindling fuel. Wings began to ice up, the crews were becoming frozen in their cabins, controls were more difficult to operate. It was essential they remain together so that the Senior Observer could navigate them safely to landfall. But Fate was to deal these intrepid flyers a cruel blow: less than an hour from the Shetland RAF base two aircraft collided. There was a vivid, sun-bright flash as a massive explosion devastated the aircraft. It was shortly after this that Lt. Cdr. Plugge was believed to have hit the sea without warning. Fourteen Albacores landed at Sumburgh between five and six o'clock that morning, the crews shaken by this experience.

A mission of high promise had turned into a totally fruitless endeavour. Braving the worst possible elements, the air crews didn't even have the satisfaction of finding and attacking the German ships. Clearly the abysmal meteorological forecasts, wrong in every aspect, contributed heavily to the debacle. Additionally the lack of proper intelligence from the Royal Air Force and Coastal Command, who had been over-flying the area for several days in succession prior to the operation, was also a major factor.

I knew, from my work in the Captain's Office, that Captain Bovell was extremely distressed about most aspects of this tragic failure. He made it clear that had he known the real conditions pertaining over the coast he would not have allowed the strike force to take off. He expressed concern over the loss of such experienced flight crews who, at this stage of the carrier war, were in short supply.

It became clear as the winter ran its course and we continued to operate in Arctic waters that the weather cycles almost defied prediction. Clear skies could, and did, within minutes, become virtual 'white outs'; keen winds became roaring gales and modest seas raging tempests.

The despondency of the ship's crew was slightly relieved at the news that an ambush force of four submarines, located near Trondheim, had torpedoed but not sunk the *Prinz Eugen*.

We returned to our anchorage at Scapa Flow in sombre mood, none more so than the Captain who proceeded to send highly critical observations to the Admiralty and Commander-In-Chief, Home Fleet. He almost demanded to be supplied with better intelligence so as to offer his flight crews at least an even chance of success.

Forty-two sacks of mail came on board the ship. Extra duty men were seconded to the Regulating Office to assist in sorting the letters, postcards and parcels. It was an odd paradox that whilst many a sailor was opening a parcel containing balaclavas, mittens and thick socks, only hours earlier he had been packaging silk stockings, make-up, hair grips and the like, obtained from the store in Iceland.

By this time supplies of provisions were reaching our ships from America. There was of course, Spam (tinned pork), canned milk, and bewilderingly, sweet potatoes. Jolly Jack Tar is renowned for his adventurous spirit ashore, but not in matters of cuisine. When reaching port and being allowed shore leave, Jack's first inclination was to seek 'Big Eats'—this to provide him with the energy and drive to pursue his second inclination. 'Big Eats' can best be defined as vast quantities of plain and simple food. Steak and chips, steak and kidney pie, fish and chips. Meat and three vegetables, all followed by a heavy pudding, such as 'Spotted Dick' etc.

It mattered little where 'ashore' might be: China, Jamaica, Port Said, Capetown or Portsmouth; the 'Big Eats' menu offered by local cafés in those places featured these homely dishes. What was never requested, nor even remotely considered, was Sweet Potato.

Of course the chefs in the Galley treated it as any other potato: fried, boiled, mashed or chipped. When the metal trays containing this delicacy arrived in the messes they were looked at quizically by most, knowledgeably by some. 'That's mashed turnip or swede,' they nodded with wordly-wise superiority. 'Haven't had any in months; makes a change from spuds.'

The first fork-full, taken boldly by the knowing and tentatively by the cautious, produced a mixed reaction. The former, quick-witted as many sailors are, remarked that 'Cook has dropped a f-----g sugar bag in the turnip;' the latter simply spat it out.

There was a complaints procedure regarding food. It entailed verbal opinion, objective of course, being offered to a Duty Officer who, on rare occasions,

actually walked into a Mess at meal times and boldly asked, 'Any complaints?'
Sullen silence meant 'Yes,' continued eating and chatter meant, 'Yes but it won't
do any good!' These were the only responses.

Sweet Potatoes were not served again in British waters on board *Victorious*,
an act of foolish self-denial when various alternatives appeared.

CHAPTER FOUR

Northern Waters—the Russian Convoys

Convoys to Russia, usually Murmansk, were designated PQ and those returning westwards QP. Although the Germans had taken a lively interest in these convoys, it was not until the late winter of 1941/2 that this interest became extreme aggression. It dawned on them that one of the reasons for the very stiff Russian resistance they were encountering on the land battle-front was possibly due, in part, to the supplies reaching Murmansk and Archangel from the USA and Canada.

These convoys normally assembled in an Icelandic fjord where they were briefed by the convoy Commodore and informed of the route plan and protection to be afforded by the Navy.

On 1st March, 1942, PQ 12 left Iceland and, simultaneously, QP 8 departed from Murmansk bound for the UK.

At 1030 on the morning of the 4th we left Scapa Flow with a heavy force consisting of battleships *King George V, Duke Of York*, battle-cruiser *Renown*, cruiser *Berwick* and nine destroyers.

Almost immediately we encountered rough weather and two boats on our weather deck were smashed almost to pulp-wood. *KGV* and *Duke Of York* wallowed, rolled, cork-screwed into the enormous swells whilst we pitched and tossed until the propellers, lifted free of the sea, raced madly in the air before being plunged back into the ocean.

Late on the 6th we were advised that it was almost certain the *Tirpitz* was sailing north, probably to attack the convoy which had by now reported it was being shadowed by enemy aircraft.

Spirits rose, the noise level on the mess decks reflected the excitement once again that we were about to carry out some positive action, hopefully to rid the merchant ship convoys of the ever present threat of destruction at the hands of possibly the most powerful battleship in the world. No-one under-estimated the problems. It was still winter, very limited daylight, the mercurial Arctic weather, strike aircraft of very limited capability and, most of all, the strength of the *Tirpitz* itself. Its fore-runner, *Bismarck*, had been torpedoed, shelled for hours at a virtual standstill, yet she sank only when the German crew eventually opened the sea-valves and exploded charges to ensure she went down quickly.

The following day news was received that a photographic reconnaissance flight revealed positively that *Tirpitz* had left her anchorage with an escort of destroyers.

We were at Action Stations all day. The weather was now its customary mix of snow, gales and heavy seas. Sometime that day, 7th March, the two convoys crossed, it was even thought that they sailed through one another without knowing—in a virtual 'white-out', whilst less than 100 miles away, three and a half hours high speed steaming, the *Tirpitz* was looking for the merchantmen.

It was now like a game of Blind Man's Buff, none of us knew where the others were and attempts by *Victorious* to fly search aircraft were thwarted by the wretched weather.

Eventually *Tirpitz* came to the conclusion it had missed the convoys and decided to return south to base in Norway. It had not been steaming for home very long before we received news from the Admiralty of its movements.

Tirpitz was bound to pass a position where we could attack her. Once again there was a feeling of 'at last'. But what of the weather? Experience had shown, even on this voyage, that flight operations in this desolate area were at best dangerous, at worst treacherous.

This time it was decided by the Admiral to fly off a search party of six Albacores, on differing tracks, in the hope that one or more would find *Tirpitz* and report her position accurately. Thus, early on the 9th, in miserably cold weather with wretched visibility, the Albacores set off on their search mission. Less than an hour later a force of a further 12, armed with torpedoes, flew into the low clouds with high hopes of being ultimately advised where *Tirpitz* could be attacked.

Remarkably it wasn't long before news came in from the search aircraft that *Tirpitz* had been sighted. She was clearly observed by two aircraft as she steamed south at very high speed. This remarkable ship was capable of travelling at some 30 knots, and an aircraft, such as the slow Albacore, chasing her into a wind, had a very poor closing speed. Nevertheless, just before 9 a.m. Lt. Cdr. Lucas sighted the mighty ship and her one escorting destroyer.

On board *Victorious* we were unaware of this, but from the most humble boy seaman upwards, we were praying for our airmen to prove that their dedication and bravery would avenge Lt. Cdr. Plugge and his colleagues. Subsequent events proved that the loss of the 832 Squadron commander was to have a critical effect on the operation now unfolding. His replacement had not had any practice in this type of situation for over four years—in a peacetime training mode. His inexperience forfeited any advantages which might have been gained by attacking from cloud cover, with a strong wind behind him—thus improving his aircraft speed.

His aircraft, battling into a head-wind and in clear sight of the *Tirpitz*, denied both surprise and speed, were heavily engaged by miscellaneous anti-aircraft fire. Two were shot down almost immediately, others were damaged, and none of the torpedoes found their target. The accompanying destroyer laid a thick smoke screen and the last sighting of the battleship was as she entered the smoke and continued her voyage safely to the shelter of a fjord.

When the remaining Albacores returned, crews de-briefed, and news percolated through the ship of their failure, there was an immense surge of disappointment and depression onboard. The bane of the Home Fleet had slipped through our fingers yet again. Here was a single ship tying up a very heavy force of the Royal Navy, plus aircraft from Coastal Command and the Royal Air Force, and with seeming impunity.

There was, of course, sadness too. More airmen lost. Those ship-board personnel who were in daily contact with the flight crews experienced a type of family grief. The mechanics who worked on the planes to ensure maximum performance, the flight deck crews who marshalled the aircraft into position, saw them leave and welcomed them safely back, supply and stores staff, administrative workers who manned the Fleet Air Arm office.

Plus the other crews, who knew that 'there but for the Grace of God go I'. These men could be forgiven their slight excesses when, missions over, the ship bound for base, they felt it appropriate to over-indulge in drinks and pranks in the Wardroom. When would the next operation dictate their own death, courted so selflessly in aircraft which would not have been allowed on an American aircraft carrier? The contest was manifestly unfair.

We were now being hunted—by the Luftwaffe. A shadowing flying-boat was seen and a flight of Fairey Fulmars launched. These planes were the carrier-borne version of the Fairey Battle, no longer in RAF service, and almost museum pieces. They attacked the German aircraft, drove it off but could not report its destruction.

In fact the shadower had managed to get a radio message away because late that afternoon three JU 88 fighter bombers were sighted approaching the fleet.

Visibility was reasonable by now and I watched with some trepidation as our Fulmars tried to shoot down the three raiders. The Germans seemed quite impervious to the presence of our fighters and came closer. At this point anti-aircraft fire was commenced by most of the ships. The noise was deafening, black puffs of exploding shells blossomed in the sky and slowly spread into thin smoke. Two aircraft broke off their mission but the third, braver and possibly more foolish than his fellows, made an attack direct on us. I viewed this with some alarm, protected only by a steel helmet. Bombs away. I watched them float free of the JU 88 and then lazily arc towards us. Even I, with only nine months in the Navy, could see that his aim was hurried—really more of an angry gesture than a determined attack—and the bombs dropped harmlessly alongside without causing anything but two splendid geysers of frothy white foam, tinged with light brown.

A message from the Commander-in-Chief praising the action of the Fulmars who had protected his ships but not destroyed the enemy was met with a pithily phrased reply from Captain Bovell. 'Thank you, but you can't catch hawks with sparrows,' a message which neatly summed up the difference between our sea-borne aircraft and the German land-based opponents.

It was some indication of the general view on the disparity between the forces that we were escorted part of the way back to Scapa Flow by five Beaufighters of the RAF!

News reached us soon after we had anchored that in the Far East, HMS *Exeter*, of the sinking of the *Graf Spee* fame, HMAS *Perth*, along with cruisers from the Dutch and US fleets had been sunk by Japanese naval forces. In a bitter battle four Japanese cruisers were destroyed but this again was another damaging defeat leaving Java exposed to invasion; possibly Australia itself in the none too distant future. Was there to be no end to the grim tidings?

We remained anchored in Scapa Flow for just over a week. A busy few days, storing, fuelling, aircraft spares and a new type of torpedo for our Albacores. This version, allegedly two and a half times more powerful than the old one, yet only just over one hundredweight heavier. The aircraft stores staff smiled as they winched the weapons onboard.

'A couple of these into the *Tirpitz* and she'll know what's hit her.'

'With a bit of luck she might never know,' replied his companion. They laughed aloud. They also hoped that soon we might have something stronger and faster to deliver the torpedoes.

On 22nd March we sailed again, this time to cover PQ 13, assembling in Seydisfjord, Iceland. *KGV, Duke Of York* and the ever present *Berwick* were with us once more.

I used to have a regular visitor to the Captain's Office, especially in the evenings. At that time the office was usually peaceful, ideal for writing letters or reading the Intelligence Bulletins we used to receive. Lt. Beer, RNR, would sometimes drop in for a chat. He was an Albacore pilot, a pre-war member of the Naval Reserve, called up on declaration of war. Tall, well built, he sported a luxurious beard and presented an imposing figure as he strode about the ship. We occasionally talked of the kind of society we would hope to see at the end of the war. He believed that pre-war Britain was class-ridden and unequal and listened to my stories of poverty-stricken childhood with avid concentration and interest. My parents were solid Labour Party supporters. Lt. Beer expressed no political allegiance, just a perceptive awareness of social injustice.

It was early evening of the 23rd, we were well on the way to Iceland and he popped in the office.

'I'm off on anti-submarine patrol soon. Another boring few hours in miserable conditions trying to find U-boats.'

'But we need you to find them,' I said, 'they're as big a menace as the *Tirpitz*. We also know for sure that they are at sea—just where is the problem.'

He laughed. 'Tonight I'll put your mind at rest. We'll find one, that's a promise.'

He got up from Mac's chair, stretched to his full height, about to leave.

'You look like an advertisement for the pipe tobacco you smoke,' I joked. He was hardly ever without a pipe jammed firmly between his teeth and jutting pugnaciously above his beard. He smiled.

'I'll say cheerio then. Pop in again some other evening.' With that he walked to the door, slid it open, turned, took his pipe from his pocket and put it in his mouth. 'Must be properly dressed for the advert.' He shut the door.

I was still in the office when his aircraft took off on patrol. As it roared down the flight deck it veered slightly to the right and the extreme edge of the starboard wing caught the island structure. The impact pulled the Albacore further to the right, control was lost and the plane careered over the side and into the dark, inhospitable water. Shortly after impact with the sea the depth charges exploded with a violence which shook the ship. The Albacore and its crew were blown to pieces. My bearded philosopher friend was dead, together with his colleagues. I was deeply saddened, the personal cost of the war was so very real. In my three brief months onboard I had witnessed the rank of those intrepid men, the carrier borne flight crews, reduced by 10%. It required an almost fool-hardy courage to be Fleet Air Arm aircrew yet there was no lack of volunteers.

We arrived off Iceland and our destroyer escort went to re-fuel before resuming our convoy protection patrol. With the Convoy under way we steamed eastwards and slightly south to cover the flank exposed to surface attack by the German warships still holed up in their fjord lairs.

The weather deteriorated rapidly. Fierce winds and high seas whipped at a fine angle across the front of the fleet. The destroyers were the first to feel the effects and began pitching, tossing and rolling to an alarming extent. Waves lifted their bows clear of the water for almost a third of the ship's length and, as the vessel plunged down into the ocean, the entire forecastle became submerged and huge cascades of freezing water rained down on the open bridge. Speed was reduced because they could no longer make normal progress through the mountainous seas.

The gale worsened and the sea became a raging tempest, frightening in its ferocity. Ahead of us the *KGV* was rolling, twisting, wallowing like a hippo in a mud bath. Occasionally she would disappear and we would watch for her emerging, shaking herself free of water, from another gigantic trough.

As it reached almost 100 miles an hour the wind began to bring real danger. Our bows, 40 feet high, began to dip into cavernous swells and enormous waves, rising up to 70 feet, thundered over the front of the flight deck. The pressure on the bow plates was intense and each time the ship shuddered, her 35,000 tons almost stopped in its tracks, we wondered what damage we would eventually suffer. Already, in the sections immediately inside the bows, the steel was buckling out of shape. Shipwrights were busy shoring up the plates with strong timbers. Their work conditions were appalling, even frightening as the thunder of the massive waves hitting the bows reverberated around the working space and the rise and fall of 60 to 70 feet produced nausea and disorientation. Water was seeping through as rivets sprang and eventually when the timber props were in place the water-tight doors were clamped closed to isolate that part of the bow section.

There was still an opportunity for that famed nautical humour—the practise of sending signals ship to ship which had characterised the Navy for years.

One of our destroyers, now looking like an Hawaiian surfer riding a huge crest, flashed a message to us: 'Good to see you leaping about like a spring lamb.' An amused Bridge signalled in reply: 'You keep clear or you will get jumped on.'

Aircraft were ranged on the flight deck, armed with torpedoes. Flight deck crews were at full strength on deck, ensuring the aircraft remained secure in the atrocious conditions. These men hung onto chocks and securing lines whilst being virtually torn from the aircraft. Wet and piteously cold they performed heroics. At the forward end of the ship we were equipped with wind shields. These were hydraulically raised and when in position were intended to deflect the wind and protect parked aircraft.

Suddenly, without warning, these massive steel shields were uprooted, lifted clear of the deck and became airborne. It was an amazing but terrifying sight. Had they been swept back at deck level the effect could have been catastrophic. In the event they landed near to the *Duke Of York*, astern of us, like two small missiles. Standing above the Bridge was alarming. At that height those of us up there rolled through the widest arc of anyone onboard. It was dizzying. We were regularly listing to either port or starboard at up to 15°, it was almost impossible to stand. Then came a prodigious list of 21° and I felt we would just carry on over and capsize. The hairs stood up on the back of my neck, my heart seemed to pump to bursting point and my stomach turned to water. Would the roll ever end? Slowly the list began to reverse and the ship returned to its proper attitude. Down below there was pandemonium as lightly secured objects were thrown about. Galley staff were unable to man the cooking ranges, we had no hot food.

I saw Carley floats being swept by on the crest of waves towering as high as our flight deck. The floats had been ripped off the *Duke Of York* which had changed station and was now ahead of us.

Sustenance was provided in the form of 'Kai', the sailors slang for cocoa. It was not Bournville Super Fine or Rowntrees Dark. No, it was made up into thick, almost black, blocks of cocoa and oil. Each block sub-divided into squares. Preparation was to pour boiling water into a mug containing one square and liberally add sugar. Frequently it was made in large, shiny metal cans into which you dipped your mug.

Its scalding, chocolatey sweetness provided warmth and energy. The cry of 'Kai' was always welcome.

Slowly the gale abated and the seas, though heavy, were a distinct improvement. The temperature plummeted and we ran into snow storms, it dropped to 25° below freezing.

By the morning of the 27th, *Victorious* was encrusted in tens of tons of ice. On the open decks by the bow, where the sea was still rough enough to be shipped onboard, it froze as it landed on the deck, ropes, chains and lockers. Soon the weight of the ice became a problem. Unless it was cleared or at least prevented from increasing, it would make the ship top-heavy. It was everywhere. All the guard rails were now four inch thick necklaces of solid ice, gun turrets were jammed—frozen solid—the flight deck was covered by almost a foot of snow and ice. The forecastle was encrusted with ice 15 inches thick. Emergency parties were assembled to combat the threat. Poor old flight deck crews were provided with shovels, brooms and anything helpful, to clear the deck. Piping steam jets were directed at the gun turrets so that they could traverse and elevate. As each became freed it would be fired and so loosen and disperse any ice still clinging to it. The bitter wind was no help and, even though the parties were clad in everything warm they could rustle up, they had to be thawed out below every half hour or so. It was dangerous to place a bare hand on the ship's surface. The intense cold glued your flesh to the steel and in prising yourself free it was easy to rip the skin off. Blisters rose up as though the hand had been placed on a hot stove. Breath was almost crystalised in the air and frost-bite of feet, fingers and ears was a real danger.

The Gunnery Officer and I looked at the scene below.

'God what a run this is Barker. I pity those poor devils in the merchantmen to the north of us and just look at that destroyer to starboard.'

It was decorated like a wedding cake, iced up everywhere. Men held safe by securing lines were diligently chipping, hacking and hammering the ship free of its Arctic dressing.

I had found that my eyes watered in the cutting wind, and as the tears rolled down my cheeks they froze. Worse still eye-lids would freeze closed and this meant a brief spell down the companionway to the Bridge level where the comparative warmth defrosted them. Wearing goggles was helpful but they misted up after a while.

It was pointless to patrol any longer. There was no prospect of operating aircraft, flying conditions were impossible. Furthermore our bows, which had suffered damage in the savage battering two days earlier now required urgent repair.

The fleet turned thankfully south, steamed into Scapa Flow on 28th March, there to assess the total effects of the dramatic Arctic voyage.

It was decided that we should proceed to Rosyth, the Naval Base on the Firth of Forth. A quick examination at Scapa had revealed that the ship was in urgent need of attention.

We passed under the Forth Bridge at 1030 and moored in the dockyard basin just before noon. The *KGV* had sailed with us from Scapa but anchored in the stream.

It is worth recording the experience of Phil Davis, Leading Seaman (Radar). *Victorious* had recently been equipped with Radar, Type 279, the aerial for which stood proud of all other masts. As we approached the Forth Bridge Phil recalls: 'We struck down (lowered) the aerial and I was *asked* to climb to the top of it to see by how much we cleared the under-side of the Bridge. As we neared it, at what seemed to me to be an alarming speed, I had visions of having to hang onto the Bridge and remain dangling until rescued. We actually cleared it by about 12 feet but it seemed very, very close.'

The old battleship *Nelson*, sister-ship of *Rodney*, was nearby, being re-fitted after damage by a torpedo. I had not been onboard a battleship so I took the opportunity to do so. I found her to be oddly dark inside and, by our standards, dirty. Captain Bovell and Commander Surtees would not have tolerated the grime and untidyness.

Rosyth, an extremely busy naval base, located on the northern shore of the Forth, was well placed to offer a run ashore in civilised style. Across the river, accessible by regular ferry was South Queensferry from which it was possible to reach Edinburgh.

George Plant had been to Edinburgh once; I had never seen it. One afternoon we made our way there and headed for Princes Street. To me, at that time, Edinburgh was quite the most beautiful city I had seen. The Castle astride the great mound, the Palace, Old Town with its alleys, minute squares, wrought iron lamps with echoes of Johnson and Boswell. A truly historic city, cultured, well planned, Edinburgh offered recreation and civilised pleasure. In the evening we wandered into a bar which, to me, was the height of sophistication. Discreet lighting, soft recorded music, solid but attractive furniture and tartan lined walls. My friend, older and wiser in the ways of such places ordered two Pimms No. 1's.

This simple, provincial soul was suddenly confronted by a tall glass of lightish brown fluid from which sprouted a miniature allotment. I gazed at it in amazement.

'George what on earth is this?'

'Pimms No. 1 dear boy, it's our customary social tipple in Ludlow.'

'But what is in it, and why the bunch of greenery?'

'Mainly gin, bitters, lemonade, and the jungle, plus cherry, is for effect. Dazzling don't you think?"

To be frank I felt a cissy. A couple of now blooded naval men, recuperating from the rigours of the Arctic, sitting in what could have been viewed as a 'peculiar' bar with even more peculiar drinks.

I was about to say something when George said, 'I say, look at the talent that has just walked in.'

Raising my eyes from the hypnotic Pimms I saw two young ladies, attractive and well dressed. Both were brunettes, one was taller than the other.

'The tall one is mine,' said George, positive and definite.

'How do you know she will even speak to you?' I queried.

'Where have you spent your time Ray? Watch me.'

With that George walked over to the bar where the ladies were ordering their drinks. He was a six foot, ruggedly handsome chap. Curly-ish dark brown hair, strong jaw, aquiline nose, brown eyes and very white well formed teeth.

Immediately he engaged them in conversation and in less than a couple of minutes, armed with two further Pimms, he escorted them to our table.

'Ladies, this is Raymond Barker, colleague of mine, all round good fellow and a volatile deck hockey centre-forward. Ray, this is Yolande (the tall one) and this is Molly.'

The introductions over they sat down. Molly sat next to me.

'My name is Molly Dolan,' in a charming Scottish brogue. 'I live in Prestonpans on the outskirts of Edinburgh. Where's your home town?'

'Lytham St. Annes in Lancashire. It is very near to Blackpool.' I believed everyone had heard of Blackpool. 'But it is much more select than Blackpool—no Pleasure Beach or Golden Mile of entertainments. By the way my ship is HMS *Victorious*, an aircraft carrier,' rather proudly.

'Yes, George told us at the bar.' We remained silent for a short while.

'Your name sounds Irish.'

She laughed. 'I know, both Molly and Dolan, but I can assure you I am pure Scots. There are many in Scotland with Irish names—and vice versa. We Celts and Gaels have moved continuously between the two countries.'

'I suppose you have a girl friend at home,' she ventured. I thought it was rather a direct and personal question on such a brief acquaintance. What should I say?

'Yes I do, her name is Barbara, we have known each other since we were sixteen.'

'What does she do?' Another question.

'She's just gone to do her bit for the war by working in a munitions factory.' That seemed to put a damper on the questions. We then joined in the general conversation with George and Yolande. I could see he was absolutely smitten and she was attracted to him. He had never mentioned if he had any affiliation in Ludlow or Church Stretton.

The radiogram was playing 'Jealousy', a non-vocal version. George and I laughed out loud, we were well aware of a sailor's version of the song, sung oft, loud and long at Flotta. The girls looked at one another, smiled, and adjudged we were slightly drunk. Truth to tell I did feel a littly hazy and light-headed. Nevertheless we had more Pimms and the evening seemed to fly by. The bar was now busy but with very few servicemen. I wondered why the two girls had come here unescorted—was it a regular practice? I decided not to ask as I saw no point in starting up a line of questioning that was really of no great concern to me.

At ten o'clock George announced he was taking Yolande home. Molly looked hopefully at me so I volunteered. It took about an hour by tram and bus and although it didn't matter what time I returned to the ship I was worried about transport. I saw Molly to her door.

'Shall I see you again?' she asked.

'I don't know. Do you have a telephone?'

'No, no-one has a telephone in these flats.'

'Well give me your address. I can always send a telegram. In any case whether I see you again really depends on George.'

'On George?' she queried, seemingly surprised.

'Well he's my friend, and if he is seeing Yolande again maybe we could all meet up.' I was not anxious to get involved, although I didn't mind female

48

company, and would always be prepared to make up a foursome with George and Yolande.

We must have been overheard talking in the hallway for a voice cried out, 'Is that you Molly?' It was her mother from the floor above the hallway where we were standing. 'It's time you were indoors. I was getting worried about you.'

'I'm coming in now, won't be a moment.'

She caught hold of my hand, gave it a squeeze, walked up the stone stairs and said, 'Goodnight, thank you for a lovely evening. It was fun.'

I caught the last tram and by a combination of walking, hitching and the all-night ferry, arrived onboard some two hours later. It all seemed a very long, exhausting exercise just to see a young lady to her door-way.

The following day George, now of soulful eyes and a strange wistfulness, told me he was utterly and desperately in love with Yolande and was meeting her again that night. I couldn't believe that George, wise in the ways of men—and I suspected—women, could be reduced to such a feeble fellow. This was not the George I knew and regarded somewhat of a father figure.

Not wishing to play gooseberry, and lacking any devastating 'love at first sight' that had smitten George, I told him I was not going ashore.

Molly and I exchanged letters for two or three weeks and then the correspondence just petered out. I suppose I was the one who broke off the letter writing, and felt slightly guilty about it, but there was no real purpose to it.

Meanwhile there were reports of a great drinking spot in Dunfermline, 'Dumps' as it was affectionately known in naval Rosyth. I went there one evening. It turned out to be an ice rink, now converted into a massive bar for service personnel.

It seemed like a throw-back to the days of prohibition and illicit drinking dives in Chicago and New York. At the door I was asked if I was a member.

'No. I've only been in Rosyth about four days.'

'Sorry, no admission without membership,' quite firmly.

I turned to leave, when the doorman called out, 'Do you want to be a member?'

'Why yes, if I can.' There had been no other reason for going except to gain entry to the 'club'.

'Show me the back of your left hand.'

Was I hearing correctly, this enormous man was interested in the back of my hand? To count the hairs perhaps, maybe only hairsute hands qualified? I thrust out my arm, left palm downwards.

Quick as a flash the man produced a rubber stamp, applied it firmly to my hand and declared, 'You are now a member, go in.'

I looked at my hand, there was a blue-black impression of blurred script and numbers. As I moved forward a further 'bouncer' asked if I was a member, I showed him the inky flesh.

'In you go. By the way, if you're coming here any other night don't wash that hand. You can't be a member twice!' Could this be true or was I participating in an Irish comic sketch?

Truth to tell when I got inside I could hardly wait to wash my hand. A seething, heaving mass of navy blue uniforms, sailors singing, shouting, cursing; a blue haze of smoke, the sharp acrid smell of stale, spilt beer. As I left, No. 1 doorman said, 'You didn't stay long.'

'No, my friend is not here,' I lied. I couldn't have found anyone anyway.

It was a joy to step out into the chimney-smoke atmosphere of Dunfermline. Resolving never to return I made my way back to *Victorious*.

By now I realised that I regarded the ship as my home, a refuge from life ashore, a cocoon of comparative security in an insecure and unsafe world. Yet those on land were happy they were not at sea. Each to his own I thought.

We had parties of WRENS come onboard to be shown over the ship. I had a group of 20 who wanted to see the Captain's Office, Pay (Ship's Office) and as much of the rest of the ship as practicable. Vertical ladders down into the Engine Room were not considered appropriate—at least by the WRENS. The girls found the visit exciting, it gave them an extra dimension to their work ashore—they could now visualise the conditions under which sailors worked and fought, and especially those who were their opposite numbers in administration duties.

On 7th April we moved out into the Stream and later sailed for Scapa Flow. On the radio the following morning we heard that *Dorsetshire*, which played such an important role in the sinking of the *Bismarck*, had herself been sunk in the Indian Ocean. Almost immediately afterwards news arrived that the elderly carrier *Hermes* had also been lost with *Dorsetshire*. Yet another carrier gone—four now, plus *Illustrious* quite badly damaged. Was our turn fast approaching? There were not many of us left!

Yet when we arrived in Scapa there was a carrier, a stranger to us, the USS *Wasp*, along with cruisers *Wichita*, *Tuscaloosa* and the battleship *Washington*. How clean and spruce they looked, only four months into their war and not having fired an angry shot. We were impressed that the cruisers carried four aircraft each and the battleship six! Swinging and tugging at their buoys they looked like a film set from Follow the Fleet. Bugles blew constantly and orders given by tannoy on each ship drifted into our hearing and were unintelligible. The same language but quite different meanings. We were glad to see them even if their presence on Flotta did cause logistic problems. The American sailors asked for beers and drinks never heard of east of Boston. US warships were totally dry, no rum for the men, no wine and spirits bar for the officers. Just soft drinks, ice cream (ten flavours) and iced water.

At this juncture it is worth recording an incident in the Flotta Canteen. 'Tucker' Carruthers, Stoker, boxer, Scouse, and a friend, were enjoying a peaceful drink—well as peaceful as any drink could be in that place. Over came an American sailor, clearly the worse for drink, jabbed his finger firmly into the chest of 'Tucker' and beerily informed him, 'I am the middle-weight champion of the US Navy.' It sounded like a challenge. Slowly 'Tucker' rose to his feet and without warning felled the American with one devastating right hand cross. He picked up his fallen likely adversary, dragged him outside the Canteen and dumped him in the mud outside. As the American regained a muzzy consciousness he heard the words, 'Well you're not champion now.' 'Tucker' and his friend continued drinking undisturbed.

Once again we left Scapa to cover another Russian convoy. We heard that Admiral Raeder—German Navy Chief—had stated quite categorically that no further convoys would get through to Russia. It was the same old naval formation, two battleships, two cruisers, eight destroyers and *Victorious*. When we arrived off Seydisfjord in Iceland four of the destroyers were detached to refuel and whilst this took place two, possibly three submarines were detected. The four remaining destroyers went hunting and tracking the U-Boats leaving the capital ships, especially *Victorious*, exposed. The *KGV* and *Duke Of York* immediately took up station close in, on either side of us, the theory being that their belt of armour protection was stronger than ours, thus they could withstand a torpedo explosion better than us. It seemed a strange formation but it gave us a feeling of security. Meanwhile the submarine search proved abortive; the 'boats' re-joined us and we proceeded east at a good speed.

We took the convoy to the entrance to the White Sea and then headed home for Scapa Flow. Uneventful is the best description of that operation. We had not been attacked, no aircraft were lost, no shipping sunk or damaged and the convoy arrived safely at Murmansk. So much for Admiral Raeder's boast. However, Naval Intelligence indicated that we should not take his threat idly. The German Navy was now devoting all its resources to the Northern Norwegian ports and fjords. In truth there was nothing else for it to do. The Atlantic was virtually a no-go area, except for its submarines, and the convoys to Russia were bound to increase in size, frequency and importance yet had no alternative but to steam at the speed of the slowest member around the top of Norway. The German Navy's prey was guaranteed if only its ships could get to it. News was also filtering through of a Luftwaffe build up and of submarines forming 'wolf packs'.

The days were lighter for much longer and within two months there would be little or no darkness. The convoys and their escorts could expect round the clock attacks by air, surface and underwater forces.

It was almost midnight on 18th April when we arrived back in Scapa, our American colleagues were still there. The following day some of us went ashore and watched the US sailors playing baseball. It looked like an adult version of 'Rounders' to us. We were invited to join in a 'Soft-ball' session, really baseball with a ball less dangerous than the cricket ball type normally used. It was fun and a distraction from the inhospitable Flotta. We found out much about our American colleagues. Firstly they were paid about three times as much as us, secondly the materials of their uniforms, shirts, shoes, coats was vastly superior, and lastly they seemed more relaxed—the relationship between varying ranks and officers was less formal than ours. We wondered about their discipline under pressure when orders had to be obeyed instantly and without question. Some of us sensed that their informality might lead to querying the necessity of an order. Time would tell.

They looked uncommonly healthy. British sailors, at least those who spent most of their time below decks, had a grey-white pallor, a distinctly anaemic appearance symptomatic of artificial light, fumes, smoke, galley odours, diesel oil smell and the like. In contrast the Americans nearly all sported a faint tan as though they all sun-bathed lightly, but regularly. How could they, we thought? There's no sun and the climate was hardly conducive to sitting up top and getting that weathered look of movie cowboys. We found they enjoyed a further luxury. Due to the lack of port-holes, considered a hazard if damaged, the US ships had Ultra-violet Ray Rooms so that crews could indulge in artificial sunshine and so acquire a tan! We all began to feel very First World War.

As we had played Soft-ball we invited a team of Americans to play us at Deck Hockey. It was not an experience they relished, probably returning to their ship to recover on Colombian coffee on tap, one of their ten ice-creams plus dough-nuts.

For two days we exercised in the vicinity of Scapa with American destroyers. They performed very well and a few days later accompanied us to escort yet another Estbound convoy to Russia.

News came through that a convoy from Murmansk had been attacked, three merchant-men sunk as well as the cruiser *Edinburgh*.

Steaming north-eastwards we ran into fog banks, many of them several miles long. It meant we could not fly aircraft on patrol but at the same time U-boats were unable to see us.

As the fog became more dense we streamed Fog Buoys. These were devices like a dumb-bell trailed about 200 yards astern. As they were dragged along the surface of the sea they threw up a plume of spray. The ship astern was to keep that plume in sight and so know where the vessel in front was stationed.

It was late afternoon on 2nd May, I was having a cup of tea in the office when 'Alarm to Arms' sounded. I grabbed my Duffel coat, binoculars and steel helmet and dashed up to the Air Defence Position. I was curious to know who would be attacking us in this fog—and how. As I arrived I could hear explosions, they sounded like depth charges.

The fog was thick, swirling and cold. It had a freezing clamminess that left beads of ice-cold vapour on eyebrows and eyelashes. I looked down at the water—almost carbon black, terrifyingly evil. There were men drifting by and, as they did so, Carley floats were cut from our Bridge structure and individual seamen threw their life-belts into the water. From their cries we knew the men were British. In no time they were astern of us and out of sight in the heavy dark grey fog. Who were they and what ship? What had happened and were the rest of us in danger too? They can't last long in that water I thought, four or five minutes at the most.

We were still in fog, the muffled 'Whoop, whoop, whoop' of our destroyers just audible.

There was no news from the Bridge and we remained closed up at 'Action

Stations' for about two hours.

Then we heard. One of our destroyers, the *Punjabi*, shifting station, possibly to pursue an echo, had cut across the bows of the *KGV*. In doing so she had been sliced in half and sank almost immediately. Remarkably only 38 officers and men were lost, the remainder of the crew being hauled out of the freezing water in various stages of hypothermia, some already in a coma.

My mind went back to the table in the Canteen at Flotta. Our companions singing loudly the praises of their ship were from the *Punjabi*. I wondered if they had survived.

Yet again we were suffering from self-inflicted damage. Not only had a famous tribal class destroyer gone down, with 38 crew members, but the *KGV* had sustained severe damage.

As we cleared the fog bank we could see a 20 foot gash into her bows. She now had the appearance of a slightly open-jawed, voracious shark cutting through the water.

Fortunately the remainder of the voyage passed without incident and when we arrived back in Scapa the C-in-C moved his flag from *KGV* to the *Duke Of York*.

We spent a week storing, fuelling, generally cleaning up. Many of us were still pre-occupied with thoughts about *Punjabi*, especially those of us who had seen those desperate, terrified faces of the men who had drifted by. The explosions we had heard were from her depth charges, detonating as they sank to the depths for which they had been primed. There was a style about a tribal class destroyer; powerful, aggressive appearance yet sleek and lithe, the epitome of the small fighting ship. They enjoyed exotic names too, *Eskimo*, *Mashona*, *Matabele*, *Zulu* and others, signifying dignity, bravery, self-reliance and courage. Their crews matched this image.

Suddenly we put to sea at 0400 on 15th May; our departure had all the hall-marks of panic. The cruiser *Trinidad*, homeward bound from Russia with PQ 13 had been torpedoed. She had returned to Murmansk, been patched up and departed again to Scapa Flow. This time she was dive-bombed and very severely damaged. Escorted by the destroyer *Amazon* she was limping westwards, we steamed at full speed to provide cover and protection. It was no use, she was a sitting target and a danger to her escorts, proceeding very slowly, gradually shipping more and more water and with a fire still burning just forward of the Bridge. On the following day her crew was taken off and she was sunk by gunfire and torpedoes.

The last convoy we had covered, bound for Russia, consisted of 123 ships—a massive enterprise—and only one was lost.

Nevertheless there had long been complaints about the inadequacy of Fleet Air Arm aircraft—both bomber and fighter planes. Our experience had shown the bombers were too slow and vulnerable as well as carrying a practically ineffectual load; the fighters were totally unable to cope with enemy fighters and, in some cases, bombers.

The Americans had been showing the way. Since Pearl Harbour there had been crucial air-sea battles, waged almost entirely by carrier based aircraft, Japanese and American. The latter had proved their superiority in actions where carriers had been sunk on both sides, the Japanese suffering most. Both fleets were now virtually bereft of carriers as a result of this war of attrition but the huge building programme in the US, mainly of the 'Essex' class carriers, had a spin-off effect on aircraft development. The Americans were now turning out advanced planes, both fighters and bombers, we were almost a decade behind.

We had one visionary Admiral, Arthur Lumley St. George Lyster—not every sailor's favourite—who had persistently and consistently campaigned for better carrier aircraft. With powerful new carriers now commissioned, or in the final stages of fitting out, it was essential to equip them to the highest standard if they were to play a meaningful role in the naval war now unfolding; in particular convoy protection.

Admiral Lyster was the Commander of Home Fleet Carriers. Soon there would be a significant Battle Squadron; *Victorious, Indomitable, Illustrious, Implacable, Indefatigable,* modern, fast, with well armoured flight decks and capable of housing up to 60 aircraft each. But what aircraft?

When Norway was evacuated in June, 1940, the elderly carrier *Glorious* embarked a number of land based Hurricanes, unable to reach England because of fuel problems. These modern, fast fighters landed on *Glorious* without the customary arrester hooks to bring them to a halt. They were brought safely onto the deck by brilliant RAF pilots, proving that such an aircraft with a hook to latch onto the hydraulic wires could be a viable carrier based plane. Unhappily *Glorious* was sunk by a heavy naval unit of the German fleet and so the RAF effort was in vain.

But not entirely, and on 17th May, a Spitfire, fitted with a hook and called a Seafire, had landing trials on our flight deck. Armed with two cannon and four machine guns, this plane would be more than a match for the land-based bombers from Germany and Norway, as well as being able to cope with the fighters it had fought with such distinction in the Battle of Britain.

Standing on the ADP I watched, fascinated, as the RAF Wing Commander approached us. Because of the mid-plane placement of the cockpit it was very difficult for the pilot to see our flight deck on a long run in from astern. Therefore he had to fly the aircraft crab-wise and then straighten up at the last moment. All of us prayed for a successful trial. We need not have worried, the Seafire landed safely, picked up the second arrester wire and was hauled to a halt. The flight deck crew cheered and clapped.

Then the take-off, a circuit, landing again perfectly. Finally the Seafire was attached to our hydraulic catapult on the port side forward and launched off the deck at speed. It dropped immediately it cleared the bow but, as we anxiously scanned the sea ahead of the ship, we saw the aircraft flying, some 20 feet above the waves and almost creating a wake!

We were, therefore, going to have a new fighter in the Fleet Air Arm but, like all compromise solutions, it had its weaknesses. Most of all the fragile landing gear. We would discover over the months and years to come that more Seafires would be written off by heavy landings than ever destroyed by enemy action. Other disadvantages were difficulty of maintenance, its very limited range, a positive handicap at sea when the 'landing field' was mobile and sometimes speeding rapidly away from the action.

The trials lasted two days then it was back North once more for convoy cover. The crew found this duty very wearing, with long periods of boredom occasionally interrupted by brief interludes of hair-raising action. But the work of protection for the life-line to North Russia was vital, especially as the war in that ravaged country was using munitions and equipment at a prodigious rate.

On May 18th we rendezvoued with American ships in Hvalfjord and the following day, whilst on Gunnery exercises, the convoy passed us heading east. There was almost 70 ships, American, British, Russian and French, with an escort of four cruisers, six destroyers and four corvettes. Proceeding slowly, at about 10 knots, they took almost two hours to pass. Every ship dipped its national flag and their crews lined the rails and cheered us! I found it a profoundly moving experience. Here were men, headed for the gates of hell, torment by bomb, shell and torpedo, cheering us for our efforts in trying to protect them. I felt we should have called all available men on deck and saluted them, unsung heroes of many nationalities, some seeing land for the last time, others to perform feats of bravery and courage so inadequately recognised, especially by the Russians.

Back in the fjord we had one day of relaxation before steaming after the convoy. It was a glorious sunny day and I went ashore alone and climbed slowly up a small mountain of about 2000 feet. At the top I found a plateau of thick, green grass which was now warmed by the strong summer sun. I lay down and looked up into the clear blue sky, stretching into ultimate blackness millions of miles in space. What was this life all about? Men clustered in metal containers afloat on an unfriendly sea being maimed and killed by other men in aluminium machines flying in the very sky at which I was gazing. How long would it last? Would I see the end of it? What of my friends onboard, who among them would never see the end of the war? Sitting up and looking about me I saw the rugged, stark beauty of Iceland. Mountains with their snowy mantles glistening in the bright sun, pure clean air free from the pollution of bomb, shot and shell. What manic desire drove men to set man against man with death the only victor? I thought of my father, country-loving Dalesman, wounded three times in the holocaust of the Great War, to prevent me and others like me, ever having to endure something similar. His efforts were in vain, would ours be the same?

Great excitement today. Douglas Fairbanks Jnr came onboard, peaked cap on the back of his handsome head, a nonchalant air about him—ready to swashbuckle with the Germans, I wondered? At least his ship, the *Washington*, sailed with us on convoy cover—two battleships, two cruisers, nine destroyers and old faithful, *Victorious*.

An enemy surface raider was reported north of the convoy. There is a suspicion it is a decoy to draw us from the south and so leave that flank exposed. We don't accept the bait and another small force is despatched from Iceland to frighten the raider off. Meanwhile the convoy was attacked by 40 aircraft from Norwegian airfields but they are driven off after dropping a near miss bomb on SS *Carlton*, fracturing a steam pipe and causing her to be taken in tow. The German effort spent, at least temporarily, we then covered the Westbound convoy.

Tragically, the Russians, who were then to protect the Eastbound vessels, until they reached Murmansk, failed to do so. They had Hurricanes and American built Tomahawk fighters available but, inexplicably, gave the Germans a free hand on the last 100 miles into Murmansk. As a result seven ships were sunk and many badly damaged. A sad and terrifying end for so many of those men who had cheered us to the echo a few days earlier. I felt a depressing sense of impotence. We were to suffer more grievously from lack of endeavour and poor intelligence by the Russians in days to come.

They did not trust us and believed only what they saw. When a convoy arrived in Murmansk they did not accept that 50 had set sail and only 40 arrived. To them only 40 had sailed.

Provisions were scarce in Murmansk and for ships returning westwards they had to accept whatever was available. On one occasion tins of red caviar were provided and eventually appeared on the mess decks. Labelled only in Russian the tins offered no clues as to the contents. One mess complained bitterly that the 'strawberry jam tasted strongly of salted fish!'

The scene was set for one of the most inglorious episodes in the annals of Russian convoys.

We arrived back in Hvalfjord on 29th May; the next convoy was assembling. This procedure could take up to a month as merchant men arrived from Canada, America and Britain. After two weeks of idleness, except for storing and cleaning, we set course for Scapa, arriving on 17th June. Our hopes had been pinned on *Furious* being sea-worthy again. She had spent five months in Philadelphia being refitted and modernised and was now at the end of her second month in Rosyth. It was time for *Victorious* to be relieved, have a minor refit, her hull scraped free of barnacles etc. which caused drag and so reduced speed. No news of either relief or assistance so we stayed on station awaiting to cover PQ 17, the convoy we had witnessed assembling in Iceland.

We left Scapa with *Duke Of York*, *Washington*, two cruisers and 14 destroyers. Vice Admiral Bruce Fraser hoisted his flag on *Victorious* and, for the first time, we embarked a squadron of adapted Hurricane fighters. The convoy, enjoying close cover of four cruisers and three destroyers was now extremely well protected. In all 25 warships were under way to guard 33 merchantmen. This convoy was comprised of fairly fast vessels and the cargoes including tanks, aircraft and other vital war supplies were probably the most valuable yet sent.

This time the Germans made a positive move, their warships left their sheltered anchorages and assembled near North Cape. This fleet included

Tirpitz—our old adversary—as well as pocket-battleships and destroyers. We learned later that their plan to engage the convoy and close escort in surface combat was only to be implemented if the Home Fleet aircraft carriers—that meant *Victorious*—were sunk or put out of action.

At some point we heard that a Russian submarine had sighted the German force at sea, nearer to the convoy than ourselves, and headed for PQ 17 guarded only by its much inferior close escort vessels. The cruisers and destroyers would be no match for *Tirpitz* and her two pocket-battleships.

No confirmation was ever received about the veracity of the Russian report but, acting on this information, the Admiralty ordered the escorts to withdraw and the convoy to scatter. This meant that 33 merchant ships, some equipped with a single gun, were left alone and advised to make their own way to Murmansk as best they could.

The German fleet did sail but it had now no need to place itself in danger. Each merchant ship could be bombed or torpedoed, almost at leisure by aircraft and submarines during the 22 hours of daylight each day. Thus *Tirpitz* returned to port and the systematic slaughter of the convoy began. Only 11 of the 33 ships were to reach Murmansk; the losses of men, ships and material were staggering. This butchery took about four days, by which time we were back at Scapa Flow—having done exactly nothing to aid our merchant comrades.

The mood onboard was sombre; there was a disciplined anger throughout the ship. Why had we left these men to a violent fate—helpless in an action which pitted great strength, ruthlessly exercised, against pitiful weakness, gallantly borne. Somewhere there had been base misjudgment. If the blame lay at the door of the Admiralty why had not the C-in-C Home Fleet challenged the orders he had received and requested authority to move his heavy units nearer to the action? The German battle fleet was ready to risk its ships, surely we could have sailed to a point where the enemy would have been obliged to divert some of its forces from attacking the convoy to ships better able to defend themselves.

A deep sense of shame was prevalent on the mess decks. Yet again we had failed to use our full potential against the enemy.

I doubted whether we would ever again by cheered by merchant seamen. The testing time for that opinion was nearer than I might have imagined.

CHAPTER FIVE

The Santa Marija Convoy—'Pedestal'

On 10th July in company with two destroyers we left Scapa Flow, flying the flag of Rear Admiral Lyster, and sailed down the Irish Sea to Liverpool where we arrived on the 12th. Immediately some of the crew were given shore leave, only three days. It was clear that something important was in the offing. We lay out in the River Mersey for 24 hours, being circled continuously by a destroyer, before moving into a large dry dock, Gladstone Dock. The water was quickly pumped out and *Victorious* was, at last, going to have the long promised bottom scrape.

The reference to bottom scrape leads me to relate one of the hazards of ship-borne life when your vessel is in dry dock. This means that the toilets onboard cannot be used and facilities on shore utilised instead. Those at Gladstone Dock were of a primitive yet radical design. A long row of toilets, brick built and soundly constructed, would be flushed by a continual flow of water running underneath each toilet. In order to facilitate proper clearance of waste, the channel along which the water ran was slightly angled downwards thus ensuring a constant flow. Those in the know would wait until the first, (the toilet from which the water flowed under all the others) was vacant. The occupant would then place two or three newspapers down the toilet, light them and make good his escape. Slowly the burning newsprint made its way to the next toilet, and the next. The agonised shrieks, as backsides were singed, had to be heard to be appreciated. Doors were flung open, men in various stages of undress jumped up and down in a fury of pain, anger and embarrassment. Workers on the ship's open decks, who had seen it all before, found it as hilarious as ever.

I had never been to Liverpool before. The dock area was, in part, devastated. One large dock, Brocklebank, had been virtually vapourised when an ammunition ship, bombed in an air raid, had exploded and disappeared. Burned out buildings, heaps of stone and rubble, patched up roads, repaired tramlines were the symbol of this war torn port. A unique city, a blend of Irish, Welsh and Lancastrian English, it boasted a character of which humour and wit were the prime elements. On the buses, trams, overhead railway, cafés, bars and pubs one heard the English language decimated into virtual unintelligibility but nearly always with a round, robust sense of fun or caustic sarcasm.

We were in dock for five days before sailing at 1300 on 18th July. Torrid romances, nurtured in the security of the black-out, had to be terminated—as ever with undying love and devotion. One old stripey said to me, 'The first turn of the screw repays all debts.' I was urged to adopt that as a philosophy if I found myself romantically 'enmeshed' at any port of call.

Back at Scapa Flow the activity was intense. Stores of all description, more members of the Admiral's staff, and most significantly, tropical gear, was hoisted onboard, along with special boxes of medical equipment.

On the last day of July we put to sea, flew on fighter planes so that we now carried a mix of Sea Hurricanes and Fulmars—24 in all.

All personnel were summoned in regular groups to the Hangar. Here, in a cleared space, the Ship's Doctors innoculated the entire complement. One of my duties was to endorse each Pay and Identity Book with a rubber stamp confirming that the holder had, in fact, been innoculated. Taking advantage of being in the team I had one of the first injections—whilst the needle was still sharp! It was interesting to look at the faces of the men lining up for their jabs. Brawny seamen, muscle bound stokers, lithe and fit flight deck crews, their faces being transformed as they neared the make-shift surgery. Bravado, outright laughter and bold talk gave way to nervous giggles and whispered teasing remarks to the one in front. Every now and then the line would dissolve into temporary commotion as colleagues lifted a fainted friend. Then there were those who, in strong and clear tones, said 'Give me a good one sir'; 'Will this prevent clap, sir?' 'It's my 27th sir'—from an old stripey.

Tropical (white) gear was issued; we were bound for the sunshine and warm water climes. But where? A few of us knew, but in the main, mess-deck gossip was rife.

At this time the situation on Malta had become parlous. Of almost 300 fighters delivered to the island in the past four months less than 100 remained, two thirds having been lost mainly as the result of non-stop bombing by German (especially) and Italian air attacks. It was calculated that at the present rate of attrition the island would be defenceless in about five weeks. Furthermore, the people of Malta were on reduced rations, vastly inferior to those available in the UK.

Convoys from both the East (Alexandria) and the West (Straits of Gibraltar) had suffered severe losses. It was clear that only a massive relief operation from the West, with carriers, battleships, cruisers, destroyers in force, would enable Malta to resist collapse and possible capitulation.

The operation, code-named Pedestal was now under way. This meant that *Victorious* had to be withdrawn from Russian convoy cover and so these convoys were stopped for the next two months. In the light of the disaster to PQ 17 it was not surprising that the Admiralty came to that decision.

On August 1st we met up with *Argus*, an old aircraft carrier, really unsuited for modern war conditions, and four destroyers. The aircraft carried by *Argus* were for 'topping up', to ensure that we had our full complement when we arrived at the position where serious operations would begin.

In Atlantic waters, not far from Gibraltar, the great assembly of ships came together. It was a formidable fighting force. Two battleships, *Rodney* and *Nelson*, four aircraft carriers, *Victorious, Indomitable, Eagle* and *Furious*, seven cruisers and 20 destroyers. Thirty-three warships in all, to accompany 14 especially selected merchant ships—all chosen because of their speed. One of their number was the tanker *Ohio*.

Furious was not to travel with the convoy beyond a certain point in the Mediterranean where she was to fly off about 40 Spitfires who were to make for Malta and so bolster up the defences of the beleaguered island.

Indomitable was a virtual twin of ourselves. Some old sailors regarded her as a likely unlucky ship as rumour had it that she had virtually launched herself and so missed the customary benediction of: 'God Bless this ship and all who sail in her.'

It was very early on 10th August when we passed through the Straits of Gibraltar and into the Mediterranean. There was no doubt that our movement was observed at La Linea, the Spanish near neighbour of Gibraltar, which harboured several intelligence units of the Axis powers.

The plan for the enemy was simple. They knew we were there, why we were there and where we were going. It was a simple matter for both the Italians and Germans to lay ambushes of submarines and minefields, to move aircraft from Italy to Sicily to launch bombing raids on the convoy, and to alert their forces in Tunisia that action was imminent. We were sailing into a series of traps, to be sprung as we progressed eastwards.

Our total fighter aircraft force was about 70, some of which were the obsolescent Fulmars. We believed that the enemy might range as many as 500 or more planes against us, in a series of continuous attacks, allowing us little respite from battle. Had we been in their position we would have so timed our attacks that there would be little opportunity for the carrier planes to re-fuel or their crews to rest.

All this was conjecture, as we steamed east we speculated on when the first evidence of enemy intentions would be revealed.

Spirits were high, here at last we were sailing literally into the dragon's mouth. He was going to throw everything at us in a stand-up fight to decide the future of Malta with its remarkably resilient citizens and absolutely indomitable airmen, ground crews and anti-aircraft batteries. There could be no better choice of battleground or prize over which to fight.

Everyone was alert, at Action Stations, waiting for the first broadcast messages of what was happening or likely to happen. For those of us above deck, at the heart of the Gunnery control and aircraft direction it was essential that we were aware of events as they unfolded. For those in the bowels of the ship, engine room, galleys, damage control centre, hospital, ammunition stores, it was judged proper that whatever information we had should be conveyed to them succinctly, calmly and clearly.

Loudspeaker announcements usually emanated from the Bridge. Occasionally the Capain would speak to the ship's company, usually it was the Commander. Messages were preceded by a call 'Do you hear there, do you hear there.' This to draw attention to the fact that vital information or instructions were to follow; the crew would stop their activities, muster around the loudspeakers and listen. 'Action Stations' or 'Alarm to Arms' (a sudden, unexpected call to Action Stations) was usually anounced by an imperious bugle call which set everyone running to their appointed station.

As the day broke, the weather was perfect. Clear, pale blue sky, sun coming up warm and fast, the water like an ocean pond. As I looked down at the sea, its flat surface disturbed only by the foaming bow waves and wakes of the ships, I thought how inviting it seemed. A deep, aquamarine blue, from which dolphins leapt in playful mood, keeping pace with us and with what appeared to be cheery, friendly faces, glistening and wet. You'll be the only friendly faces we are likely to see I thought.

Oddly enough, Day One passed off quietly. We were in a constant state of readiness, fighters and their crews available at a moment's notice, 4.5 inch guns and Pom-Pom weapon personnel elevating and traversing turrets in simulated defence postures. It was very hot, the only breeze being that created by our own momentum and forced warm air through the ventilation trunking to the perspiring crew members below.

A destroyer came almost alongside and loud-hailed a message to the Bridge. I gazed down at the open bridge of the destroyer. There the Commander was sitting on a swivel chair. He was wearing white shorts, plimsols and what appeared to be a Harlequins Rugby football jersey—the whole ensemble being topped by a steel helmet with CDR white painted on the front. Wondering what Admiral Tovey might have thought, I contrasted his appearance with that of our Captain. There, in the centre of the Bridge stood Captain Bovell. Immaculately clad in freshly laundered, impeccably pressed tropical uniform. His shoes were a brilliant white. He was the epitome of naval style.

It all seemed ominously quiet as we pressed on, the assembly of naval and merchant vessels a brave and impressive sight, perfectly on station, zig-zagging to a pattern in order to make range-finding difficult for U-Boat captains. Those members of the crew who were able to indulge in a breather from the heat below came out onto the flight deck and sunned themselves for a few minutes. The fighter planes were ranged for take-off, aircrews near-by awaiting the call that would herald the flight to battle. The ship was calm yet vibrant with expectation. Soon we would be able to expunge our shame and debt to the merchantmen; this time we were with them. They presented a noble vista, their leader *Duecalian*, upright, solid, fast, carrying food and stores—needed as never before.

During the night we encountered light fog but by the early morning of the 11th it had cleared. The sky once again azure blue, no wind, the sea flat and glassy like an enormous sheet of lapis lazuli. How peaceful and beautiful.

About mid-morning the first enemy reconnaissance aircraft were picked up.

Some had come to find us and report sighting, others would remain to shadow us from a distance. Fighters were scrambled and we heard that those from *Indomitable* had severely damaged a four engined enemy plane. One of our Fulmars crash-landed in the sea, the crew were rescued by a destroyer. Luckily the calm sea was to prove a boon to aircrews obliged to ditch; it also made it very easy to spot the fast, foaming wake of a torpedo.

Before noon several more enemy shadowers were identified, keeping a respectful distance but able to monitor the convoy movement without difficulty. As soon as fighters were despatched to challenge them they made off, only to re-appear when the danger appeared to be over!

I was standing on the starboard side of the Air Defence Position scanning the horizon with my binoculars. My gaze fixed on the *Eagle*, on our starboard quarter, aircraft ranged on her flight deck, looking quite regal and untroubled as she steamed steadily on course. As I watched an enormous column of smoke and water shot into the air; momentarily she was almost obscured then, as her impetus carried her forward, she steamed clear. At this time a series of explosions shook *Victorious*, three or four, and the ship shuddered quite heavily. I could not take my eyes off *Eagle*. She began to list to Port—to the side at which I as looking, and as she did so her aircraft started sliding across the flight deck and into the water. Smoke was billowing out from her twin funnels, she now looked a pathetic sight. The list became more and more pronounced and *Eagle* now lay on her side, doomed. To me it was like a technicolour dream, surely this couldn't be happening. By this time we had put on speed and began to zig-zag more quickly and heavily in case we were in the submarine's sights.

Eagle was now partially submerged and, when she slid under the water shortly afterwards, only some 500 seconds had elapsed after her being hit. The spread of torpedoes had torn the bottom out of the ship and some 150 men died that early afternoon. Mercifully, and probably due to the remarkable conditions, over 900 men were rescued.

Petty Officer Gunner Frank Short remembers fixing his very powerful binoculars on *Eagle*, in particular on one man who had slid down the stern as the ship rolled on its side. The man refused to jump, despite the obvious pleas of his shipmates already in the water. He was still hanging on near the ship's screw when the carrier took him with it into the steely blue depths of the Mediterranean.

Destroyers were milling about in what appeared to be 'wild abandon', depth charges, lobbed into the sea in a slow, deliberate arc, began to explode. The sea surged and boiled as it was rent by continuous underwater detonations.

The sight I now surveyed was so incredibly different from a quarter of an hour earlier that I could not come to terms with it. What had I done since my gaze fixed on *Eagle*? I recall shouting out, loudly, to the Gunnery Officer, '*Eagle*, sir, for God's sake look at the *Eagle*.' It was a cry both of excitement and bewilderment. That great armada seemed invincible. Now one of the carriers had gone, the first 150 men dead. What next? In a strange way I felt detached and without emotion for those men, I was safe and secure onboard *Victorious* and, as a ship's crew, we would ensure its survival—didn't everything always happen to others?

In practical terms we had lost about a quarter of our fighter aircraft, the enemy had struck the first vital blow. The submarine ambush had been sprung successfully.

To those below decks, aware only of the thundering explosions, the surging increase in speed and sharp zig-zags, an announcement was made, calmly and somewhat matter-of-fact that 'Eagle has been torpedoed and sunk, destroyers are busy depth-charging and these are the heavy explosions you can hear.'

It wasn't long before a torpedo was seen coming in on our starboard bow from a position slightly astern of us. A fairly sharp turn to port ensured that it crossed slight ahead—'Hard-over Cecil' at his best.

Within minutes the look-out on my left called out that he could see a periscope—in the glassy sea the feathery wake was very clear. In the knowledge that we would probably be attacked an additional look-out was posted from the port side. Sure enough another torpedo was seen, burrowing quickly, just below the surface on the right hand side of the ship. It slid harmlessly by.

The worrying factor was that despite our escort of 20 destroyers the enemy submarines seemed to be operating with impunity. How many were there? Was this the work of one of the renowned German Wolf-Packs, up to 10 submarines operating as a team to a well rehearsed and clearly defined pattern of attack procedures? We knew that they had wrought havoc in the Atlantic.

As the afternoon wore on cruisers and destroyers kept reporting contacts and sightings. We were well aware what the submarines were after—the carriers. The merchant fleet would be attacked from the air nearer to Malta, meanwhile it was critical for the enemy to sink or disable the aircraft carriers. Furious flew off the Spitfires she was carrying and they made tracks for Malta, now within their flying range.

There was some speculation that she might assume the role of Eagle, four of whose fighters had landed on our deck. This led to overcrowding especially as the Sea Hurricanes did not have folding wings. In the event Furious swung round, turned west and headed for Gibraltar at high speed. I watched her intermittently until, hull down, she disappeared over the horizon. It was now down to Indomitable and ourselves, sisters-in-arms. Would fortune favour us?

We ploughed on. No more submarine alarms, just an uneasy calm we knew could not last. Our exact position was known, as was our course and destination, there were no alternatives for the enemy to consider. Late afternoon turned into a glorious early evening, the reddening orb of the sun was slipping down astern of us and darkness was falling.

The ship was at full Action Stations, some of the men had eaten soup, biscuits, chocolate bars—those of us in the ADP had eaten nothing. Down in the blistering heat of the engine rooms the stokers and engineers, sweat rags round their necks, climbed the hot steel ladders to gain a few minutes relief and drink iced water, laced with oatmeal and salt. Dehydration was a real danger.

Flight deck crews were on full alert. They were probably the fittest men on the ship, sometimes running as much as 20 miles in a single operational day. Pilots in, or nearby their aircraft, waiting for the inevitable call, chock-men lying in the diminishing warmth of the day ready to endure the full blast of turbulence and fumes from their aircraft as the engines revved to full power before they pulled 'chocks away' and rolled to safety.

Pom-pom crews nearby shouted good-natured banter, a little bravado to re-assure themselves and those around them.

Indomitable was the first to launch her fighters; her Hurricanes had been successfully directed by Fighter Direction Officers, listening to information generated by Radar Mechanics sitting blinking before their green screens. Blips indicated aircraft—'bogeys' unidentified, 'bandits' when positively known to be the enemy.

At last our aircraft were started up, the roar of the engines shattering the peace of the late evening languid scene—a picture post-card sunset. It was now darkening fast, the tactics of the enemy were clear. It would be difficult for our fighters to find them in the gloom, and dangerous to land back on the carriers in the dark. Meanwhile the Axis bombers would have an opportunity to attack us in the brief half-dark that preceded total night.

We had heard that some 40 German bombers were in a running battle with fighters but that despite interception and attack by the Hurricanes, some of the enemy were now near the convoy. Quite quickly two bombers appeared on our port side, making their way to our stern so that they could turn and attack us from behind—offering themselves a 250 yard long target. Although the sun had now disappeared there was a residual glow in the sky, only faint, but it was sufficient for us to see clearly the two planes begin their bombing run and dive towards us.

The pom-poms, just abaft the bridge, particularly the one whose crew had been calling out to the flight deck handling party, commenced a rhythmic thud-thud-thud as their eight barrels fired in a pumping sequence. Tracers, armour-piercing, high explosive, a mixture of 2lb shells spewing out at 960 rounds a minute.

Captain Bovell, well aware that we were under direct attack, began once again to exercise his renowned manoeuvres—'hard a port' then 'hard a starboard' as *Victorious* began to snake in the water. I found it amazing that 35,000 tons of ship was so responsive, heeling this way and that and so quickly.

Bombs away. Under the intense blanket of anti-aircraft fire the German planes seemed to wilt in their determination. The bombs fell almost directly astern but short of the flight deck. We felt a slight shudder from the explosions. The bombers themselves were hit, repeatedly, by pom-pom and 20mm guns; the first came down almost to sea level, flew straight very briefly, then crashed into the sea. The second was on fire, a spectacular sight in the semi-darkness, flames flaring out from the fuel tanks before it too plunged into the still calm Mediterranean. Cheers echoed around the ADP, we clapped each other on the back. 'Guns' was smiling and shouted his congratulations down the inter-com to the guns' crews.

Within minutes it was dark and coming home to their base were the fighters we and *Indomitable* had launched earlier. A fighter from our sister-ship was so low on fuel that it had to land on us. Unhappily for him we were still turning into the wind when he came on deck. His plane hit another Hurricane parked near the Pom-pom gun unit which had just performed so effectively, careered sideways into the heavy wire crash barrier and immediately burst into flames. At that point our special fire-fighters moved in. These men, usually two on duty, clad in asbestos suits and helmets with heavy visors, had foam extinguishers to deal with such incidents. It was only a matter of a few minutes before the flight deck was cleared—how splended a team were the aircraft handlers—but two fighters less to face the morrow.

The 'batsman', the officer who stood on a platform located on the edge of the port side of the ship, was now using his fluorescent 'bats' or 'paddles' to guide the fighters onto the deck. If his arms were held aloft, as a 'V' it signified that the aircraft was to go higher, arms held down, an inverted 'V'—drop lower. As each plane came over the end of the flight deck, in a correct landing attitude, he would cross his arms, then uncross quickly to indicate 'cut power'. His was a very responsible duty, occasionally dangerous. He usually had flying experience. Below his platform, and extending outwards was a strong rope net into which he could dive or jump if the aircraft veered off the flight deck towards him!

Some of our aircraft had landed on *Indomitable*, possibly because its Captain had put on his deck lighting system to assist his weary pilots. These lights, about 30 on both port and starboard sides of the flight deck were housed in small steel mounds allowing their welcoming glow to be seen only from the stern approach to the carrier.

It was now dark enough to give us some respite. I looked at the Gunnery Officer, he smiled and said, 'Today has been the easy one, tomorrow we will be for it. You know we have only about 50 fighters between *Indom* and ourselves; the guns will have their share of defending this convoy when daylight comes. Go and get your head down for a few hours.'

He stood down some of the guns crews, it was essential that whilst we remained vigilant throughout the night, the maximum numbers of gunners should be fresh to face the forthcoming challenge.

I lay on my camp bed, fully clothed, having quickly wolfed a corned beef sandwich and hot cocoa, and tried to sleep. My mind was full of kaleidoscopic images—*Eagle* listing over and sliding into watery oblivion, an aircraft becoming a flaming bonfire of death on such a benign sea, the pilot of the crashing Hurricane leaping out of his burning wreck, and the fearsome flare of spume denoting a running torpedo. I was not sure, at 19, whether I was able to accept these incidents within the philosophy of 'it's war'. But then I was no different from hundreds of thousands of others, service and civilian, who had been confronted by extraordinary war-time experiences.

It was just before 0500 when I went back up to the ADP. 'Guns' was there.

Full Action Stations was soon called and, as dawn became full day, we flew off our first patrols.

Our close proximity to both North Africa and Sicily meant that we would be under constant attack before long.

The very early morning brought a success when one of our much maligned Fulmars found a Savoia Marchetti shadowing aircraft which it promptly shot down into the sea.

Not long after 0800 the Radar screens revealed a group of aircraft some miles away and at about 8000 feet. Fighters from *Indomitable*, well positioned above the Germans, attacked approximately 24 aircraft. Some immediately dropped their bombs and tried to make good their escape, two more were shot down and a further two fell to our fighters as they fled for home; it was essential that we were kept briefed so as to know where and when to expect the bandits should they break through the fighter cordon.

As the day wore on the activity was intense. Both *Indom* and ourselves launched and landed patrol after patrol. The aircraft handling parties were working non-stop in fuelling, arming, cleaning windscreens and the like. We knew from the information percolating up from the Radar Room that the enemy was never really off our sets. Not remarkable when considering our proximity to the Axis airfields.

It was not until the late morning that a formation of Italian torpedo bombers appeared low over the water and performed strange manoeuvres which seemed to us like 'you go, no you go' series of feeble attempts to come nearer. Eventually, and to our utter surprise, not to mention theirs, the *Rodney* fired two 16 inch shells in their direction. They caused no damage, but the very gesture of an old bull-dog growling to protect its pups put them to flight. Some wag remarked that 'it might have shaken the weevils out of their bread'— referring of course to *Rodney*.

Sometime around mid-day we were steaming fast into the wind, preparatory to landing on an exhausted fighter patrol. The Gunnery Officer turned to me and said:

'Barker, you were in the Observer Corps, what are those two aircraft on the port quarter?'

I fixed my binoculars on them.

'They look like Hurricanes with an extra fuel tank.'

He looked at them again. 'But we have no Hurricanes with fuel tanks.'

As he finished his sentence they were now amidships on the port side and flying towards us at about 200 feet above the sea and at high speed. The 'extra fuel tanks' were jettisoned and performed a shallow downward arc.

'They are bombs,' shouted 'Guns'.

I was virtually transfixed at the sight of the missiles. The aircraft banked and shot overhead at what seemed like mast level, one of the bombs dropped in the water and exploded causing little more than a modest fountain of water. The second fell on the flight deck, failed to explode and broke into several pieces. The fragments, large and small continued their way across the deck and into the sea near a pom-pom battery by the island. A score had been cut into the armour, to a depth of about half an inch and about five feet long. The Leading Gunner on the pom-pom later told me that he shut his eyes and shouted 'Mother' as the bomb landed. The aircraft were two Reggio fighters of the Italian Air Force.

Alan Belcher, Petty Officer Air Mechanic, recalls: 'Chalky White, RAF Sergeant Armourer and me were in the Flight Deck Party. We were keeping a sharp look-out because of what had happened on the previous day. We saw two aircraft in formation speeding over the fleet and in our direction. We assumed they were Sea Hurricanes because no-one was firing at them. Suddenly "Chalky" shouted "They're not bloody Sea Hurricanes!" As he did so I saw a large elongated object, with tail fins, leave the underside of the aircraft. This "object" quickly made its way towards us. We (and others) plunged face down onto the flight deck and vainly tried to scratch a hole into the three and a half inch armour. The waiting seemed like an age. There was a loud clang, the deck shook, we lay there waiting for a four second delay timed explosion. None came. We slowly got to our feet. Fifteen feet away was a nasty groove where the bomb had skidded and broken up before hurtling over the starboard side.'

I felt I had let everyone down. Observer Corps trained as I waited to go to Chatham, and with a certificate of proficiency in aircraft identification, I had failed to spot the Reggio fighters. The trouble was that in England we were well versed in the head-on, plan and silhouette views of ME 109's and JU 88's but no-one anticipated spotting an Italian fighter over Britain!

Admiral Lyster was not best pleased and let his feelings be known to 'Guns'. I was apprehensive that the displeasure would filter down to me but it didn't.

We began to feel we were lucky, that our crest 'Flying Angel' was indeed a 'Guardian Angel'.

Meanwhile a near miss, very near, had disabled the lead merchantman, *Deucalion*, she was unable to steam at convoy speed, fell behind, eventually lost power and was later sunk by Axis aircraft. We had lost our first charge.

By this time we were only about 60 miles south of the southern Sardinian airfields; the Mediterranean had now narrowed considerably between Sardinia and Tunisia—an ideal position for another submarine ambush.

So it proved. The destroyers were picking up echoes on their ASDIC (Anti Submarine Detection Indicators) and depth charges were being flung from their stern batteries at regular intervals. Suddenly, and within 400 yards of us, the bows of a submarine shot upward out of the water, levelled out and there it was totally surfaced and in full view. One destroyer started firing its guns at the submarine. It was shooting very wildly and without accuracy. Shells exploded everywhere but on the enemy. Others joined in, equally ineffective. It seemed that the gun's crews were so excited, maybe even angry, that they fired in frantic haste. Eventually one destroyer could stand it no longer, she put on full power and steamed directly at the submarine. We watched as she rammed it very hard, almost riding up on top of it. Badly holed the submarine sank in minutes, the last sight like the first, being the bows, but this time slipping back into the water for ever. Some slight revenge for the *Eagle*.

I did not know until later that it was an Italian submarine. Somehow that made it feel less of a prize—it was a U-boat which sank *Eagle*.

The early evening of the 12th August was the time for a determined and concentrated effort by the enemy to sink the convoy and, if possible, its escorting warships. It seemed they had dredged every airfield, within range, of its serviceable aircraft and the force that came out to do battle that evening was composed of bombers, fighter-bombers, fighters, torpedo bombers. There was no doubt we were in for a torrid time.

The various groups were intercepted, some driven off easily, others only after stern and testing dog fights. But the attacking force, however mixed in type, nationality or function was disciplined and well co-ordinated.

Suddenly the air seemed filled with enemy planes and our fighters, wheeling, twisting, diving, turning over the convoy. The crackle of machine guns and cannon could be heard, occasionally tracer fire was seen flashing across the sky. A group of very determined German aircraft broke through the fighter cover and were engaged by anti-aircraft fire from the warships. Both *Indomitable* and ourselves had a light cruiser astern of us, equipped with 10 5.25 inch anti-aircraft guns and other smaller weapons. The carriers had 16 4.5 inch guns as well as the multiple pom-poms and oerlikons.

The JU 87, the German custom-built dive bomber, was a formidable weapon. It had been used to devastating effect in Poland, France, Rotterdam, Dunkirk, Crete and North Africa. It was able to dive almost vertically, dropping on its target like a stone. Eight of these now fell into their dive onto the luckless *Indomitable*.

As I watched our sister ship, on our starboard side and about 1000 yards distant, she became totally enveloped in enormous columns of water and huge clouds of light brown smoke. It was clear that she had been hit, and badly. The sky was a mass of small black puffs, hundreds of anti-aircraft shells exploding over what seemed to be every available square inch of air space. The noise was deafening. The heavy bark of the 4.5's, thumping chatter of the pom-poms and long sustained bursts from the 20mm's.

It seemed like an eternity before *Indomitable* emerged from the smoke and water, on fire and beginning to steam at high speed. Her funnel was pouring black smoke, her deck littered with wreckage and debris.

Over 40 of her crew were killed and more than 50 injured; she was unable to function operationally, her flight deck out of commission. Her aircraft in the air had to land on *Victorious*, we were the sole fighting survivor of the three carriers that entered the Mediterranean those few days earlier. It seemed like light years since we passed through the Straits.

The action was not over. A lone Stuka, its pilot probably seeking the Blue Max medal, attacked us. As he did so he was jumped by one of our fighters and the dive-bomber, ablaze all over, plummeted into the sea.

The Axis attack was now spent. It had lasted almost an hour, had seen feats of

68

great gallantry by our fighters and almost suicidal determination by the German bombers.

Throughout all the action, the merchantmen, except *Deucalion* remained unscathed. Now as night fell on this long, exhausting, frightening, exhilarating day, we left the convoy. It was just over 120 miles to Malta, much of which would be steamed under cover of darkness. In the morning, the RAF from Malta which we had re-inforced, would now be able to provide fighter protection.

In company with *Indomitable* we headed at speed, back to Gibraltar.

Other warships had been sunk; the cruisers *Cairo* and *Manchester* plus the destroyer *Foresight*.

Unhappily the convoy of merchantmen was to be partly decimated by submarine attacks plus determined torpedo operations by fast motor boats, based on the tip of Tunisia near to the point where the cargo ships had to pass. Only five, including the tanker *Ohio* reached Malta; eight were lost in those final 120 miles. It seemed scant reward for the effort and losses involved—but the Island was saved.

The supplies would last over two months, by which time the war in North Africa would swing the Allies way and the seige of Malta be finally lifted.

Onboard there was relief, pride and total exhaustion. The flight deck crews had worked like galley slaves, operating a 17 hour day of pushing aircraft, handling chocks, releasing arrester hooks, fuelling, assisting aircrews, manning starter motor units, striking aircraft down into the hangar then up again. Here, amid the volatile stench of petrol, oil, ethelynglycol; mechanics, fitters, storemen, armourers had sweated off pounds as they worked in the enervating heat, clad only in shorts and sandals. It was reckoned that many of them had run more than 20 miles that day.

There were heroes galore, but none more than the remarkable young men who, flying a mix of three types of fighter, had taken on forces at least five times their number, often with superior equipment, and had emerged victorious by at least three to one in terms of aircraft shot down and lost. This time we had truly played our part.

The 14th August was distinguished by one of our aircraft bombing a submarine and bringing it to the surface—whereupon it bombed it again. It disappeared. We never knew if it was mortally damaged. *Victorious* rattled and shook as we thrashed westwards at high speed to reduce our vulnerability to submarines. The weather was still perfect.

It was 1600 on the afternoon of the 15th when we arrived at the mole in Gibraltar. There we embarked about 500 survivors from *Eagle, Manchester* and *Foresight*. By coincidence one of the survivors I registered onboard from the *Manchester* came to work with me in Thomas Cook some nine years later.

We left Gibraltar to return to Scapa Flow where we arrived on 21st. Just before passing through the boom defences all of the crew not required for anchoring duties had to line both sides of the 250 yards long flight deck. We steamed slowly past the *King George V, Anson, Kent, Suffolk* and *Renown*. As we did so the latter's Royal Marine band played 'Here the Conquering Hero Comes' and all the ships, with their crews lining the rails, standing on gun turrets, cheered us to the echo.

We felt humble and embarrassed. My friend Les Vancura, our deck hockey goal-keeper, wrote in his diary, 'I felt so very sheepish.'

I went on leave, the first since joining the ship just over eight months earlier. I had left home a youth, returned a man.

Sitting with my fiancée in the cinema in Lytham I saw part of the convoy story unfold on the News Reel; it suddenly seemed unreal after three days in this leafy, seaside backwater of Lancastrian gentility. The audience cheered and clapped as the chauvanistic tones of the commentator spoke of our 'brave boys against the dastardly and treacherous enemy'. Thus ended 'Pedestal'.

CHAPTER SIX

'Torch'—North Africa Landings

Quite a lot of work was being carried out on *Victorious*, new emergency lighting generators developing 150 hp, more escape hatches in crucial areas and extra fire-fighting systems and equipment. I assumed that these steps were initiated as a result of the sinking of *Eagle* and severe damage to *Indomitable*.

We learned with sadness of the sinking of the *Wasp*, our erstwhile US carrier companion, torpedoed in the Pacific and sinking in five hours. The US Navy was now critically short of battle fleet aircraft carriers, so many having been lost in the Midway and Coral Sea battles.

It was 21st September when we arrived at Scapa Flow once more, this time at 0330. A vast amount of stores came alongside, it seemed as though we were being set up for a lengthy period at sea.

Over the next few days we carried out more Deck Landing Trials with the Seafire and Grumman Martlet. The latter, an American aircraft, small, like a stubby cigar, also possessed a relatively weak under-carriage.

We also received a new aircraft to replace the Albacore; the Fairey Barracuda. When it first landed on it was greeted with amazement, amusement and not a little astonishment. This torpedo bomber, more than five years in the making, looked less like an aircraft and more like a kind of flying Meccano model. Single in-line engine, high wing profile—broken by the cockpit—tail fin adorned with tail planes, strutted from the end of the fuselage almost to the top of the tail fin. It was assuredly designed by a committee. Was this to be our weapon of vengeance? None of us, and few of her aircrews ever believed it.

Yet the Barracuda would prove to be both famous and infamous as the months and years passed by.

The weeks progressed, constant Deck Landing Trials, Speed Exercises and Gunnery Shoots. One day 'B' Turret of four 4.5 inch guns shot down a practice Drogue—towed behind an aircraft—and the Captain ordered that each man be given 5/- reward.

Great excitement on the Mess Decks, word had got round that Winston Churchill was coming to see us. He arrived, accompanied by Sir Stafford Cripps, the Lord Privy Seal and Mr. Alexander, First Lord of the Admiralty.

The ship's company was assembled and Churchill with his penchant for dressing up, wore a naval peaked cap, with a tiny Trinity House badge, and a short Naval greatcoat. There was an entourage of Admirals. He gave us a pep talk, spoke of our 'valiant and glorious deeds' on the Malta Convoy, and reminded us of how much remained to be done to rid the world of the 'Nazees' and Japanese aggressors. New and daunting tasks lay ahead but he knew that drawing inspiration from our Naval forebears we would triumph and bring greater glory to the Royal Navy and Fleet Air Arm.

It all went down very well and the old man was cheered to the echo.

Yet more exercises, this time with *Biter* and *Avenger*, two of the new light fleet carriers based on a merchant ship conversion.

We sailed for the Clyde, wondering slightly about the efficiency of our Seafires as carrier aircraft. During the exercises with the 'Woolworth' carriers, as we called them, three had crashed on landing, ruining undercarriages and bending propellers.

The run to Greenock was punctuated by yet more 'working up', this time around the Isle of Arran and Kyles of Bute. Many of us just gazed at the magnificent scenery as up to 200 aircraft covered a Combined Operation Commando exercise. The wise-acres nodded sagely; there was going to be an invasion somewhere and we were to be involved. The messes buzzed with rumour and speculation.

Looking about it was the only logical conclusion. The Clyde had a large assembly of troop carriers, all full, and we had 61 aircraft onboard—our greatest number ever. Stores were everywhere onboard, even replacement mainplanes were lashed to the sides of the hangar because the deck-head storage was full.

On 30th October at 1330 we got under way; in company with *Formidable* and some of the new Escort Carriers. Ahead of us had sailed the troop ships previously anchored off Greenock. The game was truly afoot.

We were joined by old 'friends', *Rodney, Renown, Duke Of York*, cruisers and destroyers. There were those onboard who predicted another Malta convoy, but when challenged as to why the Island needed troops and not supplies, they fell into sulky silence. In any event we didn't have to wait long before the familiar 'Do you hear there' presaged an announcement from the Captain.

He said we were going to Gibraltar, that most of the rest of the Fleet would put in there, but we would carry on into the Mediterranean whereupon 'our movements would depend on events.'

This vague information would have been better left unsaid. There was gossip about invading the South of France, Sicily, somewhere in North Africa. I felt the crew should have been told clearly what our intentions were. They were well known in the Cypher Office—where all who worked did so under an oath of secrecy. As we were not going into Gibraltar there was no risk of the information being whispered outside the ship—it was too fanciful to think we would be sunk and survivors captured.

Clues kept mounting up. We were going into heavy action, grab lines were being rigged up all over the ship—in case we were to take on a heavy list these would facilitate movement about the vessel. Food dispenser points were being erected at various strategic places in case we suffered damage to the Main Galley. All the messes were crammed with tinned food, up to a week's supply and any provisions below the water line were brought up and restored above it. All water-tight hatches above these now emptied store rooms were firmly and permanently closed. Some of this had been done for the Malta Convoy but on a much smaller scale.

Horror of horrors—the roundel markings on our aircraft were being replaced by the American Star symbol.

The ship's radio disseminated BBC World Service news and as this spoke of the great offensive in the desert it was assumed on the mess decks that we were bound for the Eastern Mediterranean to give support. Back to the submarine ambushes and through 'E' Boat Alley off Tunisia's Cap Bon. Sailors have a tendency to predict the worst possible scenario—they then feel charged up if it materialises or relieved if it doesn't!

Every amateur prophet and strategist was in his element, even the 'card' and 'tea leaves' readers were busy predicting the future—consisting mainly of 'dire events' as we 'steamed into the jaws of the enemy'. I had many a wry smile. Of course I was interrogated, in a casual, almost disinterested fashion, as to my views on the situation but declined to be drawn.

We were not in the Mediterranean at this point, but cruising off French Morocco awaiting for the massive force to be assembled before proceeding through the Straits.

On 5th November, Captain Bovell told the ship's company that an invasion of North Africa was to take place, landings would be made at Oran and Algiers by both British and American troops. We would be deployed, as Force H, as a covering force to protect the invasion fleet from attack by Italian or French surface vessels. He went on to say it was probable we would be no further than 20 miles from Algiers to give constant air support to the sea-borne landings there.

We could see the lights of Tangier and Ceuta at 0530 on the morning of the 6th, as the huge assembly of shipping slipped into the Mediterranean. We later learned that some 400 vessels were involved in the greatest invasion fleet ever gathered. It was an incredible sight.

We wondered what the on-shore Axis spies were making of this. Perhaps they too were reading cards and tea leaves! Gibraltar itself was a gigantic airfield with every square inch of space given over to planes, both British and American.

All day long on the 7th we operated fighter patrols whilst the invasion vessels were assembling into their planned groups ready to launch the landings in the early morning of the following day.

By this time we had been seen by enemy aircraft but they gave no indication as to their intentions—possibly waiting till they could be sure of ours. The weather was warm and visibility good.

It was now less than five hours to Zero Hour and we, together with *Formidable* were stationed some 80 miles off the North African coast.

One look-out shouted that he had spotted the wake of a torpedo on the starboard side. No-one else confirmed his sighting, it was noted but not regarded as positive—maybe just nerves. We were on full alert in the ADP but nothing further suspicious was observed and our tiny Radar, with a 9" screen, and in my charge, was clear. More importantly, the large sets located down below and manned by fully trained men, were also clear. My set was housed in a small shelter, partially roofed to provide some shade so that I could see the 'blips'. Above the set was a large perspex display panel. The ship was considered to be the 'dot' in the centre of this panel and the circles and lines which radiated outwards represented bearing and distance indications. Anything I picked up on my set I placed as a small 'X', in chinagraph pencil, on the plot, moving it closer or further away as the 'blip' indicated.

'Guns' would pop his head under the shelter, read off the bearing and distance of aircraft. Beside the 'X' I would write A10 (Angels 10—10,000 feet) or whatever was appropriate. I would plot them until visual contact was established. The range of my set was about 15 miles, give or take a couple. This was a technological leap of gigantic dimensions—so we were told—but woe betide if a glimmer of sun got onto the screen.

The 'escort' carriers were positioned off Algiers and Oran, and as dawn broke news began to filter in that troops had landed successfully although some fierce resistance was encountered from heavy gun emplacements and forts.

One of the tasks allotted to our fighter aircraft was to patrol the two airfields near the Algerian coast and especially that of Blida, 20 miles or so from Algiers. These airfields were manned by Vichy French forces; one of the reasons we had changed our roundels to stars on our aircraft—the French roundel being virtually indistinguishable from the RAF and Fleet Air Arm markings.

A pilot of the second flight of Martlets, despatched to neutralise any flying or opposition from Blida, witnessed a number of military personnel waving what seemed to be a flag of surrender—a large white piece of cloth. After reporting back to us, and circling the airfield whilst a decision was being made as to the wisdom of allowing him to land, he was finally given permission to do so. The remaining three aircraft of his section were instructed to give close cover in case of any treachery. It had to be remembered that many French were embittered by our bombardment of Dakar when heavy casualties were inflicted on French servicemen.

Thus, with some trepidation, but with a sense of history—it was rare for an airfield to be captured by an enemy aircraft—the Martlet landed.

On taxi-ing to a standstill, and sliding back his cockpit hood, Lt. Nation was handed a signed document of surrender. It was a strange situation. Here he was, a single member of a vast Allied force, performing the role normally reserved for a dashing tank commander breaking through the perimeter fence and, by sheer bravado, forcing an enemy surrender.

Not surprisingly he again radioed back to *Victorious* to seek yet further advice. Told to sit tight he did so until a Commando unit arrived to take charge. Whereupon he flew back to us.

Meanwhile our old Albacores were dropping 250lb bombs on troublesome forts and gun emplacements still holding out.

The afternoon was busy but peaceful. Aircraft were taking-off and landing on in rapid succession. We had been at Action Stations since 0200, the flight deck crews were exhausted—their work was immensely physical and required deep stamina and resolve.

Escort carriers *Argus* and *Avenger* now moved very close to the Algerian shore and we took up position about sixty miles off. *Argus* received a bomb hit, not severe but enough to prevent flying operations for at least 24 hours. We had escaped scot-free. Until dusk, when many of us, bleary eyed and with positive hunger pangs, were thinking of sustenance and a nap. A small group of JU 88's approached us. They didn't seem to have the heart or the determination of their colleagues who plagued us in August, but one broke through and made straight for us. He was met by a curtain of anti-aircraft fire, pressed on resolutely and dropped his single bomb nearby.

'Guns' believed that the weight and strength of our gunnery, plus its accuracy, created so many problems for enemy airmen that they could not sustain their attack at its crucial moment—bomb release. Hours and hours of practice and drill paid dividends and *Victorious* was renowned for its anti-aircraft capability as well as the bravery and dedication of its flying crews.

We stood down as darkness fell and resumed Action Stations at 0500, as dawn was about to break.

Our aircraft were now almost fully engaged in providing support for the army onshore. It was impossible for the RAF to do so as they had no fuel reserves available at the captured airfields and Gibraltar was too far away from which to operate successfully. Unhappily the Seafires and Sea Hurricanes were very prone to self-destruct on landing. Time and again heavy landings wrecked undercarriages and aircraft skidded along the flight deck on their bellies and into the crash barrier. We were writing planes off at a rate which would have delighted the enemy.

It was unjust to blame the pilots who were so remarkable in their dedication to the Fleet Air Arm that they accepted, without question, equipment which was manifestly unsuitable. The sturdy little Martlet, robust and carrier friendly, coped well with continuous operation but we always had the feeling that an accident was in the offing with the Seafires.

As another day passed, without incident to the main fleet, it was clear that the landings had been a complete success. There would be no surface confrontation from the East—the Italian fleet was not renowned for seeking battle—so we turned west and headed for Gibraltar.

The escort carrier group had not been so fortunate and we heard with regret of the sinking of the *Avenger*, less than 20 men saved out of a complement of 800. The frailty of these vessels had been demonstrated yet again.

The Germans had not been inactive over the previous five days and a submarine force had been assembled to cover the western approach to the Straits. A fierce battle between destroyers and U-boats ensued over the next few days. A Dutch destroyer was sunk, four submarines reported destroyed plus one discovered beached on the North African coast.

Within a short while of our arrival in Gibraltar the destroyer *Marne* came in with her stern blown off. A stores ship *Hecla* was torpedoed and the destroyer *Venomous* claimed to have sunk four submarines within two days.

When we left the Rock the battle was still at its height and we steamed East for a couple of hours—in an attempt to mislead the watchers in la Linea—before doubling back and proceeding at high speed out of the Mediterranean and into the Atlantic.

Off the Bay of Biscay, and only two days from the Clyde, yet another submarine was found. This time by one of our anti-submarine patrol aircraft. Bombs were dropped, the U-boat surfaced badly damaged. It was scuttled by the crew and the destroyer *Opportune* picked up the entire crew except one. The German Kapitan, Hartwig by name, in post-war years became C-in-C of the German Navy. It was his lucky day to be captured and spend the rest of the war in safety in Canada.

All in all some ten German submarines had been accounted for; they, in turn, had sunk *Avenger, Martin*, a Dutch Destroyer, *Hecla* and severely damaged *Marne*. The encounter off-shore had taken more lives than the invasion of North Africa itself.

Captain Bovell broadcast his congratulations to everyone onboard. Listening to his precise, clipped tones it was impossible to detect he would be leaving us at Greenock. He had been appointed Captain when *Victorious* was still a Dockyard Job No. in Newcastle in October 1940. During his two years the crew had found him an efficient, fair, somewhat remote Captain.

Reading Les Vancura's diary on Operation Torch, his abiding memory was not of odd bombs, anti-submarine successes, deck crashes, long hours without proper food, but 'Went ashore at Gib. today 17th November, tried to get a silk dressing gown and or pyjamas but the troops had cleaned the shops right out!' Righteous indignation.

My own was of standing, head under my shelter, looking at my mini-radar screen and then at 'Guns' also staring at the 'Tube'. Our faces a sickly green. 'Hell's bells Barker, we look like a couple of frogs.'

It was 28th November when Captain Bovell left us. The Marine Band formed up on deck, played 'Auld Lang Syne' and he was rowed ashore in the Ship's whaler, our cheers ringing out as it pulled slowly away.

Commander Ross recalled, 'I joined *Victorious* in the Clyde. I found myself facing a pretty tough Admiral (Lyster) and a Captain (Bovell) who had never seen me before and wanted somebody else. Yet inside a couple of weeks everything changed. Away across the world, in the Pacific, the Americans had been losing carriers quicker than even they could build them. President Roosevelt appealed personally to Churchill for the loan of one. It was to be *Victorious*. Away went Captain Bovell and Admiral Lyster. Command of the ship was taken over by the finest Captain you could ever want—my old friend and shipmate Lachlan Mackintosh.'

CHAPTER SEVEN

'USS *Robin*'

We now had a complete change of senior command. Our new Captain, Lachlan Donald Mackintosh, the Mackintosh of Mackintosh, Chief of his Clan, and now to be our 'Chief'. Our new Commander, Richard Cyril Vesey Ross—a character, as time would reveal. To those of us who had only experienced Captain Bovell and Commander Surtees, the change was to be remarkable.

At the time of his appointment we were not to know that Captain Mackintosh, who had been in command of the *Eagle* as I watched her sink on the Malta Convoy, had been selected for his diplomatic skills as well as his undoubted other abilities. All would be revealed in due course.

Our stay in the Clyde was marked by frantic activity of storing and de-storing. One had to determine from these clues what might be afoot. For example we had sent all our Rolls Royce Merlin engines ashore—clearly we were not going to carry Barracudas. Added to which about 25 tons of miscellaneous stores—some, very suspiciously, not fully labelled, were housed in the hangar.

The remainder of the hangar space, now clear of aircraft, was decorated with Flags and bunting to welcome 150 Wrens coming onboard for a Dance, music courtesy of the Royal Marine Band.

Despite our being in a British port and obvious to all ashore, it was an offence to either telephone home or post letters ashore. Mail to us was nearly always addressed c/o Royal Naval Post Office and that was our address until advised to the contrary. The temptation to post a letter ashore was hard to resist—after all who would know? Occasionally members of the crew did so—it avoided having letters censored.

A very close watch was kept at Greenock in case anyone had deduced from the various clues what our destination might be. My friend Les could not resist posting three letters—to his beloved Beth—he was especially anxious that they reach her as quickly as possible as they were at the point of having the banns for their marriage called for the second time. His letters were intercepted and he had to be punished, probably in front of the entire ship's company, 'pour encourage les autres'. At that time he was a Leading Stores Assistant; his obvious punishment would be the loss of 'rate' to Stores Assistant. This would also incur loss of pay and he would not be able to apply for re-instatement for at least six months. So it proved, it was my melancholy task to record his punishment at Defaulters. The lower deck was cleared, the charge read out, the punishment announced and indignity and ignominy heaped on his head. 'Van' was the most loyal, dedicated and hard working man on the ship; he was also very popular and everyone was sad to witness his public humiliation.

In the event it was not difficult to work out our probable destination. Various personnel, including a few civilians, started arriving onboard. Their documentation, on occasion specific destination orders, were processed through the Captain's Office. I was handling papers for individuals destined for Washington and New York. Clearly we were not bound for South Africa.

Captain Mackintosh, maybe as a consequence of Les Vancura's misdemeanor, recommended we all write home and tell our wives, sweethearts and mothers not to worry if there was a gap in the mail. He was stretching the rules somewhat—I could not have imagined Captain Bovell making such an announcement.

Quiet discussions among my close friends resulted in the conclusion that we were bound ultimately for the Pacific. Just a year after Pearl Harbour the US Fleet was boasting only one fully operational aircraft carrier—the *Saratoga*—the *Yorktown* having been lost on the 30th September. It was our reasoned view that we were being seconded to the US Navy, just as *Washington* had worked with us out of Iceland.

Those others, who believed that we 'were in the know' used all their naval guile and wit to persuade us to give them the 'gen'—an RAF expression for information, which was now common currency onboard.

We sailed on 20th December, and that evening Captain Mackintosh told us we were making for Bermuda. As there was an area of the Atlantic off that island, known as 'Torpedo Junction' there was some slight apprehension. But thinking back only six weeks, with U-boats almost as numerous as dolphins in the Gibraltar Straits, shoulders were shrugged, palms outspread and 'so what' was the now considered response. There were in fact at least 40 U-boats, grouped in packs, strung across the Atlantic to intercept convoys and troopships. It was the hey-day of submarine warfare and they wrought terrible havoc in the central area of the Atlantic which was the least subject to air patrols due to the distances involved.

The Captain was a profound personality change from Captain Bovell. He was less formal, had a wry sense of humour, and communicated more readily. In a broadcast on 22nd December he told us we were 300 miles off Iceland, there was going to be a heavy storm, subs were everywhere and we should wear our life jackets at all times. The penalty for not wearing a life jacket was 'drowning'. There was thus the prospect of sea-sickness and a possible swim in the Atlantic. A straw poll revealed a marked preference for the former.

The weather had indeed deteriorated and, at times, it was difficult to see our escorting destroyers. Rumour now had it that we were Pacific bound—so 'Jolly Jack' had reasoned it out. Still no official word.

On the day before Christmas Day the gale was consistently recorded at 95 mph. The ship was being battered unmercifully. Most of the Galley staff were ill, the combined effect of the heaving and rolling of the ship and the smell of food and oil in their confined workspace.

Volunteers were called to help bring up the Xmas Puddings from the stores. One wondered if anyone would be eating them. The effect of the constant accentuated movement was very debilitating. Apart from the stomach-wrenching emptiness at the rising and plunging, the problem of maintaining a proper balance as the ship also rolled and cork-screwed, brought on headaches and nausea. There was a sullen, suffering, silence onboard; everyone hoping to witness an improvement soon.

The destroyers were undergoing absolsute torment, almost halted at times by the enormous seas. Continuous shipping of water meant that conditions onboard were atrocious, the crew working and resting in wet clothes and eating cold, tinned food.

There was a slight respite on Christmas Day. The gale dropped to 50 mph and the galley staff were able to operate again. It was remarkable what they produced in the conditions. Dinner was Tomato Soup, Roast Turkey, Ham, Roast Potatoes, Parsnips and Peas, Christmas Pudding. We had a 20lb+ Turkey between 29 of us and 'Taff' our messman performed brilliantly as carver. There was a sing-song with marvellous Welsh voices, and the choruses leavened by those non-vocalists who had been saving their rum and were now in full, discordant voice. ·

The Captain popped his head in for a few minutes, wished us a 'Merry Christmas', laughed when such destinations as New York, Pacific, even Panama were called out. 'You'll be wiser on New Year's Day,' he said.

Our escorts were running short of fuel, the wretched weather having resulted in a heavier consumption than normal. On Boxing Day the decision was made to attempt to re-fuel them from *Victorious*. At the same time, now in mid-Atlantic we commenced anti-submarine patrols by aircraft. Landing back onboard was fraught.

On the 27th, with the seas still running fairly high, we attempted to re-fuel the destoyer *Redoubt*. For some time we ran parallel but just too far distant for the fuel line to be passed from ship to ship. Eventually a determined effort was made and as both vessels edged towards each other a heavy swell took control. The fuel line was carried away and *Redoubt* bumped firmly into us, or us into her. Standing in the ADP I could look straight down the destroyer's smoke stack. Her crew, in oilskins, gum-boots and roll-neck jerseys were being drenched—yet again. Momentarily she became slightly entangled in our radio masts, which projected horizontally from our flight deck, and a catastrophe seemed inevitable. Slowly, and with a great display of seamanship, *Redoubt* cleared our side and re-fuelling was called off. As a result we had to proceed at reduced speed to conserve oil; this increased the danger from submarine attack.

Once again our bows had suffered slightly, our most vulnerable part of the ship when steaming head-on into huge seas.

By the 29th December we had begun to receive American programmes on our radio. Most of us had never heard a radio 'commercial', except perhaps those who were 'Ovaltinies' with Radio Luxembourg.

We were amused and intrigued to discover that I V O R Y, Ivory, was the 'soap that floats'. Do you spend half your bath time looking for the soap? Get Ivory, it floats right into your hand!

Morning was also 'Griffin time to shine', the best shoe polish in the US would be ours when we arrived at where-ever we were to dock on that blessed land.

The following day we anchored off-shore at Bermuda. It was ten o'clock in the morning, all our meat was unloaded—this to avoid the possibility of our importing 'foot and mouth' disease into America.

The water, almost emerald green, was as flat as a pond.

As an indication of the attitude of the new regime, we heard an unusual pipe on the ship's system. 'Hands to bathe.' In no time sailors, marines, airmen were diving off the Boat Deck, Weather Deck and a few intrepid souls—like my friend 'Van', off the flight deck. Men were bobbing about and splashing like dolphins. The reason, mainly, was the icy cold of the water. Well, not icy, a fresh 51°. It was impossible to believe that not so far back east was a raging tempest.

Our arrival brought out every curious islander, and visitor, to see us. All kinds of craft were circling—motor boats of all sizes, yachts, large rowing boats and even a couple of small seaplanes which landed on the water nearby and just sat looking at us.

Their inspection period was relatively brief for at 1600 that day we weighed anchor and set course almost due west. As we headed directly into the pale, watery winter sun we knew for certain our destination was the central eastern seaboard of the USA, maybe Norfolk, the giant Navy yard and base.

All personnel were told, in a broadcast by the Paymaster Commander, who always said, 'Pay attention to this broadcast—it will not be repeated!', that from now on our currency was the US Dollar. We would be paid in dollars until further notice and at the rate of 4.25 dollars to the £.

The Captain then told us we were proceeding to the Navy Yard at Norfolk, Virginia, and from there to go elsewhere to form part of the US fleet. We would have extensive modifications; in particular more defensive weaponry would be added. Our Albacores would leave us. We would be supplied with Avengers—which we called Tarpons—a fine torpedo-bomber, especially designed and constructed for carrier operations.

On New Year's Day we sighted the US coast early in the morning and entered the estuary of the Elizabeth River. As we proceeded up river we were cheered by Ferry boats, ship's sirens and whistles were blown, flags waved. All the while our Royal Marine Band played American tunes and marches. Our Albacores had taken off, one with a bicycle strapped to a wing, we mused on what the Americans might think of that! The crews would eventually return with new aircraft. We later learned that their arrival at the Naval Air Station was greeted with amusement, amazement and not a little outright laughter.

Looking for all the world like predatory grass-hoppers, and not much more effective, they seemed like a footprint in the sands of time to the Americans.

At 1800 we moored at the Navy Yard not far from the new US carrier *Essex*, the first of an entirely new class, nearing completion. By the time the war ended there would be as many as 48 of these vessels.

On the morning of 2nd January, each member of the crew was given $10 until we could arrange for a much larger supply of dollars to be obtained. The first personnel went ashore at 1600 and headed for the Naval Canteen a short distance away.

The difference between that establishment and the Canteen on Flotta could not have been more marked. Instead of being almost permanently awash with spilt beer, and with visibility impaired by a thick tobacco fug, this place was spotless. We had all noticed that America smelled of cigar smoke, not heavily so, but just the pleasant, rich aroma of a decent leaf, probably Cuban, and smoked by hundreds of people—even dockyard workers.

There was another smell too, the sweet, syrupy scent of Coca-Cola—of which we had never heard. Ice cream with up to 25 flavours was available, but who would risk Pecan, Maccademia and Maple? With the 'Limeys' ashore there was a very predictable run on Vanilla, Strawberry and Chocolate.

The on-shore cinema had a different film every night and entrance was about 5d.

Then there was no black-out. As soon as darkness fell the lights blazed on, coloured neon, flashing signs, floodlights in the Dockyard where the work never ceased. It was indeed the New World. On the jetty there were stalls selling waxed cartons of milk—what no bottles?—Honey Dipped Doughnuts and Hershey chocolate bars, just in case the night workers needed a little extra sustenance.

Within a few days an Avenger was hoisted onboard so that measurements could be made for new mooring rings to be welded onto the flight deck. The Avenger looked a formidable aircraft, able to carry a 21" torpedo in a bomb bay, up to four crew, including two gunners, and with an extra 270 gallon fuel tank enabling it to fly for up to 16 hours! Unheard of.

The people ashore were remarkable, always wanting to talk, to offer hospitality, to be friends. The 'Jolly Jacks' found the Drug Stores amazing. With not a drug in sight, but refreshment of all kinds. One had to learn about 'Sunny side up', 'Over easy' when ordering fried egg, 'grits' tasted just as translated into English. It was living on a film set and waiting for Mickey Rooney and Judy Garland plus friends to come bowling in.

We were now allowed to write and say we were in the US—not where exactly—just America. Letters were going air mail, we presumed via Iceland.

Serious work now started on the ship and we went into a Dry Dock. To ease the pressure onboard—there were hundreds of workers all over the ship—leave was arranged.

The USO had liaised with 'Bundles for Britain' movement to offer hospitality to British sailors. There was a choice of going to Washington, New York,

Baltimore, Richmond, Lynchburg or Charlottesville.

Three of us, George Plant, a colleague named Bill Monteith, a quiet rather dour Scot with a wry wit and a banker's caution, and myself, elected to go to Richmond.

In the event we were the only three to do so, many having decided to seek the bright lights of New York. We caught a train, mis-named the 'Cannonball Express', after a deal of negotiating for return tickets. Our terminology was as foreign as Greek and eventually we left the Ticket Hall with a Round Trip ticket.

On arrival in Richmond we made our way to the 'Bundles for Britain' shop. There was a queue outside; we were delighted that so many people wished to donate bundles for our homeland. They were not there for that purpose at all—they were waiting to offer hospitality to the host of British sailors due to arrive.

We went inside the shop and announced ourselves.

'Are you the first to arrive?' asked the lady in charge, smartly dressed, rather too many jewels I thought.

'No,' I replied. 'I'm afraid we are the only ones.'

There was utter consternation.

'But some of these people have been here since 7.30 this morning, what am I going to tell them?'

'You could say that there will be another group due in three or four days and that we are the forward party.'

She looked unconvinced.

'I don't suppose you three want to split up do you?'

'Not really, we came as a trio and would like to remain so.'

'Don't you speak real nice. So different and so clear, like Ronald Coleman types in the movies.'

We stood embarrassed. Bill had not spoken, I doubt she would have been able to understand half of what he would have said.

'Well I will just have to tell the folks that more will be coming out next week and they should be here early. The USO office will let us know when your friends will be arriving.'

We nodded in agreement. We were going to be 'allocated' as a three-some.

'I think you should go with Mr. and Mrs. Cliff Weil; they were the first here this morning and I know they are able to take all three of you.'

At a sign, Mrs. Weil stepped forward. Dressed in a heavy fur coat, head-scarf and fur boots, she introduced herself.

'I'm Lizzie Weil, call me Lizzie. This is my husband Cliff, and this is our chauffeur James.'

Cliff, about 5'6", thin, with sharp features and bright eyes, was immaculate in a Navy blue cashmere top coat, shiny black ankle boots and a dark Homburg type hat. He took off a glove and shook hands with us. As we gave our names, Ray, George and Bill, he said 'Call me Cliff' and took a pull on an enormous cigar held in his gloved hand.

He spoke to James, 'Take these gentlemen to the car. Don't drive too fast as I will be driving behind you.'

They had come in two cars. Maybe one wasn't large enough for the Weils, chauffeur and we three. I couldn't have been more wrong. Parked nearby were two enormous Cadillacs—his and hers—and James took us to the farthest one. It was like a small, luxuriously appointed coach. Cocktail bar, iced water dispenser, foot rests, rugs and an electric dividing window between the driver and the main seats.

James, in a very dark grey uniform, was black. Shiny skinned, tall, with laughing eyes, deep voice and warm Southern accent. He told us that his wife Bessie was the cook and that there were two house-maids.

As we glided clear of Richmond, with Cliff and Lizzie in close attendance, James told us that 'Mr. Weil is a senior Vice-President of a large tobacco company, and Mrs. Weil does a lot of good work for the poor black folk in the area.'

By now we were being driven down a magnificent tree-lined avenue and past houses like small mansions. We turned into a drive and eventually came to the Weil's residence. Large, colonial style, with marble pillars, it looked like a film set. As the two cars stopped at the front door Bessie and the housemaids, all in uniform, waited to greet the Weils and us.

We were introduced all round, Bessie just looked for all the world like a prototype for the film cook who bounced piccaninnies on her lap whilst watching pumpkin pies cooling on an enormous kitchen table.

There was an air of homely luxury about the house. Heavy, dark American furniture, bright chintzy covers and curtains, thick carpet and total comfort.

We were shown to our rooms. We each had a bedroom with its own private bathroom. On my bedside table was an envelope with 'Ray' written on it. Inside a welcome note and $100 in $10 bills. I wondered how my name got onto the envelope. I could only assume she had telephoned from the 'Bundles for Britain' shop.

At dinner that evening I was intrigued to see that we three had knives and forks but our hosts only forks. I had not known that Americans, many of them at least, do not use knives. They watched us with some interest as we ate using both utensils.

Cliff told us he would be taking us on a pre-arranged programme of excursions. To Richmond to shop, to Yorktown and Williamsburg for sightseeing, and one evening into Richmond to go to the cinema with three nurses who had volunteered to be our companions. No wonder this man is a Vice-President I thought.

We had an incredible three days and my memories are a kaleidoscope of remarkable hospitality, the soft beauty of Virginia, the pride in historical and so well-preserved Williamsburg, the fantasy of shopping in Miller & Rhoades store, and the kindness and courtesy extended to us everywhere. In the Departmental Store we were taken from counter to counter and asked 'to say something'—like a 'pome' or 'recite the British Oath of Allegiance'. This was a problem. I only knew two poems, The Highwayman by Alfred Noyes and

Tewkesbury Road by John Masefield, plus the first verse of The Hound Of Heaven by Francis Thompson. Bill weighed in with a piece of Robert Burns, never understood but loudly applauded. It was truly amazing, as though we were visitors from another planet. Yet deep down these people acknowledged that their roots were represented by we three from the old country and were truly fascinated by our presence.

When we left the Weils to return to *Victorious* Lizzie took our home addresses and every month from that day on my mother received a food parcel. They wrote regularly to one another until Lizzie died in the late 1960's, Cliff having died some years earlier.

We returned to *Victorious* with boxes of cigars and a bottle of Jack Daniels, as well as packets of candy and chocolate.

Two other members of the crew had a different approach to their brief leave. Tony Sagar and Roy Harris looked at a map of the Central East Coast area of the US. Tony picked up a pin, spun around, closed his eyes and plunged it in the centre of a Cherokee Indian Reserve in North Carolina. They debated on whether to try again, but no, fate had decreed and they would observe.

They had to choose a town both as a place to stay and a spot they could reach by public transport. Ashville was the nearest to the pin-prick, so Ashville it was to be.

Comprehensive research revealed that coach travel was the most convenient and economical. At the Bus Station they went through the familiar one-way, round-trip routine; single and return was Martian language to the ticket clerk. The tickets were a remarkable testimony to the fact that the US had a surplus tree problem—each ticket being almost two feet long, to be worn around the neck rather than carried!

There were three passengers on the coach when Tony and Roy boarded. Two middle-aged ladies, blue-rinsed and with diamante-studded spectacles, and a be-medalled US Army sergeant, immaculately clad in finest olive-green serge uniform, knife creases in his trousers, an advertisement for military sartorial elegance—but he was black. The coach driver, brawny, short-necked and blessed with supreme sensitivity towards his coloured brethren, shouted 'Hey Buster, back seat for you.' The sergeant continued, untroubled, to read his 'Life' magazine.

The driver put his hand on the soldier's shoulder, it was brushed quietly, but firmly away. This simple act of preserving the smart neatness of his uniform acted as a catalyst for confrontation. The driver abandoned his coach, only to return a few moments later with a denizen of the law, a Broderick Crawford look-alike, who, brandishing his revolver, advised all onboard—the ladies, Tony and Roy—that the coach would not leave until the sergeant sat in the section reserved for non-whites. The ladies, to whom this was obviously a daily occurrence, remained oblivious to the scene about them. A policeman, an apoplectic driver, two foreign sailors, a drawn gun—an explosive situation. Prodded by the revolver the sergeant moved to the back—followed by Tony and Roy who, in expressing sympathy for the soldier, were now sitting in a 'nonwhite' section. This was as offensive to the driver as the sergeant sitting in the white area. He ordered the coach to be cleared and to be re-boarded in 'accordance with State Statutes'. This time everyone sat in their designated area and the coach moved off.

Stops were made at 'comfort stations' to enable those onboard to go to the lavatory. These facilities usually housed a 'flasher', slyly opening his long overcoat to reveal a flask of whiskey; it was prohibition territory.

Almost 22 hours after departure from Norfolk, the coach drew into Ashville. It was six o'clock in the morning, pitch black and pouring with rain. The intrepid duo made their way along Main Street and came across a club for members of US Forces. They rang the bell, no-one answered, and then stood in a quite luxurious, brightly lit hall. A sign, pointing towards a downward flight of stairs, indicated baths and toilet facilities. In true US traditions these were quite magnificent. Baths, showers, lashings of hot water, soap, clean towels, after-shave and towelling dressing-gowns. After bathing, shaving, and annointed with fragrances, they returned to the Reception Lounge. Still no-one in sight. Finding two comfortable settees they stretched out and fell sound asleep.

Roy was awakened by something cold, hard and hurtful, pressing into his neck. It was a revolver, held in a large, threatening hand of an officer of the law. Another policeman had his gun firmly pressed into the nape of Tony's neck. At this point it has to be understood that British servicemen had not been encountered previously in Cherokee territory; the rumour was rife down Main Street that two German 'spies' had been discovered in the US Forces Club. Our two heroes, still held at gun-point, then produced their Pay Books and Station Cards—they were British, allies in the Great Cause, defenders of freedom, far from their homeland, offering their skilled services and battle-gained experience to the American people. The atmosphere was transformed. Guns holstered, hands shaken until arms ached and fingers felt crushed, backs slapped, welcomes proclaimed. No greeting was more tangible than the mountain of food which suddenly appeared—ham, eggs, 'hash browns', 'grits', fruit juice, coffee, toast. Life had taken a pronounced turn for the better.

Months earlier, a Mrs. McGuire, British born but married to an American, had advised the Centre that if any British servicemen should, by some amazing mis-chance, visit Ashville, then she must be advised. And so it was. The said Mrs. McGuire appeared within minutes and announced to all and sundry that Tony and Roy were her personal guests for their entire stay.

Mrs. McGuire was in business. She ran a large private hotel. It was currently home to some 80 evacuees from Washington—a 'danger' area—all were female, aged between 18 and 25, and engaged in Government administration. Could this be true? Two handsome, well-spoken British sailors, in their mid-20's, at their physical and intellectual prime, unwillingly thrust upon 80 ladies, lonely, away from home, seeking mental stimulation, trans-atlantic charm and possibly physical comfort. It was the stuff of Hollywood—if only Roy could dance like Gene Kelly and Tony sing like Frank Sinatra.

The car that took them to Mrs. McGuire's was roomy enough not only for them but for many of the 80 females too. By the time they arrived at the hotel the local radio had announced their arrival and advised Ashville citizens to give them a real Carolina welcome.

Mrs. McGuire drove them to the local Fuel Officer—there was petrol rationing of a sort. This official had total domain over who had what fuel and the purpose for which it might be used. He listened to Mrs. McGuire and then issued a written permit, part of which read, 'Can obtain fuel for and can drive the two British sailors to any place she damn well pleases.' So much for fuel rationing.

Radio interviews were arranged. Tony, actor and raconteur, was a sensation. His suave, cosmopolitan style charmed the locals to the extent that everyone wanted to be a part of this remarkable event. Invitations poured in, back to back, two hours at a time, during which Tony and Roy were passed from host to host to host. Steaks, oysters (the aphrodisiac properties of which could have been invaluable had the boys been permitted the company of any of the 80 young ladies at Mrs. McGuire's), pumpkin pies, Budweiser beer—these exotic delicacies were thrust upon them at each and every location.

Photographers were everywhere, even taking pictures of the 'peculiar manner' in which these Englishmen used their knives and forks—the skill employed in utilising both at once was digital dexterity at its highest level.

Tony, in his thespian element, fortified by food and alcohol, recited long excerpts from Lear, Richard III, Julius Ceasar and Macbeth. Hosts and their friends were enraptured, shouting their delight and pleading for more. As Roy recalls: 'I have seen and heard Shakespeare many times but never before recited from the top of a beautiful polished dining table by an actor holding a plate of oysters in one hand, a large glass of beer in the other, and at four o'clock in the morning!'

One of the dates arranged for the duo was with a pair of sisters of the Vanderbilt family. What an honour, an assignation with two of one of America's dynastic families, a brush with North American wealth and culture, a glimpse into the lives of the surrealistically rich.

A magnificent chauffeur-driven car was placed at Tony and Roy's disposal. The appointment was for 2000 hours until midnight. The car drew up at the magnificent porticoes of an enormous southern mansion—the drive-way had taken almost 10 minutes to traverse—dead on time. A uniformed flunkey took them indoors and, in the time-honoured manner, announced their arrival.

One of the sisters aristocratically enquired, 'Which of you creeps is my date?' When they heard the cultured response from Tony, the other sister graciously asked, 'Jeez, which corn cob did you guys crawl out of?'

It was not surprising that the susceptibilities of our two sensitive sailors were offended and they remained at the mansion for only two hours of the allotted four.

Roy and Tony were 72 hours in Ashville during which time they never went to bed. They were handled like extra-terrestial visitors who looked human, spoke an odd version of American, and had to be seen and heard to be believed.

The visit ended in an alcoholic haze of physical exhaustion. There is no recollection of the journey back to Norfolk. Roy vows to return to the scene, acknowledging that it can never be the same. He looks upon the episode with much joy; his most profound recollection being of Tony taking the inhabitants of Ashville by storm with his excerpts from Shakespeare, rendered in his immaculate English accent. 'It could never happen again,' he says, 'but it did once, I was there and regard it as a most remarkable experience of American generosity and hospitality which I shall never forget.'

Our experiences were not unique; they were replicated by those who went to Lynchburg and Charlottesville. What remarkable, open, generous and kind hosts the Americans turned out to be.

Back at the ship we noticed various changes—even in four days. The stern end of the flight deck, formerly curved and known as the 'round down' had been almost straightened. A battery of 20mm guns was ranged across the width of the stern. Bofors guns, 40mm, were being installed everywhere there was a space, the arrester wires were strengthened to cope with heavier aircraft.

On shore a favourite recreation for many of the brightest chaps onboard was to go to the USO Club and make up a British Quiz team to play against an American foursome. Night after night they won $10, free meals, stationery and pens, chocolates and candy.

Those who had been to New York regaled us with tales of their adventures. 'Van's' notes read: 'Went to Radio City Music Hall where we listened to a Philharmonic Orchestra, watched a Ballet, a stage show with the famous "Rockettes" dancing chorus and then saw a film. At midnight we went to the Stage Door Canteen—there was Katherine Hepburn, Edmund Gwen, Al Jolson and Monty Woolley. The following morning we caught a ferry to the Statue of Liberty, climbed up to the Torch, met Les, came back and strolled up Broadway, bought a wedding ring (had to guess the size, they have numbers not letters) then went to see Sonja Henie skating in "Icecapades" '—New York was well and truly done!

January slipped into February. Oddly enough we were now anxious to get to sea again. *Victorious* was now bristling with armaments, stored to the hilt. Everyone was broke—some in debt—there was so much to buy ashore. Lockers bulged with presents although no-one knew when we might be able to give them.

Gunnery and Flying Trials were held as we sailed in Chesapeake Bay. The latter were proving very difficult and troublesome. We now had to adopt the US landing signals—and these were the exact opposite of ours. The uplifted arms of the Batsman now indicated not 'go higher' but 'you are too high' and arms down 'you are too low' not 'drop lower'. Additionally the landing technique was vastly different. Whereas the Fleet Air Arm employed a nose up, low speed almost level approach, the Americans would fly flat at about 40 feet above deck level, cut the engine and drop onto the deck. We gasped as we watched planes almost plunge down, shaking the aircraft and crews almost to destruction as they thudded against the armoured deck.

Small wonder we had accidents and the loss of both pilots and aircraft was very distressing.

On 3rd February we steamed out of Norfolk and south towards the Bahamas. Everyone had been innoculated against Yellow Fever so obviously we were en route for the Tropics.

One day out and we practised 'Abandon Ship'—now renamed 'Boat Stations'—is nothing sacred we thought. We were confidently told that *Victorious* would list to 50° without sinking—a prospect which did not fill us with untramelled joy!

A week after leaving Norfolk we arrived at San Christobal at the Atlantic end of the Panama Canal. It was here that when a US battleship enquired of our identity she was informed we were the USS *Robin*. A likely story with the White Ensign flying proudly from our mainmast!

CHAPTER EIGHT

Pacific Mission Number One

The Panama Canal presented a slight problem. We were too wide to go through the locks! The minimum width through the three sets of locks was 110 feet. With overhanging sponsons and other appurtenances we were wider than this. Two days were spent burning off and removing these obstacles. No shore leave was permitted, both Colon and San Cristobal having dubious reputations for safety and security.

The mess decks were buzzing with rumours about 'the Pacific' as well as chatter about having seen the coast of Cuba, shoals of flying fish, sharks and a first sighting of the Southern Cross. Few of us believed this. We were told we were using 180 tons of water a day, or 23 gallons per head, and that care had to be exercised.

The NAAFI shop was filled with fruit—oranges and apples being 1d each. 15,000 bananas were taken onboard as the storing party joked about monkey food.

On the 13th February we got under way and headed for Gatun Locks. We took on a Pilot, several officials, and, strangest of all, a number of US marines who stationed themselves in the Engine Room. Each lock had 12 'mules', electric beasts of burden. Six on either side of the ship, the forward ones pulling and the aft mules holding us back if we moved too quickly.

It was inevitable that we should cause damage, both to the lock-sides and other equipment. With about 12" to spare on either side it was an extremely delicate operation. It took more than four hours to get through the first set—each set contained three locks.

There was a deal of Spanish swearing and many a sailor's vocabulary of oaths was widened extensively that day. We anchored for the night in Gatun Lake, 165 square miles of water and small islands, teeming with alligators and water snakes. A few hopeful matelots appeared in bathing trunks, eager for a tropical dip. A couple of beefy Marines armed with both alarming information and weapons had no problem in dissuading them. It was a quiet, steamy night, with the odd jungle cries and howls.

At 0600 we were away, sailing 23 miles across the Lake to the renowned and infamous Gaillard Cut. An 8 mile channel carved and hacked through a mountain, this Cut cost thousands of lives when the Canal was constructed. It was here that the French engineer De Lesseps, builder of the much simpler Suez Canal, quit and it was left to US engineers to complete the Canal and commandeer the land on either side to ensure safe passage for their vessels sailing from East to West coast ports and vice versa.

By 1400 we had successfully negotiated the Pedro Miguel and Miraflores locks and tied up at a pier at Balboa.

The following day we were allowed shore leave. Before-hand was a lecture to the ship's company by the senior doctor onboard. He vividly described the evils and ravages of venereal disease and recommended that 'those unable to resist the urge' should attend Sick Bay and collect a 'preventative'. There was a queue.

As the sailors jostled at the top of the gangway before proceeding ashore, the Master at Arms read out details of 'places to be avoided'. This was, in fact, the Red Light district of Panama. The names of the streets were instantly burned into the memories of those who had queued at the Sick Bay. As they boarded the buses for Panama City you could hear them shouting 'Does this go anywhere near . . .?'

We were not allowed to take cameras ashore so there was a brisk trade for the post-card sellers.

I found old Panama interesting and attractive. It was fascinating to recall that the town had been sacked by Captain Morgan, Welsh-born pirate and brigand of the seas.

During our two days in port the various sponsons and overhangs which had been removed at San Cristobal were replaced. It was in the late morning of one of these days that a US Marine officer presented himself at the Captain's Office. He had an envelope containing a message for Captain Mackintosh and would await an answer. The envelope was taken into the Captain's Day Cabin. He looked at the message. It was, in fact, an invoice for damage caused to the locks as our vast bulk was hauled through. Several thousand US dollars. He smiled wryly, wrote 'LEASE LEND' in capital letters, signed it, and replaced it in the envelope. The Marine officer accepted it, departed, and we heard no more.

At 1230, on 18th February, we left Panama in company with three brand new US destroyers; sleek fast, well armed the *Bache, Converse* and *Prindle* were to be our escort to our destination—PEARL HARBOUR. As we sailed clear of Panama we had simulated attacks by Aerocobra aircraft and Mosquito Boats (almost an equivalent of the German E-boat).

For two weeks we sailed WNW to the Hawaiian Islands. We carried out regular flying exercises and suffered some unfortunate accidents because the arrester gear was still unable to cope with halting the very heavy Avenger if it picked up any of the wires more than a quarter of the way along the deck.

Now we had an American 'batsman'—Lt. Tommy Thompson. He was known as 'Mickey Mouse', often sporting clothing with that cartoon character's likeness on it. He also had a wide and varied range of headgear. He was extremely popular because of his technical expertise and thorough outgoing friendliness. His was the most difficult task onboard, after all he was using contrary signals to the Fleet Air Arm batsmen.

The tremendous pull exercised by the Avenger on the arrester wires, and their failure to stop within a short distance, led to new procedures such as lowering the first crash barrier as soon as a hook caught a wire, so as to lengthen the stopping distance. It was not a long term solution and Pearl Harbour would need to provide one.

The weather was benign, many of the crew slept on the open Boat and Weather decks, some, especially flight deck parties, slept on the flight deck. Excitement was intense as we neared Pearl Harbour; after all was not this group of islands once British, did it not still sport the Union Flag in the corner of its own, and did not Captain Cook make an impression here—albeit by being killed by the natives. We felt certain they would be more friendly on this occasion.

Two days before arrival one of the American liaison officers onboard gave us a talk about Pearl Harbour—Ford Island where we would moor alongside—about local transportation and the local curfew. All shore leave ended at 1800 each day and there was a Black-out! Gas masks were being carried by some servicemen and civilians!

It was 4th March when we arrived off Oahu and steamed slowly past Waikiki Beach and Honolulu before tying up at a jetty alongside the air station on Ford Island. There were crowds of US servicemen on the banks, thousands of them cheering and waving. A large naval band played the Hawaiian welcome music plus as many British tunes as it could cull from its repertoire.

The jetty was teeming with US sailors, all frantic to get onboard and see this 'Limey flat-top'. Hundreds of them were soon swarming all over *Victorious*. This was the relaxed regime of Captain Mackintosh and Commander Ross, both very skilled at PR as well as their naval duties. The Americans I spoke to were fascinated by the Pom-pom batteries and the three and a half inch armoured deck. US carriers had a thin steel flight deck with a wooden planked surface. This gave a resilient platform for landing aircraft but offered virtually no protection against even fairly small bombs.

Just onshore was a Canteen, another marvel of US logistics. It featured a Beer Garden, Swimming Pool, souvenir and clothes shops, candy store and soda fountain.

Honolulu was seven miles distant by bus after taking a free ferry from Ford Island. Looking round the smiling, and in many cases, tanned faces onboard I sensed that we were going to enjoy our stay at Pearl.

Our first mail for six weeks arrived onboard. Sacks and sacks littered the gangway by the Regulating Office. As soon as it was distributed a curious silence fell on the ship as news from home was eagerly assimilated. There were even Christmas Cakes—having braved and withstood a 10,000 mile journey, parcels, cards and a few 'Dear John' letters, the recipients of which were sometimes to be found pouring out the stories of broken romances to the Padre, or Sky Pilot as he was known. Our address was now c/o Naval Post

Office, Washington, USA and a new letter type, called a 'V' Mail, single sheet self sealing air mail letter form, had been introduced for our use.

Commander Ross recalls an important development on the question of naval dress. 'When we started working with the Americans I was very much impressed with the neat appearance of their everyday uniform. What we called Working Dress had always been a problem. We were then wearing "whites"— our tropical gear—or those ugly, untidy blue overalls. The Americans didn't like our wearing white at sea—they said it made our ship more conspicuous at night! One day alongside Ford Island, I sat at my desk and wrote a report to the Captain headed "US NAVY FORM OF WORKING DRESS', describing their neat, well cut blue jean shirts and trousers. To make a long story short, the Admiralty quickly approved of our being fitted out with these garments for trial—then eventually the whole Navy got them. And now? Well just look— everyone from Royal Princesses to the Gas Board man seems to wear the identical rig and I sometimes wonder if it all really started with that report of mine which Captain Mackintosh sent from Honolulu.'

One day six of us went into Honolulu, including George Plant, RPO Tucker, PO Rogers and the NAAFI Manager. People stopped us in the streets, shook our hands, took our photogrpahs, yet again asked us to speak, and offered hospitality. We took a bus to Waikiki, sat on the beach by the Royal Hawaiian Hotel—like a pink palace—and savoured the good life. I wondered if Bill Webb would now change places with me!

A couple of days later I stood on the flight deck and watched the *Oklahoma* being raised; only the *Arizona* remained as evidence of the treacherous Japanese attack, and we were told that it would remain a tomb for the many men who died when she sank. A very tall, about 6'5", American civilian approached me. He told me he was a Naval Architect, very interested in the ship, would I show him around and explain certain things. I told him I was hardly qualified to point out the merits and de-merits of our naval constructors, but I would be happy to take him round. His name was Basker, Hal Basker, his mother Betty came from Hull, his father was a Californian. I showed him as much as I could and he invited me to spend a week-end at his family's beach cottage. As there was a Curfew I could not accept but I requested Captain Mackintosh's permission to do so.

'Is the object of this exercise furtherance of good Anglo—US relationships?' he asked.

I was not slow to grasp the significance of his question. 'Indeed sir,' I replied.

'Then I believe you are doing a very good job in that direction. You have my permission to take a week-end leave at the Basker family home. Leave the address at the office of the Master-at-Arms.'

It was arranged I would go the following week-end. Meantime the crew were having a marvellous time, eating, drinking, shopping, swimming, sun-bathing. But above all the shopping. This extract from Les Vancura's diary:

'Today I bought two blouses for Beth, plus a head-scarf and a small shell necklace. Another necklace, wooden, for June, a handbag for Beth's Mum, wallets for Charles and Harold, and two pram pillow cases for Elaine and Jane!'

In those days I was a 'swing band' fan, as were many young men. Dorsey, Goodman, Ellington, Herman—but my favourite was Artie Shaw. On 19th March, Lt. Cdr. Artie Shaw and his Band came onboard *Victorious* and gave a two hour Concert. Absolutely stunning, with the favourites 'Frenesi', 'Traffic Jam' and 'Begin the Beguine'. There was a five minute ovation at the end. A troupe of Hula-hula dancers kept the temperature high, whirling, swirling, gyrating in their grass skirts. Sailors were shouting for scissors and boxes of matches, one enthusiast a 'lawn mower'!

The war seemed a million miles away. Trips were arranged to prevent boredom. There were coach journeys into the mountains, a visit to the 'Dole' pineapple plantation and factory. I didn't know that pineapples grew out of the ground! They sent a ton of pineapples to the ship, everywhere smelled of them. Civilians onshore were intrigued by our short sleeved shirts and shorts—we had not yet obtained our denims—and many a restaurant refused payment for meals or drinks.

The dockyard staff were working 24 hours a day. We had never seen such a disciplined, productive work force. They concentrated on the arrester wires, our armaments and safety measures. All the 'cortesine' was stripped off our decks, all carpets and rugs removed. The inflammable enamels and paints were burned off and our stores cleared of any non-essential flammable material. Our defensive power was now 65 20mm, 22 40mm, 48 pom-pom and 16 4.5" guns—we believed we were the heaviest armed carrier afloat. At this time our impression was that we were being prepared for something big and probably rather nasty.

The hospitality went on. I had my week-end at the Baskers; their 'cottage' was a four bedroomed, four bathroomed bungalow on the edge of its own private beach! Hal and I went out regularly in a small, dug-out canoe, from which he would dive, disappear, emerging what seemed to be minutes later with an octopus. This he threw into the canoe where it wriggled and writhed to frightening effect. He swam like Johnny Weismuller. It was an unforgettable two days in every way. (He came to see me in London and Marlow in 1950 and 1956, then disappeared without trace.)

As the days went by we regularly went out for the whole of daylight to test the new equipment. The new arrester wires, only 11/16ths of an inch thick could now halt an aircraft weighing up to 20 tons. They were ideal for the Avenger.

All our weapons were tested, old and new. We had simulated attacks by radio controlled aircraft—Drones. The noise as our guns opened up was shattering, it was impossible to speak to 'Guns' even standing shoulder to shoulder. We shot down a 'Drone', the first time it had been done; they, the Americans, decided not to repeat the exercise as the equipment was too expensive to lose. Once again our gunners had done us proud. The US observers were very impressed.

The ship was now one colour, no longer the camouflage previously sported but the blue grey favoured by the US Navy. Our conversion to an American vessel was almost complete and USS *Robin* was almost ready to leave Pearl Harbour.

Before we did, many of the crew went ashore on 1st May, 'Lei Day'. There was an enormous procession, flowers everywhere, all of us with at least one garland around our neck. Singing, dancing, music, and the overpowering perfume of tropical flowers—it all seemed somehow incongruous. One day we were blasting the heavens with shells and cannon, the next dancing in the streets, garlanded with flowers in 95°. What a paradoxical war.

3rd May. We had three icecream and one Coca-cola machine fitted today—now we were truly an 'American' war-ship. My mind went back to Flotta, the sailors from the *London* singing their parody of a hymn—what would they think of us now?

Our long denim trousers and blue shirts had been supplied—long sleeves—as the Americans insist that long trousers and long sleeves offer more protection from flash burns.

Admiral Chester W. Nimitz, C-in-C, US Pacific Fleet, came onboard to inspect us. As Commander Ross recalls: 'some wretched ordinary seaman left a bucket of dirty water at the bottom of the gangway; it was retrieved only moments before the Admiral stepped onboard.' He wished us well, thanked us for being there. A charming, elegant man, a true believer in the role of carriers, he was most impressed by all he saw.

As we left Pearl Harbour on 8th May, it was clear from the Band onshore that we would not be back for a while. It played Hawaiian and British tunes which all had a farewell theme. The US battleship *North Carolina* accompanied us, as did our faithful trio of destroyers which had escorted us from Panama. A few hours out and Captain Mackintosh informed the crew that 'We were bound for Noumea, New Caledonia, in the South Coral Sea, the main US Naval South Pacific Base. The town has about 10,000 inhabitants, mostly French speaking, and has very few facilities for shore leave.' Atlases were retrieved from lockers and drawers—no-one had heard of New Caledonia—and why French? It sounded Scottish to us.

It became extremely hot as we steamed south. We could not work in the office between 1300 and 1700, the temperature being about 98°, sweat and perspiration dampened papers and service records. The evening, slightly cooler, was worked from 1700 to 2100. Liberal supplies of salt tablets were stacked by the drinking water fountains as a measure to prevent dehydration. The weight, so easily gained in Honolulu, was being shed even more quickly.

The extreme heat caused rashes, prickly heat especially. There was also sunburn but that was an offence, and a sailor could be charged with 'self-inflicted injury' and lose pay and leave privileges if his sunburn prevented proper pursuit of his duties. My friend Van decided to grow a beard. For this you needed the Captain's permission—not to grow a beard but to 'discontinue shaving'. The Navy does not acknowledge that you can grow a beard until one appears. Of course, they were right; many, ambitious to have Capstan cigarette

Hero type beards, finished up with straggly wisps like Ho Chi Min and anxiously sought authority to 'recommence shaving'. But Van's beard prospered, luxuriant and impressive.

As we passed about 80 miles from Fiji two more US destroyers came to join us to offer additional anti-submarine protection. On 17th May, after passing several Coral islands, we took on a pilot and anchored in the Bay of Noumea. George described it as 'Scapa Flow with palm trees, sun and a few houses'. Anchored nearby were three new US battleships and the famous aircraft carrier *Saratoga*, the largest in the world, and at that time the only US carrier to survive the war with Japan. (She did indeed survive the war and was later vaporised at Bikini Atoll in an H-bomb test.)

An oiler came alongside, USS *Sapela*, armed like one of our cruisers! We had only just finished fuelling when we were put under two hours notice to steam, and at 1400 we left. A very strong force; the three battleships, two carriers, four cruisers and eleven destroyers. A report had been received that the Japanese battle fleet had left Truk and we were to steam north, at fairly high speed, to protect the hard-won Solomon Islands.

Admiral Ramsey was onboard *Saratoga* and anxious to do battle with the Japanese. The two carriers had almost 140 aircraft to deploy and it was to be an interesting spectacle as we competed in take-off and landing times against the very experienced old war-horse—mind you we were not inexperienced ourselves.

Saratoga was the first to show and, in an impressive display of disciplined circuit formation and landing, retrieved 60 aircraft in 45 minutes. We landed fewer but our performance was slick and controlled; we had passed our first test well. There was an unhappy incident later in the day when one of our Martlets accidentally fired its guns on landing. It sprayed the Command Platform of Commander (F). 'Guns' and I were face down on the ADP as soon as we heard the burst—far too late of course. The bullets hit some ten feet below our level and three people were slightly injured. Characteristic of US aircraft— electrical operation not pneumatic like British—thus prone to inadvertant firing when extracting fuses and accidentally shorting circuits—Corsairs and Avengers had this problem.

In the early evening the destroyers depth-charged two submarines and promptly sank them after they surfaced. We wondered if they had radioed our position to their Fleet HQ.

On 20th May we sent out 20 aircraft on anti-submarine patrols. Apparently the Japanese Fleet had returned to its base and so we too headed back to ours at Noumea. We carried out dummy attacks on one another with a high degree of efficiency and superb flying. We were learning a lot from the Americans.

Admiral Ramsey allowed us to lead the fleet into Noumea; it was a signal honour and we were very proud. He came onboard the following day and spoke to us in the hangar. He was complimentary: he also told us that the tide had turned, we were now positively on the offensive against Japan and would fight them relentlessly until they agreed to Unconditional Surrender.

With the mail came a load of different games sent with the compliments of Coca-cola—some wag offered the view that 'We had never received Tombola from Tizer'.

Admiral Ramsey returned onboard and came with us on exercises. He brought with him the Captain of the *Saratoga*. They were impressed, and this against the background of the enormous belief by the US senior naval commanders that their fleet was the only sea-borne fighting machine to equal the previously ridiculed Japanese Navy.

At this time an order was received from the Admiralty instructing *Victorious* to carry out a further 'tilt' test to prove the stability of the vessel under conditions created by heavy flooding following torpedo damage. Water and fuel was shifted from the starboard tanks to those on the port side. Slowly the ship began to list heavily to port. An urgent signal was flashed to us from a US warship asking if 'we required assistance', they were alarmed that we appeared to be slowly sinking in a peaceful, protected anchorage.

Commander Ross had decided that we should hold an 'Abandon ship' exercise at the same time. What more realistic opportunity would there be? None, we hoped! 'Boat Stations' was piped and we all jumped into boats or scrambled and slid down ropes to Carley floats. I found the slide from the dizzying heights of the ADP quite hair-raising but clearly entertaining to those on the Bridge who were smiling as we went past at hand-scorching speed. Commander Ross felt it would be proper for him to abandon ship too. Obviously he had no intention of standing resolutely on the Bridge with the water lapping around until it rose to engulf him for ever in the classic sacrificial tradition of the Navy.

Down the dangling line he slid. A noble figure, the most senior 'dangler' on that memorable day. But what was this? As if by some of his own magic the boats and rafts had disappeared. He was left alone, unsupported, on a line not far above the water but over 40 feet from the flight deck. Where were his trusty seamen? They were all around the starboard side laughing their heads off! After some minutes one of the boats chugged steadily around to the port side and, without the batting of a guilty eyelid, the crew ranged their craft below Commander Ross and relieved his now aching arms—he was no light-weight. He smiled wryly as he stepped onto the gangway. One up to the lower deck.

There was little to do ashore, indeed the numbers allowed to go were very limited. There were Australian and New Zealand troops in Noumea. We raised a Rugby Union team to play them and they beat us out of sight. I accompanied our 15 as Reporter and that evening I broadcast the sad story of the five push-over tries scored against us.

We challenged the US Fleet to a game of deck hockey. The Administrative Staff were undefeated having won 15 consecutive games. In their wisdom the Americans declined but sent Basket Ball and Soft Ball teams who won as easily as if they were playing Girl Guides teams. Where they found the 6'6" sailors for Basket Ball we never knew.

There were many deserted beaches within a few miles of our anchorage so

Van, George, myself and three others took the whaler and rowed off to an idyllic strand about four miles from the ship. We had assembled an appetising picnic and afer dragging the boat ashore we sat on the sand like a party of Robinson Crusoes. Food and drink were quickly set out and we lay back in the warm sunshine reflecting on life's cruelty and misfortune. Then we had company. Not Man Friday, but scores of land crabs. About 18″ across their shell, they moved nimbly around us, balanced upright, with fearsome claws opening and closing in a rhythmic but threatening click-click-click.

'Ignore them,' said Van, as though these creatures were an everyday spectacle on the Gower Peninsula. I used to go crabbing with my father off West Scar Rocks at Redcar and knew from experience that some crabs could not be ignored. They closed in to form a ring around us. If we moved they danced out of danger in the blink of an eyelid. Obviously they had smelled the food, we learned later that these crustaceans particularly relished fruit and we had plenty of that with us. We did ignore them, but they remained with us as we consumed our picnic. In truth it was uncomfortable, they watched every mouthful we ate, like the family dog at the dinner table. We decided to return to the boat.

The tide had receded, the boat was now high and dry. We pushed, shoved, sweated, heaved, even prayed. After about half an hour we managed to refloat her and flopped exhausted onto the thwarts. The land crabs, fortified by the scraps we left them, watched us with what appeared to be cynical amusement, from the water's edge. There must have been over 100, in random formation, click-clicking farewell.

In the middle of June we left for four days' exercises, swapping aircraft with *Saratoga*. She took on Avengers and Martlets from us and we accepted Dauntless, Avengers and Wildcats. These latter fighters were 370 mph aircraft, slower only than the new Corsair, the world's fastest carrier combat plane.

This exchange of squadrons between *Saratoga* and ourselves worked very well. The US airmen onboard us were especially pleased to have access to a bar; their own ship being completely 'dry'.

We were informed that the Americans were going to land on New Georgia island in the Solomons, north of Guadalcanal. We sailed on 28th June and steamed quickly northwards to patrol an area about 350 miles off the Solomons. The purpose both to protect the landing force as well as endeavour to entice the Japanese Fleet to leave Truk and do battle.

Two further destroyers joined us and a heavily armed fast oil tanker accompanied the fleet to top up ships as required. It seemed we were to be at sea a long time.

We closed to about 250 miles off New Georgia, the battleships some 50 miles closer but under our aircraft protection. We were patiently trailing our coat before the Japanese, but to no effect. The landing went smoothly.

It was time to oil. Commander Ross recalls: 'Of course we had to have oil. Fuelling at sea was the new fashion. One day after flying off our air patrol we were steaming, sedately, head on into the long Pacific swell. Up alongside came the beautiful great US Navy tanker, almost as long as a battleship, and steadied down just clear of our starboard side. Up tumbled the Gunner's Mate and his party, over went the Coston Gun lines, then the headrope, the fore spring, the distance line, the stern rope, the petrol pipe and two great fat metal oil pipes slung in a big W between the two ships. The pumping started and from where I stood, abaft the funnel, I could see a party of Royal Marines skilfully tending a large hemp steadying line on the after oil hose.

'Up on the Bridge all was peace. On one side, unnoticed by all, sat an electric Helm Indicator. Never used. Quite forgotten. Someone—I won't say who—just happened to give the handle a little push. Six decks below, in the Lower Conning Tower, "Ting" went the little bell under the Chief Quartermaster's nose. A pointer jumped to PORT FIVE. The first thing I noticed amiss was those Royal Marines. One by one they were slowly rising off the deck—becoming airborne. Now when a Royal Marine is ordered to hold on, he holds on. Just in time I ordered the Sergeant Major to tell the men to "Let Go". Slowly, inevitably, the two ships were drawing apart. I rang the Bridge—they thought it was the Oiler. Then, one by one, the lines started to part; the Headrope, the Distance Line, the Breast, the Spring and the fat six-inch oil hoses spurting out into the sea best quality Texas oil—plus, for all I know, an icecream line too. A very angry tanker finally drew clear and once more, like the Ancient Mariner, "we were alone".'

In view of our long period at sea I decided, with Lt. Jealous, to publish a news sheet of information about home and Europe which the Wireless Telegraphy Office picked up from the BBC World Service. Bernard Jealous was a reporter in peace-time, now a junior Gunnery officer. Tony Sagar provided the information from the W/T office. We wrote and edited the information into what we believed was daily newspaper style. We had a cartoonist, Writer Neal, and when the layout had been completed we would 'Ormig', in vivid purple ink, the resultant news sheet and distribute copies to the various messes. Thus the crew read of the Sicily landings, the Dam Busters, the new Mosquito aircraft and the beginning of the surrender by the Italians.

By the time we had been at sea for 21 days we had run out of potatoes. To anyone familiar with Naval cuisine this was tantamount to an Italian restaurant without pasta. We advised *Saratoga* of our problem, maybe she might have some spare potatoes. She declared she had the answer. Within an hour an Avenger left *Saratoga* and landed on our flight deck. As it was released from its arrester wire and rolled up to a parking position we noticed the white chalk graffiti—'SPUD SPECIAL' 'TATER TAXI'. Its cargo was dehydrated potato. Now this offered a new challenge to those masters of the art of cooking—our Galley staff—being a technological breakthrough of mind-blowing dimensions. They mixed it with warm water; it cooked solid into brick-like portions. Very cold water, hot water—it mattered not—the result was still unbelievably appalling. A further plea went out to *Saratoga*. This time the Avenger, styled 'CHEF'S CHARIOT', had a US Navy Chef onboard. Why the answer was simple, add plenty of butter and milk—the result a tasty, nutritious, horrendously expensive dish. The Paymaster Commander, who had to ensure that we were fed three meals a day for the equivalent of what the US Navy would allow for breakfast, reluctantly acquiesed and endeavoured to recoup some of the costs by selling fresh bread to the US destroyers!

I believe each ship has an awkward squad. These are sailors who don't break the rules but challenge them, who reckon to know naval regulations and bend them as far as is possible within the bounds of legality. One of the most notorious onboard *Victorious* was Gordon Langley. Langley was a Leading Coder, a very intellient, articulate man who, in civilian life, was a Chartered Accountant. He had been offered a commission on joining but had refused, on the basis that 'you have conscripted me—do not expect me to make any effort to change anything'. 'I will do what I am told but no more' was his philosophy. His friend was Charlie Minett, also a Leading Coder and he recalls the following incidents: 'When Gordon joined he was asked what his religion was. He replied "None"—which was true—but of course we all had to be pigeon-holed so the Recruitment Chief wrote down "Church of England". At Sunday Divisions onboard ship he would listen carefully to the Chaplain's Sermon. He would then go back to the Mess, write a long letter home, shredding the sermon to pieces in a dry, desiccated critique, then deliver the letter to the Chaplain for him to censor it! He would sit in the Mess wondering what he could request next which would test the system to its limits. One day he decided to request a change of Religion. From Church of England to "Rationalist". He had done his homework because there was such a regligious order and its President was a Vice-Admiral! The request went to the Signal Officer, the Commander and ultimately to the Captain. Langley duly appeared as Captain's requestman and the Master-at-Arms read out the request. "Does anyone know what a Rationalist is?" asked the Captain. "Some sort of Atheist," commented the Master-at-Arms. "I don't believe so," said the Captain, "and I don't see why I shouldn't grant his request. If he wants to be a Rationalist why not." He then added "Request Granted". Thus Langley became the only Rationalist onboard. When the Master-at-Arms came round to clear the Mess-deck on a Sunday morning for Divisions and Church Service he would shout "Everyone to Divisions and Church, Stand Fast that bloody heathen." Langley had bent the system and no longer had to attend Church compulsorily.'

The second incident concerns both Langley and Minett.

'We were working in the Signal Distribution Office, on tasks normally carried out by Signalmen. This evening they were short of Signal ratings and the Chief Yeoman of Signals came into the SDO and said to Langley and me "You two go Aft and do Sunset." This is the ceremony, carried out every evening, when the ship's ensign is lowered. As we were in harbour, the flagstaff was situated at the after end of the flight deck. Normally two signalmen and one Royal Marine bugler are on the deck and, when the Officer-of-the-watch pipes "Attention on the Upper Deck, Face Aft" the Marine blows "Sunset" on his bugle and the two signalmen slowly lower the flag so that the bugle call and flag being lowered to deck level are accomplished at the same time. We protested—well Langley did—that as we were not signalmen this was not our job; indeed we had never carried out "Sunset". "You can either get Aft and do Sunset or get Aft and report to the Officer-of-the-Day for refusing a lawful command," said the Chief. We looked at each other and decided it was simpler to carry out "Sunset", and made our way to the end of the flight deck.

'When we arrived there Gordon untied the rope and commenced to lower the flag. I told him to wait until the Royal Marine bugler arrived. He replied, "I am a Coder, not a Signalman," and carried on lowering the flag quickly until it was a heap on the deck. At this juncture the Royal Marine arrived. He suggested we should raise the flag again so that he could play "Sunset". We pointed out one very serious objection to this. As we were the senior ship in harbour all the other vessels present had taken their cue from us and lowered their ensigns. Gordon thereupon folded the flag and returned it to the Chief Yeoman. The Royal Marine reported back to the Officer-of-the-Watch—who had clearly not heard "Sunset" being sounded. We then sat in our office waiting for the telephone call from the said Officer as to why, for the first time since Nelson expired on the Victory, the "Sunset" ceremony had not been properly carried out. We heard nothing. I have often wondered if it was because had we raised our Ensign again every other ship in the harbour would have had to go to panic stations to raise theirs and carry out "Sunset" twice. Langley entered the Naval Hall of Fame that evening.'

On our 24th day at sea, and steaming through a very heavy rainstorm, the *Saratoga* failed to zig-zag and by continuing a straight course cut across our bows. We heeled hard over, with our Port Engine racing Hard Astern to accelerate our turn, and avoided *Saratoga* by about 70 yards—less than a third of our flight deck length. Admiral Ramsey signalled congratulations to Captain Mackintosh for his seamanship—we had expiated our tanker misdemeanor.

It was 25th July when we arrived back in Noumea. We had set a record for a Royal Navy vessel of 28 consecutive days at sea yet we had not fired an angry shot or sighted the enemy. Well over 600 flights had been made by our aircraft. We had received and been able to send mail by means of a US destroyer especially designated for the purpose. Another example of American welfare care for its servicemen.

There was unbounded joy displayed by 832 Squadron when it returned from four weeks of enforced abstinence from John Barleycorn and the Juniper. A party to end all parties.

Already our role with the US Navy was ended. The *Essex*, whom we had been alongside in Norfolk, was now worked up and a whole new class of carriers was coming on stream. They were, in fact, almost running ahead of the provision of aircraft and fully trained air crews.

As we steamed clear of Noumea, almost all of us lining both sides of the flight deck, the band of the *Saratoga* played loudly 'California here I come'. Wherever we thought we might have been headed, there was now no doubt. What chatter, gossip, speculation. Would it be San Francisco, Oakland or San Diego. Our decyphering had specified San Diego with a call at Pearl Harbour en route.

We had a Stoker onboard named 'Tansy' (a nick-name). He was slightly eccentric and also determined to get out of the Navy, or at least off *Victorious*. On occasion he would eat soap, drink scalding hot tea and report immediately to the Sick Bay. Of course he had a raging temperature and irregular heart-beat. Shipborne doctors were familiar with such behaviour and would ask the 'patient' to return in two hours and 'not to eat any soap in the meantime'. Tansy also had a 'horse'. He would walk through the ship's corridors, left arm extended behind him and holding the 'horse's bridle'. He would issue clear directions to the 'horse' to avoid various obstructions and promise 'we will soon be where the hay is stored'. Other members of the crew complained about the 'horse manure' deposited about the ship. It was all good natured. Tansy was always thinking of new devices to be put ashore. Not long out of Noumea the Master-at-Arms came to see me.

'It's Tansy again,' he said, with resignation.

'What's he done now?' I asked.

'I have put him on a charge and he will be a Captain's Defaulter,' in other words a miscreant.

'What's the charge Master?'

'Shall I read it out so that you can check the proper wording?"

'Please do,' I could hardly wait.

He started to read from the charge sheet in his right hand.

'. . . did commit an act to the prejudice and good order of naval discipline in that he did prefer a frivolous request to the Captain, namely, TO BE SHOT AT DAWN ON THE QUARTER DECK.'

I burst out laughing; he couldn't forbear not to join in.

'You're not serious,' I said.

'Absolutely. He demanded that I put the request to the Captain or, alternatively put him on a charge. I had no option. Wording OK?'

'Perfect. I don't know if the Captain will see him, it is commander's defaulters, Commander Ross.'

Commander Ross was an unusual seaman Commander. He liked to sing on the ship's radio system—once when he had been confined to his cabin ill, for a week, he wanted air time and sang, unaccompanied and with good reason 'Don't get around much any more'.

He was also a conjuror, asking the carpenters to make boxes with secret compartments.

Tansy duly appeared, the charge was read out seriously by the Master-at-Arms. I was there to officially record the verdict.

'You wish to be shot at dawn on the Quarter Deck?'

'Yes sir,' replied Tansy, smartly turned out with his cap held in his right hand neatly by the seam of his trousers. No sign of the 'horse'.

'Pour encourages les autres I suppose.' The sarcasm was lost on Tansy. The Master raised his eyes to the deck-head.

'Request denied. Five days cells'.

'On cap, 'bout turn, quick march,' shouted the Master.

'Very appropriate quote that Barker. Voltaire you know.'

'Yes sir.' I was busy writing down the punishment.

The cells were at the very forward end of the ship where it narrowed in the bows. There were five, but two were permanently allocated to VD cases. They were jointly and somewhat quaintly known as 'Rose Cottage' and frequently an inflated preventative, suitably lettered, identified the isolation units from the punishment cells. 'Clap Castle' had also appeared but was frowned upon.

Tansy served his five days, promptly set fire to his mess deck table, was charged again and this time given ninety days detention. Unhappily for him this had to be served in the Marine Brig ashore in Honolulu. That was the last we heard of him.

James Jobling recalls another Pacific criminal episode. There were a number during our period on loan to the US Fleet and it was assumed that some of the misdemeanors were due to boredom and lack of action. Whatever reasons the following incident was significant in the annals of criminality onboard *Victorious*.

'We were at Pearl Harbour when it was discovered that the Captain's Wine Store, well aft below the Quarter Deck, had been broken into. There followed some very clever detective work by the "Jaunty" (Master-at-Arms Deegan) and his brave men. It was discovered that the Stokers' Mess Deck was being governed by a "Mafia" comprised of four ex-criminals (conscription did not consider a criminal record a bar to being called into the King's service). It was a large mess deck with only the one hatch for access and, of course at sea, access was only through the man-hole. These four had terrorised the others so that they—the four—kept no watches, had all the rum they wanted, and generally lived the life of Riley. However, they became greedy. They discovered that by getting into the bilges of the ship they could go almost the entire length of the vessel. This enabled them to proceed, unseen, to a position where they could gain access to the Captain's Wine Store and leisurely select their wine for dinner—a full red or a clean, dry white. The interesting result was that when they were caught and tried summarily, they were given seven days cells. As we were in Pearl Harbour they were sent to serve their time in the US Marine and Navy Brig—a notorious penal institution. I don't know what the routine was, but when they returned to the ship from that day on they were four of the best behaved stokers that ever served *Victorious*.'

James' story recalls to mind one, very well remembered to this day, by Commander Ross. 'There was an outbreak of thieving onboard. It was persistent and caused a great deal of suspicion and unhappiness onboard. Random, without pattern, it was difficult to begin to trace the thieves. Then they struck at the Canteen Store. This was the day after I had broadcast on the ship's radio system to warn those involved that they would be caught—like the rats they were. In the Canteen Store was a note—it read "The Rats have been at it again"—printed in capital letters. We hit upon a plan which Sherlock Holmes would have been proud to have initiated—A Notice was contained in the Daily Orders to the effect that for certain administrative reasons everyone onboard had to complete a new Next of Kin form—IN CAPITAL LETTERS. In point of fact the details of everyone's next of kin was fully recorded in the Captain's Office, but what I wanted was a sample of everyone's CAPITAL LETTER writing. Obviously not too easy to analyse but with a small group of intelligent assistants we collected all the forms and laboriously went through them. Surprise, surprise, one—and only one—stood out unmistakably. It matched precisely all the features of the printing on the burglary Note. So I knew who it was—but! The formation of the printed letters pointed to one of the most blameless characters ever to have served on the ship. Had it been the Padre I could hardly have been more surprised. On the one hand I had irrefutable evidence, on the other a character of absolute probity and conscientiousness. What to do? I decided to give the benefit of the doubt, slight as it was, to this highly regarded upright person and did not have him charged. Oddly enough the robberies ceased from that day on. I still know who it was—possibly, after the next of kin form episode he knew that I knew!'

We were in Pearl Harbour for just two days. Time to attend a 'Luau', an Hawaiian feast—where a whole pig is buried in a pit of hot rocks and left to cook for three hours—with my friends the Baskers. It was marvellous.

The departure from Honolulu was very emotional. Three bands played as we cast off our mooring ropes and moved slowly into the channel. Another band was gathered in a motor boat and it ran alongside us, playing continuously as we cheered and shouted for more. There was many a misty eyed matelot as the islands slipped down out of sight and we set course for San Diego.

Two Japanese prisoners of war were taking passage to San Diego; odd that they should be the only Japs we had encountered since our entry into the Pacific in mid February. In some ways we felt we had contributed so little, taking into account the immense logistical effort to get us out there, the extensive alterations and improvements, and the retraining of our air crews. Nevertheless it was a fact that our presence had bolstered US naval morale by making a clear statement that they were not alone. And what if the Japanese fleet had come south from Truk? Maybe they knew the 'Mighty *Vic*' was on station and discretion formed the better part of valour. As my friend Tony put it in one of his poems 'Of course the bounder's yellow, you can see it in his face.' Well that's what we liked to think.

En route to San Diego we stretched our Deck Hockey record to played 25, lost 1, 127 goals for and 42 against.

We docked at 0900 on 18th August and shore leave commenced at 1300. A few of us went to Balboa Park, a most beautiful spot, and just sat in contemplation. Nearby was the US Naval Cemetery, reminiscent of those First War memorial burial grounds in Northern France.

Some of the crew caught a bus to Tijuana, in Mexico, a small village about 25 miles from the naval port.

Not surprisingly when we weighed anchor the following day we were two seamen adrift. Just as the gangway was being raised a telegram was delivered, addressed to the Master-at-Arms.

It read 'Hasta la vista, viajes con Dios' and was unsigned!

To the Panama Canal. No hanging about, straight through and hardly touched the sides, maybe the old sea warrior had the scent of the UK in her nostrils.

Steaming through the Caribbean we sighted San Domingo, Haiti, Cuba, then the Bahamas. 'Van' records it was 102° in his office.

Mail had come onboard at San Cristobal. In it were my Draft Orders. I was to leave the ship in Norfolk, proceed to New York and join the Administrative staff at Asbury Park. I was mortified. The last thing I wanted was to quit *Victorious*. Once again friendship solved my dilemma. George Plant, gallant and fairly enamoured of the US volunteered to go in my place. The only favour he asked was that I take his presents for his family to the UK and post them to Shropshire in several small parcels. I was delighted to oblige; having struggled to get onboard *Victorious* I would not leave without another struggle.

In Norfolk we found *Indomitable* being repaired, she had been torpedoed off Sicily, seven killed in the Boiler Room. This was the third time she had suffered damage—maybe there was something in naval lore about ships that allegedly launched themselves.

Two weeks were spent in Norfolk, de-storing many of the US spares which would no longer be required and replacing the guns and sponsons removed to enable us to navigate the Panama Canal locks. We also discharged some personnel, including George, who had been drafted to shore bases in Washington and New York.

Once again we marvelled at the productivity of the US dockyard workers and the generosity of the civilians; a truly remarkable country.

Our Route home was on the Great Northern Circle, to avoid U-boat packs. We put into Argentia, Newfoundland, very briefly, before pushing eastwards.

There were submarines about and we sent off a patrol of two aircraft. Within half an hour the visibility had come down to about 100 yards. For a brief while we thought we would lose both planes and everything was done to enable them to find us. We laid down a thick smoke screen—a much different colour from the all enveloping mist. Then our searchlights, fitted with fog penetrating filters were switched on and shone vertically into the sky. Finally we fired star shells in the hope that they would burst above the fog level. Eventually our two strays found us. They were as relieved as all onboard when they landed without incident.

Captain Mackintosh advised us we would be docking in Liverpool and on 26th September we steamed down the Scottish coast, flew off our aircraft to Arbroath and arrived in Gladstone dock for a re-fit and thorough overhaul.

All the crew were given fourteen days leave, in two watches, and many took the opportunity to get married—myself included.

Some more left the ship, having served over two years. Many of my colleagues were drafted elsewhere but a solid nucleus of stalwarts, in all branches, remained. Although they grumbled, many of them were secretly pleased. I was one of them.

Captain Mackintosh left us. He had been an ideal man for the sensitive task of blending us into the US Fleet. His diplomacy and natural charm overcame many potentially difficult situations. There was no doubt that not all the US Navy senior officers wanted us or even judged us to be capable of fighting alongside them. All the crew, and our Captain in particular, demonstrated our efficiency and capability. Even the most vociferous critics acknowledged we were as good as their best. The Captain ran a happy ship, that was his nature. He was a very perceptive human being with a deep knowledge and insight into his men. His ready smile communicated warmth and a generous nature; he respected his men and commanded their respect.

CHAPTER NINE

The Old Adversary: *Tirpitz*

There is little more debilitating than spending months in dock under refit and renovation. The ship is untidy, dirty, noisy and devoid of character. It seems a fact that ships only come alive when at sea, responding to the united endeavours of their crews, demonstrating their characteristics and foibles, and challenging the elements. In dock a ship must be passive, indeed inert, as if completely anaesthetised and undergoing an operation. To the crew onboard it is a testing time, there is no danger, no excitement, fear, anticipation, satisfaction or sorrow. It is boring. Thus it proved. The weeks dragged into months, Christmas came and went as did the New Year.

A new Captain joined *Victorious*, I was transferred to the Ship's Office, handling pay, allowances, ships ledgers and other cash orientated documentation.

Michael Maynard Denny was our new Captain. A short, stocky man, bushy eyebrows, stern face, puckish smile on the rare occasions we saw it. A strict disciplinarian, somewhat remote, he devoted much of his time to studying aircraft carrier history, planes, strategy and tactics, capability and vulnerability. He was a gifted seaman with an extraordinary feel for a ship, its virtues and vices.

'My name is Denny,' he told us. 'Captain M. M. Denny. The initials do not mean "make and mend" as you will learn.' 'Make and mend' was a period allotted by the Captain or Commander so that the crew might have an opportunity to get their laundry (dhobying) up to date, write letters, take some fresh air or just relax. It was generally given when the ship was clear of action zones and could be operated by minimum crew. Our new Captain made his attitude clear from the outset, there was to be little 'make and mend'.

We all had the feeling that the relaxed days of our Pacific adventure were over. We had been brought back to the UK for a specific set of tasks and those would require a Captain of the calibre of M. M. Denny.

It was 10th February before we went out on Speed Trials off Greenock. There was a 'measured course' down the Firth of Clyde to Ailsa Craig and we would hurtle along, flat out, shaking, rattling, shuddering at 30+ knots. Always enjoyable.

The Clyde was full of shipping including the Queen Mary, used exclusively as a high speed troop carrier between the US and Britain. Escort carriers were in absolute profusion, so many had been built in the past 14 months.

During the few days in the Clyde, with officials from the Admiralty onboard, no doubt checking the quality of the dockyard work, only 'natives' were allowed ashore for 'security' reasons. 'Natives' were Glaswegians and locals, many of us were puzzled why they were regarded as better security risks than their shipmates.

Back to Liverpool for more remedial work and improvement to some that had already been done. There was a general feeling that we were behind schedule. An air of anxiety and slight disquiet permeated the ship. No matter how tight the lid is kept on security the details trickle out piecemeal. The prophets and sages would then provide the composite picture.

Unhappily someone, overdue from leave, was diagnosed as having diptheria. The Doctors were busy taking swabs of our throats and checking temperatures—very concerned to prevent an epidemic so close to our time for getting back into action.

Another few days of Gunnery and Flying Trials, some of them carried out in Belfast Lough. There were rumours that we were bound for our old hunting ground in the Arctic as extra blankets were issued. The cypher traffic was enormous, lengthy top secret messages, some for the Captain's eyes only. I found he did not care to be woken at 0200.

It was 25th March when we eventually arrived in Scapa Flow. Our old escorts *Duke Of York* and *Anson* were at anchor as well as *Furious* and four escort carriers. For two days we put to sea on combined exercises—the prelude to mounting an action or, yet again, covering a convoy.

When Convoy JW 58 left a Scottish loch, headed for Russia, we moved out of Scapa Flow to position our force between them and our old adversary *Tirpitz*, known to be lurking in Alten Fjord, near Narvik and sheltered by the Lofoten Islands. This ship had done nothing, except menace our convoys and escorts from the almost impregnable redoubt of a mountain fjord. Truth to tell she didn't need to put to sea, her brooding presence commanded so much attention by the Royal Navy that she was truly 'an ace in the hole'. It was now judged time she should be attacked yet again in a bid to neutralise her completely.

Tirpitz was probably the most powerful ship in the Second World War. There are those who advance the claims of the Japanese battleships *Yamoto* and *Musashi*, but given the incredible technology of the Germans most of us believed *Tirpitz* was the ultimate fighting ship. The inferior *Bismarck* had proved virtually unsinkable, and a match for any two British battleships. *Tirpitz* was in a class of her own. She weighed almost 60,000 tons and was armoured and armed far in excess of any ship outside of the Pacific.

It was 30th March when we put to sea from Scapa in the knowledge that if *Tirpitz* came out to attack the convoy we would intercept her—if she didn't leave her hiding place, we would bomb her at anchor. Either way the die was cast for her. The anchorage was well known by now. It had been monitored daily from the air for the previous six months. The part of the fjord where *Tirpitz* lay was less than a mile wide with cliffs rising sheer out of the water and up to almost 3000 feet. Boom and net defences had been arranged around her and the inventive Germans had installed an enormous smoke creating machine, on shore, which, in a very short time, could screen the battleship in a dense, impenetrable cloud.

As we headed to the extreme north of Norway we were put on 'Dawn to Dusk' action stations. It was once again bitterly cold, about −6° with an added chill factor from the wind. On April 1st our destroyers claimed to have sunk a U-boat but there was no wreckage or oil slick. The Captain told us the convoy was now safe from *Tirpitz* and its destroyers, the attack would be launched on her on 3rd April, in a dawn bombing raid.

We were carrying about 50 aircraft, some of which had to be deck parked as the hangar was full. This not only created mobility problems but exposed those planes on deck to the cold and weather. This time we were much better equipped than on our 1942 enterprise. The Barracuda was our strike bomber and the two fighter squadrons were operating the fast and powerful Corsairs—28 of them. This remarkable aircraft, the Vought Sikorksy 4F had a speed of almost 420 mph. It weighed nearly ten tons, was heavily armed and very strongly constructed. There was no doubt it could protect our bombers and cope with any fighter the Germans might put into the air.

Two strikes were arranged, to be mounted jointly by ourselves and *Furious*, the second attack being scheduled one hour after the first. Detailed knowledge of the *Tirpitz* determined the bombs to be used and a special 1600lb armour piercing bomb was loaded onto some of the Barracudas.

At 0200, when we closed up at Action Stations, the Flight Deck and hangar were the scenes of frenzied, frantic activity. Planes were moved into pre-take-off positions, bombs pushed along on their trolleys to be fitted underneath the Barracudas, fighters were fully armed. Mechanics stood by for last minute problems. Les wrote: 'I stood in my sheepskin coat waiting for the shout that signalled a spare of some sort was needed. The thumbs up sign came from plane after plane. It was incredible to see.'

Up in the ADP we watched the sky brighten very slowly. The wind was light—that would entail a full speed run into the wind for the aircraft to take off—and the sea almost calm. Certainly the best conditions we could have hoped for. All the guns crews and control units were reported at full strength. Our latest Radar Scanners, fitted in Liverpool, were probing the skies and my own small, emerald green screen was clear as the pointer swept through 360°. As the Corsairs coughed into life and then a sustained, throaty roar, the flight deck became a bedlam of noise and turbulence. There was an air of expectancy this time, a sense that, for once, the elements were on our side. I said to 'Guns' as we looked on the animated scene below us, 'I can now imagine how the Japanese felt as they prepared to attack Pearl Harbour.' He didn't reply, just scanned the sky as if he had reservations about our Radar. 'Keep a sharp look-out,' he called to the four men sitting in their swivel chairs, eyes to binoculars. 'Especially low down,' he added, almost as an afterthought. No doubt mindful of the two Reggio fighters on the Malta Convoy.

Suddenly, on a given signal, the first Corsair moved forward to the take-off position, the FDO rotated his flag, as if winding up the fighter's engine, then dropping it as the Corsair ran on full throttle and rolled slowly down the flight deck. It was followed by others, then the initial strike of the Barracudas. All the planes, both from *Furious* and ourselves, 65 in the first launch, assembled at very low level before making for the Norwegian coast.

Our prayers and hopes went with them. In the meantime the few remaining planes had been drawn up to the ready and waiting position; the second strike being due to depart at about 0515.

We had no news. Nothing had filtered up from the Bridge or the Air Operations Room; at least they would be there about 0530. This was when we launched the second strike and immediately ran into problems. A Barracuda could not, would not, start. The crew were hastily ordered out and watched miserably as their plane was pushed, almost at a run, over the side into the sea. Another took off, sounded slightly rough, failed to generate enough power to climb and crashed into the sea. The crew died.

The first strike returned; we counted them as they joined the landing circuit. There appeared to be one Barracuda missing. The expressions of the aircrews said it all. As the bombers landed, hauled to a standstill, released from their arrester wire, then run forward beyond the crash barriers, we could see the great smiles creasing the crews' faces. Thumbs up signs, shaken fists, 'V' signs, all revealed an operational success.

By 0800 the second strike was also retrieved, again with one Barracuda missing. We heard later it had crashed in flames after completing its bombing run.

The pictures of the raid were quickly developed and these confirmed that *Tirpitz* had been hit time and time again. One photograph revealed the shock waves set up by her 'whipping' motion in the water as the bombs struck.

Victorious was buzzing with excitement as we headed back to Scapa, some retribution had been exacted on the old foe. We knew she was only disabled, but at least there might now be a breathing space of a few months during which the merchantmen could go to Russia free from her menace.

At 1400 on 6th April the Force entered Scapa Flow in line ahead. The remainder of the Home Fleet, which had stayed in the anchorage, waited expectantly to greet us. We had arranged a neat formation of our aircraft, and lining the flight deck, in their full uniforms, were the air crews. They presented a brave and proud sight. Each ship we passed, its rails lined with men, gun turrets formally arranged with gunners standing on top, cheered as we glided slowly by. The resounding hurrahs echoed across the dark water, the breeze ruffling the hair of the sailors as they waved their caps and cheered. Thirty eight inch chests became 40", each swollen with pride at a task well done and so generously acknowledged. I found it impossible not to think of those who had died, in a fireball on a mountainside or a cruel, destructive explosion in the North Sea.

When we anchored the messages of congratulation arrived including one from KING GEORGE VI, another from Winston Churchill.

Captain Denny told us we had two or three more Norwegian operations to do then these might be followed by others 'in a more favourable climate'. From our experience of Arctic weather almost anywhere was bound to be more favourable. There was certainly nothing unusual coming through the Cypher Office—at least when I was on duty—just the normal traffic about Russian convoys, U-boat movements, German naval dispositions in the fjords, and general intelligence reports.

After another brief interlude in the Clyde, exercises ad nauseam, we returned to Scapa. One facet of the Captain's philosophy was now firmly embedded in our minds; he believed in practice, exercises and more practice. Every available hour was employed on speed and manoeuvrability trials, gunnery and deck landing. If we believed we were a 'crack' ship before his arrival, he clearly did not. We became sharper, more efficient, better disciplined but marginally less happy. Commander Ross was the counterbalance. Never without his telescope, which he hugged like a baby hangs on to its 'comforter', he strode around—very visible, often with a twinkle in his eyes and a half smile on his face as if he was enjoying some private joke. Revenge on the 'tilt' test delinquent?

We left Scapa on 20th April with *Furious, Anson, Kent* and a destroyer escort. The routine was the same, dawn and dusk action stations as we pushed north to our 'favourite' area, the fjords of Northern Norway. The obligatory closing up at Action Stations at dawn and dusk, was another discipline introduced by Captain Denny. He believed that a ship was most vulnerable to attack at either or both of these times; that the enemy probably believed the ship's crew was less mentally alert and prone to error. Furthermore, half light presented better opportunities for attack than defence. Our own experience generally bore this out. It was yet another example of his attitude of being ready for all eventualities. Being at Action Stations saved up to five minutes—the time it took the crew to rush from their normal activities to defensive positions.

As ever, the weather turned against us, and with winds gusting up to 80 mph, plus intermittent snow storms, we were unable to fly off aircraft let alone send them on a mission. After the spine-tingling excitement of the *Tirpitz* raid everyone was in high spirits and anxious to capitalise on that success. We knew there was enemy shipping in the area and that our crews would be able to seek out and destroy it. The only element beyond our control was the weather. Turning south we hoped for improved conditions. The storm moderated and on 25th April at 0400 we flew off our bombers and fighters. They soon found targets, a convoy of five ships, hugging the coast for protection and shelter. The main supply route from southern to northern Norway was the sea. Coastal water traffic was quicker, more efficient and had greater capacity than the tortuous road system. Food, spares, ammunition for all German units in the northern fjords was sent by sea, so a convoy was a positive target.

Despite a low cloud base, and a deterioration yet again in the weather, the strike force pressed home its attack with great vigour and skill. Three of the five ships were sunk, the other two damaged or, as one of the returning aircrew put it, 'well and truly plastered'. A later strike force flew to the port of Bodo and attacked the harbour installations and light shipping. The results were not clearly observed.

After another night of miserable weather; appalling visibility, heavy sleet and rain, strong winds and a sea running at force nine, we separated from the other units and with *Kent* and two destroyers headed back to Scapa. It has to be remembered that whilst the cloud base may have allowed some flying, the conditions for take off and landing were positively dangerous. The flight deck pitched and tossed through 50 or 60 feet. Only dire necessity, such as an attack on a major capital ship, would have justified serious consideration of an operation.

An added risk to the fleet was the laying of mine-fields by the Germans. Although these were normally near the coast—to hazard attacks by our surface ships—the severe weather caused many mines to break adrift from their moorings and float further out to sea. We encountered a number and our accompanying destroyers would endeavour to sink and explode them by gunfire.

Scapa Flow was now becoming an invitation for most of us to remain onboard. I looked around the anchorage; seven battleships, plus cruisers and destroyers. The pressure on the facilities ashore was enormous and there was the ugliness of seeing Jolly Jack at his worst—drunk, aggressive, maudling, pathetic, tribal, depressed and mentally weary. Those of us on the large ships could not truly imagine the wretched conditions of sailors on the destroyers, frigates and corvettes. It was said of the latter that they 'would roll on wet grass', but having just witnessed the fearful battering suffered by our own escort destroyers, it put the behaviour of some of the crews into some sort of perspective.

Yet not all was despair and despondency. In one week we had an extraordinary miscellany of visitors, so completely different it would have been difficult to select such a diverse trio.

On May 7th there was a classical pianoforte recital by Pouishnoff. The bar in the Canteen was closed, the enormous place cleaned, cleared of tables, with chairs arranged in orderly rows. An odd respectful silence descended as we waited for the Maestro. White haired, slightly stooping, seemingly diffident and no doubt possibly apprehensive about his audience, he came on stage and sat at the grand piano. The applause was polite. As he played, mostly Chopin and Mozart, one could see the transformation on the faces of those who had attended—just to escape their ship or even for a cultural experience. Within 10 minutes the entire audience was his and at the end of the recital the applause was unrestrained, joyful, appreciative and emotional. Here was a man who, in an hour, had erased weary minds of fatigue and depression, and substituted happiness, peace and serenity. A cultural shock it may have been to many but I am sure they would have returned again and again for a concert of such purity and beauty.

The following day General Montgomery came onboard. The hangar was cleared and he stood on a partially elevated aircraft lift and addressed the ship's company. A small, wiry man with a slightly falsetto voice, thin in tone with a slight lisp, he thanked us for all we had done and were to do in the days to come. He spoke, like head of School, in prose peppered by expressions we had read in the Hotspur, Rover and Wizard. 'Hit the enemy for six' and the like. His dry, almost ascerbic delivery was not the stuff of famed orators but his vitality, magnetism and self-confidence raised him to a new level. Here was a fighting man who, like Henry V, identified himself with, and cared for, his men. There was a great surge of empathy, his listeners identified themselves with his cause—their cause. They believed and trusted him. It was a remarkable display verging on political jingoism—he would have been voted Prime Minister in the absence of Churchill.

It was May 11th when King George VI came onboard. He was with us for six hours as we put to sea for Flying and Gunnery exercises. He was smaller than I had imagined and obviously diffident. His movements about the ship were programmed to the minute and a schedule was posted in various places to that everyone was aware of his location and kept out of his way. I found this strange and I doubt he spoke to more than 20 people all day. Enjoy himself he did, especially the flying exercises. When we returned to Scapa we formed into Divisions and were inspected by the King.

Commander Ross recorded his impressions of the visit thus:

'I had just 48 hours notice of the King's visit. The ship was looking care-worn and a little scruffy. I arranged for a painting party to commence work and they went to it with a will. Unhappily the Provisioning Party embarked a load of flour and peas over a wet paint area—it looked almost as bad as previously. In the end I decided to paint only those parts of the ship that HM would see on his way from the Starboard gangway to the Bridge. Luckily his Barge did not arrive port side.

'Whilst we were at sea, Captain Denny decided he could not leave the Bridge so I had the privilege of escorting the King to lunch in the Wardroom. We had a small table, Engineer Commander Cronk, Lt. Cdr. Pollock (Torpedo Officer), a Squadron Commander from the morning's flying, and myself. We had Grapefruit, Fried Chicken and vegetables, Tinned Pears and Rice (The King declined this dish), cheese and biscuits, coffee. The King enjoyed a whiskey and soda.

'Later that day we had tea, with Admiral Fraser. The King, the Admiral and me, (plus telescope), crammed into the tiny lift from the Bridge to the Wardroom Flat six decks below. "May I press the button?" asked His Majesty. I graciously gave him permission.

'Wherever we went that day I had a Lieutenant scouting ahead, just out of sight, to waylay and remove the inevitable ordinary seaman with a bucket of dirty water. One was always lurking somewhere; they did it to Admiral Nimitz and they could do it to the King.

'When His Majesty left, Captain Denny—believing I had had my share of fun—banished me to the flight deck where I had to listen on the breeze for the Captain shouting "Hip Hip" as the King left, join in, then ensure that all assembled provided a good, loud, resounding "HOORAY"'.'

An interesting four days; a music man, a fighting man and a royal man. I found Montgomery shaded Pouishnoff by a short head and wondered what kind of an individual that made me.

The following day to Norway once again. It was soon obvious that the enemy's influence on the weather was far greater than ours. Atrocious conditions, no flying, just total frustration. After three days our destroyers were very low on fuel and we had no option but to return to Scapa Flow. Some of us wondered why the US 'boats' had such a greater range than ours.

Captain Denny was not best pleased. He had his heart set on a number of follow-up raids on *Tirpitz* and, if these were not possible, then against any other targets available. He believed his ship had the equipment, his crew the morale and efficiency to deal further heavy blows at the Germans, being thwarted was irritating.

After spending five days once again in Liverpool 'to be fully ready for Operational service' (causing us to wonder what we had been doing lately), we returned to Scapa Flow from where we departed with *Furious* and escorts to Norwegian waters once again. Seamen, stokers, flight deck handling parties were all becoming expert at the pronunciation of fjords and coastal towns. By now we were almost at the end of May. Even so the weather was adverse and we made our way south from northern Norway, slowly, and awaiting any intelligence which might give a clue as to the location of likely targets. In the event a Mosquito of the RAF spotted a small convoy with accompanying destroyers and anti-aircraft ships. By now the Germans had decided to send specially equipped vessels, with a bristling array of guns, with all coastal convoys. Clear evidence of the importance of such shipping.

Steaming towards the launch area we found the weather improving and by the time we reached South West Norway the sea was almost flat and visibility excellent. *Furious* and ourselves flew off a combined total of 50 aircraft. They found five merchantmen, two of which were promptly sunk whilst another one was very severely damaged. The remaining two were also hit as were four anti-aircraft vessels. The latter being heavily battered by our Corsairs.

As our aircraft returned we noted one Corsair missing; the remainder landed on without incident.

Captain Denny was convinced we would be attacked in retaliation, especially as we were in range of two German fighter bases. We remained at Action Stations from 2000 to 0300. There was only two to three hours of darkness at that time of year and for once, it was not cold. The sky, almost clear, became a succession of pastel colours as the sun set. A purple plain preceded the pale black that represented night as we shuddered our way westwards to safety and Scapa Flow.

This was our last foray from this naval fastness of the Orkneys, except for one diversionary 'operation' when we sailed close to Norway as the Allies were landing in Normandy. If it was to be of nuisance value we had no means of measuring its success. We saw no enemy and, as far as we knew they didn't see us. Our Home Fleet operations were at an end. Our future was to be the harassment of the 'wily Nip'. We were to leave UK waters, to return only when the war was finally ended.

CHAPTER TEN

Nicobar Nights and Safari to Sabang

Six days after the start of the Second Front we left Greenock and, heading south we knew that the Far East was beckoning. The Mediterranean was now an Allied sea, those desperate days of 1942 an imperishable memory for the men who had met head-on the Germans and Italians on land, sea and in the air.

Tropical rig was the order as we passed Gibraltar and at 0830 on 18th June 1944 we made fast alongside at Algiers. It was a strange run ashore there; only 20 months in Allied hands and our first visit to an Arab port. Of course everyone dashed to the Casbah, mindful of Charles Boyer, intrigue, mystery, beautiful women, yashmaks, crafty Arabs. What they found was a bewildering maze of alleys and streets, pick-pockets—dozens lost wrist watches and cash— tiny dark shops offering sweet mint tea and always somebody's daughter.

Several of us went to see the Mosque Notre Dame D'Afrique and walked the main boulevards. A cinema attracted our attention and in we went; for at least ten minutes. Sitting on the floor, with fleas for companions and surrounded by indescribable smells was not our idea of 'going to the pictures'. The film was French, dubbed into Arabic, no doubt a gem for a motion picture museum. Some sailors returned onboard with leather bags and wallets, these a curious light brown colour with a heavy animal smell and small fleas.

The following day, with *Indomitable*, we steamed east towards Suez. The weather was glorious, clear skies, warm sun and calm, limpid seas. As we passed Cap Bon, the northernmost part of Tunisia, it was strange to think that somewhere below us, in that peaceful inviting water lay the *Manchester* and *Foresight* resting, duty done, in the now friendly fathoms of the Mediterranean.

In the early evening we passed a convoy of at least 150 ships; signalled greetings flickered from Aldis Lamps. I was on the ADP with Les Vancura when we drew near to Pantellaria. An odd, rocky, volcanic outcrop, we found it difficult to understand why the Italians had been so anxious to possess it. We ascribed it to one of Mussolini's many colonial aberrations.

Just before we arrived in Alexandria at 1700 I had been busy changing Sterling into Egyptian Piastres in the hangar. The pilot boat had brought out a suitcase full of local cash and the anxiety to get ashore could be judged by the lengthy queue for local currency. As I recall it was 100 Piastres to the £. As we were secured to a buoy we had to go ashore by Felucca, those remarkable Egyptian sailing boats which had not changed since the days of the Pharoahs. I decided to go the following day as it was almost early evening.

The horse-drawn vehicles—Gherries—were all drawn up at the point where the Feluccas tied up. I had looked in vain for a submarine depot ship, couldn't see one and wondered if my trainee colleague Webb was still in the area. I recalled the words of the Draft Office Petty Officer about the sunshine of 'Alex'—he was right about that. His comments about Pension 17 also came to mind. As soon as I climbed into the Gherrie I said to the driver—he told me his name was Mustapha, but then wasn't everyone's?—'What about going to Pension No. 17?' He turned round, with a mildly surprised look on his lined, leathery face. 'You want to visit brothel? I know much better one.' So the mystery of the establishment was resolved. 'No thanks, I've changed my mind. Please take me to the city centre.'

He dropped me in Ramillies Square from where I caught a tram to Stanley Bay. A glorious swim and for a few minutes I lay on the warm sand and thought of Bill Webb, he really must have had an enjoyable war to date. Many of us had dinner that evening at the Navy club; I made enquiries about Submarine Depot Ships but was told that the last one had left some three months ago, there being little requirement for submarines in the Mediterranean at this stage of the war.

We left Alexandria the next morning at 0800 and 12 hours later arrived at the entrance to the Suez Canal. Picking up a pilot we passed Port Said and entered the Canal with a huge searchlight on the bows lighting up the way ahead. Two further lights were on the Bridge playing on the sides of the waterway.

By noon the following day we had left the Canal and anchored in the Gulf of Suez waiting for *Indomitable* to appear. In the meantime we were quickly visited by male and female members of the Royal Air Force. Strange how most of them said, "I wouldn't have your job for all the tea in China, terra firma for me.' Obviously no air-crew among them!

As we entered the Red Sea the heat became intense. At night the flight deck was littered with hammocks and bedding laid out in any vantage spot that offered the slightest wisp of breeze. The Engine Room staff were working 15 minute shifts, drinking their iced water, taking oatmeal and salt tablets. Our water consumption was 170 tons daily.

It is worth recalling the *Victorious* was constructed to accommodate about 1250 officers and men; we now had 2200+ onboard and facilities were stretched to the limit.

The daytime temperature hovered for hours around 100° and, despite forced air ventilation, it was rarely less than 110° below decks. The Sick Bay was crowded with dehydrated crew—mainly from the engine and boiler rooms— and one died as we neared the end of the Red Sea not far from Aden.

Just short of that Arabian outpost of the Empire we were met by five destroyers, they were to be our escort to Bombay. It was a brief overnight stop in Aden before departure at 0540. Those who went ashore regaled us with tales of fierce-looking tribesmen, on camels or white horses, with curved swords, jewel encrusted scabbards, ancient rifles, bandoliers heavy with ammunition, veiled women with dark, mysterious eyes. We put it all down to drink!

We were now on salt water showers only, the evaporators being unable to cope with providing enough desalinated water for our needs. As we had no salt water soap we all itched and were glad when we sweated the salt off.

On 3rd July we arrived at Bombay and anchored about two miles off-shore. The Royal Indian Navy supplied half-a-dozen large launches to ferry crew members ashore. Few, if any of us, had been to India. Some of the old 'stripeys' knew all the vices of the city and graphically described the 'joys' to be found in Grant Road, Forest Road and the 'cages'!

Three of us hired a taxi driven by a middle-aged Sikh named Atma Singh. For the equivalent of £2 he remained at our disposal for the entire period we were ashore. He also acted as Guide, Interpreter, Counsellor and Conscience. Off we drove to Malabar Hill, the Hanging Gardens, Tower of Silence, Marine Drive, the Gate of Bombay. He introduced us to Iced Tea, Iced Coffee, Papaya and Mango—which he washed and dried before cutting up for us to eat.

Tommy was anxious to see the less salubrious parts of the city, particularly those we had been warned to avoid. It was extremely disturbing to witness the squalor and poverty, especially after the luxury of Marine Drive; the continual begging, fingerless hands being rapped on the side of the cab windows, poxed and diseased faces pressed against the glass. I felt ashamed, shocked and nauseated. Was this the Empire?

As we left that part of the city Atma asked if anyone was interested in 'distinguished female company, sahibs.' 'Not me,' I replied politely. The others voted me down and we were driven to a splendid house, in its own beautifully kept gardens, in a select area of Bombay.

Our driver rang the bell and, when a stylishly saried middle-aged lady opened the door, he just said, 'I will be waiting for the gentlemen!'

We were ushered into a large lounge, exquisitely furnished with silk covered armchairs, settees and loose cushions on thick, intricately patterned carpet, and invited to sit down. Tommy smiled, the other two also but somewhat nervously. I just felt very embarrassed.

Soon 'Madam' was back with several young 'ladies', two appeared to be Anglo-Indian, one was Eurasian, one white, another almost oriental. They were quite beautiful and very expensively gowned. Tommy sat with a peaceful beatitude on his face, as though his ultimate ambition was about to be realised.

'Can I take first choice?' he asked.

In the silence which followed, he went on: 'That lady there please,' pointing to the Eurasian. She came and sat beside him on a settee. Once Tommy had broken the ice the other two made their choice.

'Madam' looked at me. 'And you, sir?'

'No thank you,' I replied, 'not tonight'—or any other night I thought.

'Perhaps a drink whilst you think about it.'

'I would appreciate a drink—but I won't have any further thoughts.'

The others left the room and I was left alone with 'Madam'. A uniformed waiter brought me some iced coffee—I wondered how he had been summoned. A hidden bell-push? We sat in silence for a while.

'My name is Olga, I am a White Russian, and I came from Shanghai where I earned my living as a high-class prostitute.'

'That would account for your excellent English,' was all I could think of saying at that moment.

'Yes but I also speak French, Mandarin and Russian.'

She must have been a beautiful woman in her younger days, I thought. I supposed she was in her forties but as a little travelled and naive 22 year old I was hardly a competent judge.

'Why didn't you choose a girl like the others?'

'I just couldn't,' I said weakly. 'I couldn't go with a "girl" unless I had genuine affection for her. The idea of casual sex is just alien to me.'

We then had a long discussion on morality, prostitution as a true profession, Colonialism, Communism, the caste system in India. It was fascinating but I was beginning to wonder what had happened to my colleagues, and would Atma be still outside. They appeared shortly, having been gone about half an hour. Odd that they all came back together I thought—no doubt they would tell me all in due course.

Tommy, with his soft East Lancashire accent, spoke first.

'Quite unbelievable. Nothing like that has ever happened to me before. I think I'm in love with her.'

I burst out laughing. 'Tommy, you can't be. You don't know her and besides think what she is.'

He looked at me quite seriously, 'She has told me she would give it all up for me. I am certain about this.'

'You've only known her half an hour. You're infatuated and I can understand that, she is quite beautiful, but there's a war on. We leave here tomorrow, you probably won't see her again. Come on Tommy, let's go and put it all down to a wonderful experience.'

He shook his head but said nothing. The three of them went to Olga, now seated at a small, antique, knee-hole desk, and paid their dues.

As we made to leave Olga called me. I walked to her desk. She stood and extended her right hand and as I shook it she said, 'I hope you will come again, you will always be welcome for a drink and a chat—we have much to discuss.'

'It's a promise. If we return to Bombay I will call on you.'

She stepped forward, kissed me on the cheek, and said, 'Good luck, may God protect you and all your friends.'

Atma was still there. He had a questioning look on his face. He wanted to know if his recommendation was sound.

Tommy spoke first. 'Incredible, you're a genius Atma. Look, write your name and taxi number in pencil in the back of my Pay Book so I can use you again if we come back.'

This done we drove back to the jetty to catch the launch to *Victorious*. Effusive goodbyes to Atma, a generous tip—he could have almost bought a new cab—and we parted. He stood and waved as we left.

The following day we sailed for Colombo where we arrived at 1330 on 7th July. We shackled to a buoy in the Grand Harbour, about 800 yards from shore. There was a lot of shipping but little sign of the Royal Navy.

Of course it was monsoon weather. Every four hours it rained as I had never seen in my life. Visibility zero, a dense curtain of the water, the ground inches deep in minutes. The locals disregarded it except those sleeping on the pavements. No wonder Ceylon was so green and lush.

Mount Lavinia and the SWOC Club were the highlights. An elderly train chuffed and stuttered uncertainly to Mount Lavinia with its marvellous beach, surf and dangerous under-tow. No-one seemed to worry, this was the stuff of South Sea Island films; palm trees, coconuts, crescent beach of golden sand, rollers sweeping in to crash, in confusion, in pure white foam. Whilst some tried to surf with makeshift boards, others of us sat in the shade sipping a cool drink and eating a plate of fresh fruit.

Shopping in Colombo was varied and an art form. Tiny shops housed jewellers whose initial anxiety was to persuade you to drink some tea; their second to inveigle one into buying jewels and stones of dubious provenance. The principal item in each shop was an old steel safe, crammed with rubies, sapphires, opals and semi-precious stones. Bargaining, good natured courtesy, even deference, could last an hour. Even without a sale at the end there was no ill-will. Many of the crew bought bracelets, rings, ear-rings and necklaces which looked fine in Colombo but were hardly appropriate for Coventry. Mess-deck tables were regularly the scene of displays of purchases and boasts of bargains. The real winners were those slight, dark men with bright, white smiles and unlimited patience who finally succumbed to agreeing a price they had always had in mind.

Trincomalee beckoned. This Scapa with palms was located on the north-east coast of Ceylon. A naval base for many years it was a safe and sheltered anchorage. We steamed there on 19th July arriving in the late afternoon of the following day. This far-flung post of Empire, that had been flung a deal too far, had one virtue—decent swimming. It was to be our base for the next six months. We were now part of the Eastern Fleet. This had been a poor relation in the Royal Naval family; in fact until our arrival, the *Illustrious* was the only carrier east of Suez.

There was genuine concern that the Japanese might detach a section of their Fleet, locate it in the Indian Ocean and menace the convoy route from Aden to Bombay and beyond. With the naval aspect of the European conflict now virtually resolved, except for U-boats, the Admiralty desired to strengthen our presence in the Far East and ultimately in the Pacific. At this time the Americans had revealed little anxiety to see a build up of Royal Naval forces in the Pacific. They were now very strong in all types of vessels, most of which were superior to our own, being based on more recent designs and specifically tailored for Pacific work. They were quite content to see us in the Indian Ocean and if we would draw off some Japanese forces then so much the better.

'Trinco' was a well equipped base. Two Depot Ships, two Floating Docks, good store facilities but a shortage of some stores. The supply line to the UK was long although South Africa was used where practicable, especially for short re-fits and running repairs. The force, now assembled for Admiral 'Slim' Somerville, was an odd mix. Elderly battleships, *Queen Elizabeth* and *Valiant*, a battle-cruiser *Renown* (whose sister-ship *Repulse* had already been sunk by the Japanese), the French battleship *Richelieu*, Dutch cruiser *Van Tromp*, plus six other cruisers and a dozen destroyers.

The task for this force, was to harry and hurt the Japanese in Java, Sumatra, Borneo, loosely described as the East Indies. The mainland of Japan boasted no oil, therefore the supply of this vital commodity to its armed forces was a prime target—most of its oil came from the East Indies.

We were in Trincomalee two days before leaving for a strike against northern Sumatra. The main purpose on this occasion being to knock out Japanese airfields and destroy, on the ground, as many enemy aircraft as possible. This would open up the area to sustained attacks later against a weakened Japanese defence.

Our onboard news-sheet had not been published since we left San Diego. Bernard Jealous was still onboard and we talked about resuming production quite soon. Meanwhile another friend, Tony Sagar, and I had been discussing the possibility of a radio programme for the ships company. We felt that morale was sagging slightly in Trinco and that half an hour of comedy, fun, wit, might improve the spirits of those onboard, however marginally or briefly.

Tony was an actor in civilian life. Born just outside Burnley, he had left the North after outstanding academic success and, for some time, lived with the Thorndike family—a dynasty of actors from whom he learned much. He possessed a dry, almost cynical sense of humour and was a considerable wordsmith. He had a love of language and people. A genuinely kind man he embodied all the virtues of a gentleman, good manners, respect for and understanding of others. He was also a fine cricketer, the game was second only to his affection for the theatre. It was his anxiety to 'tread the boards'—if only on radio—that brought him to me to talk about a programme.

By this time *Victorious* had a nick-name on the lower deck. It was Denny's Dungeon, a wry indication of how Captain Denny's strict regime was regarded among the men. In thinking of the programme, and a possible title, we took account of this. We decided to call the half-hour 'Dungeon Dust Time'.

The format was simple. There would be advertisements for mythical products—all called Dungeon Dust—sending up a lot of what we had heard in America. In the News of the World there was a weekly column, 'John Hilton Talking', a rather pompous output of jingoism, cynicism, gossip and comment. We had a 'Ron Stilton Squawking', a know-all.

The Navy had a word for anything that was genuinely in accordance with regulations; it was Pusser. We devised a character, known as Pusser Bilt, an old 'stripey' who dispensed knowledge and wisdom—most of it as fanciful as that

121

which normally was currency on the mess decks.

Tony wrote a poem for almost every programme. These, invariably, related to happenings of the previous week or period since we had last broadcast. The works were usually parodies of Chesterton and Belloc and were so popular that we eventually published all the poems and donated the receipts to the ship's welfare fund.

We were obliged to seek Captain Denny's permission to broadcast and he insisted that the scripts be submitted to him for approval. Occasionally this meant delays as it was not always operationally feasible for him to spend up to half an hour on such trivia. On one occasion, when we referred to the Spithead Mutiny, some 160 years earlier—Pusser Bilt was regaling his listeners with tales of yore—the item was heavily censored and we were admonished. On the whole he was good natured about it all.

The studio was completely make-shift, with one microphone. Two marine musicians were our engineers—:Cutler and Willis, the former known as 'Cutie' because of his Don Ameche moustache, the latter 'Slim' as he scaled about 16 stones. We had two sound effects records, each one with about a dozen sounds. The 'engineers' had to be careful which band they played otherwise the 'roaring sea' was heard as a 'farm-yard hen'. I have to say it happened on occasion and the listeners could never be sure whether it was intended or not!

The third member of our broadcast team was Jimmy Jobling, like myself a Petty Officer Writer but studying hard for a commission. He was an extremely talented man. Very intelligent, quick witted, competent impressionist and a natural comic. He not only acted a number of parts but contributed to the scripts. It was to his credit that, despite the long hours of study which filled his off-duty time, he was prepared to give some of this to entertain his shipmates. I had always found his company very stimulating and his soft 'Geordie' accent masked a sharp cynicism about snobbery and class consciousness. (Years later James Jobling wrote to me and said, 'I recall vividly our famous "Dungeon Dust Show" with you, Tony Sagar, me and the two Marine musicians. Captain Denny spoke to me about it one day—he was an avid listener—and with a definite twinkle in his eye—he said "Jobling, I do not know where you got the title Dungeon Dust from." ')

We tried to broadcast on a Thursday night at 1930, when the messes were cleared of the evening meal. Despite our best endeavours we were only able to go on air an average of every third week. This was because of operational reasons, or if *Victorious* was in a port as opposed to a naval base.

Of course we had to have a Producer to feature among the credit names at the end of each programme. He was Peter Lorne, a Lieutenant in administration. In civilian life he was in the Advertising Department of Cadburys. He had a knack of bringing out the best of scripts and situations although he was not a creative writer for our programmes. A cutting sense of humour was his main attribute as well as an ability to persuade people to undertake entertainment tasks they would normally abhor.

At 1630 on 22nd July we left Trincomalee, a strong force of two carriers, three battleships, one battle-cruiser, seven cruisers and 10 destroyers. We were bound for an island called Sabang, just off the north-east tip of Sumatra. The task for *Illustrious* and ourselves was to bomb and strafe the Japanese airfields whilst the heavy capital ships went inshore to bombard installations. Some of our fighters were detailed to provide air cover for the bombardment group, others to photograph the results of the attack.

A new development, learned from the US Navy, was the use of submarines to carry out air-sea rescue missions. The vessels would normally be positioned between the carriers and shore. Any aircrew which considered it could not make it back to its carrier base had information as to where to ditch so that rescue by submarine could be effected. It was vital to provide airmen with an alternative to crash landing in Japanese territory as the treatment of prisoners could be brutal, sometimes fatal.

We went to Action Stations at 0500 on 25th, it was oddly dark and our strike aircraft, ready for their mission, had to be held at 'ready' until it was considered visibility was suitable for launch and form up. When eventually the planes took off they seemed to mill around almost aimlessly in the dreadful half-light as they tried to form into their appropriate group and depart the carrier force for the target area.

The weather was still inclement when the Corsairs and Barracudas arrived at their respective attack positions. The results, we subsequently learned, were disappointing. From previous experience, those of us in the open positions when strike aircraft returned need only look at the faces of the most junior pilots. Squadron Commanders and greatly experienced air crew were able to maintain a sang froid, almost an inscrutability as to the success or otherwise of a mission. Others revealed elation or disappointment. On this occasion it was the latter. Yet again it seemed we lacked good pre-strike intelligence. Offensive actions were very expensive to mount, often in both men and materials, and when they took place to little purpose the effect on morale was always deleterious. This was such an occasion, indeed it seemed the enemy knew more of our intentions than we did of his.

Late in the day a squadron of Zero fighters approached the force but were engaged by our Corsairs and driven off.

Victorious had a remarkable Fighter Direction Officer. His name was Lt. Martiensen and his ability to position our fighters in a favourable attack position against enemy aircraft was quite uncanny. His interpretation of our long distance radar scanner readings, sent to him by the radar operators, was almost psychic. Time and time again he manoeuvred our aircraft above and up sun against 'bandits' with recurring success. Pilots knew that when they received directions from him the likelihood of splashing a Japanese plane was probable.

This time we shot down two Zeros and damaged others without loss to ourselves.

It was stormy as we crossed the Bay of Bengal to return to Trincomalee. Of course it was the height of the monsoon season and vast depressions came and went with torrential regularity. Not ideal weather for operations, particularly as conditions onboard were humid and sticky.

Admiral Sir Bruce Fraser was awaiting our return—he was to take over from Admiral Somerville—another indication of the high priority now being placed on the Eastern Fleet by the Admiralty. Admiral Fraser was well known to us, having directed our exploits in Norwegian waters.

Illustrious left us too, bound for South Africa and a refit. Ships, like cars, require regular servicing, especially after operating to the limit of their design and engineering capabilities. It was essential to get *Illustrious* up to scratch if we were to form a credible carrier force. Two carriers were not really adequate. The US Navy preferred four in a Group with an aircraft resource of about 250 planes.

On 31st July we cleared the hangar, put benches and seats from the messes so that about 2,000 could be accommodated and witness a concert by Noel Coward. Men came from other vessels so the hangar was crowded when the star appeared on the makeshift stage in the aft lift well.

Noel was not every sailor's idea of an entertainer. His camp drollery, acid wit, light tenor voice was in direct contrast to his film portrayal of the square jawed, resolute, fighting naval officer. It was no surprise, least of all to Noel, when there were titters of laughter in inappropriate places, shuffling of feet by those embarrassed by 'Don't put your daughter on the stage Mrs. Worthington', outright outbreaks of coughing interspersed with the odd hiss. At one point though, now discomforted by the barracking and the metallic ping of pennies bouncing off the lift well bottom, he and his white tuxedoed pianist left the 'stage'. It was taken as an 'Interval' and he had to be cajoled and persuaded to resume his act.

Commander Ross noted at the time: 'I went to meet Noel at the airfield. I was taken aback when his first words were, "Where's your Captain?" I suppose he expected red carpet, guard and band. Altogether he was rather like a Prima Donna. On the other hand he had just completed an exhausting tour of the troops in India which culminated with his being involved in a very nasty car crash. The doctors advised him to return home but he decided to visit Trincomalee and the Navy. Maybe we should have made allowances for his rather temperamental display.'

J. B. Priestley is said to have asked Noel Coward: 'Why are you called the Master?' Coward replied, 'It started as a joke, but now it is true.' That is the measure of both the wit and arrogance of an entertainment genius. By and large his concert went down well after such an unpromising start, and many found his massive talents a morale booster which surely was the purpose of the event.

Within days we had an ENSA Company onboard; they performed 'Love in a Mist' to the great pleasure of all who saw it. I had a feeling it was the presence of some rather nubile ladies that spiced the evening with sustained interest.

On 8th August, the battleship *Valiant* went into the Floating Dock, one of two at Trincomalee. During the night there was a huge explosion, or at least what sounded like one. Action Stations was sounded and when I scrambled, bleary eyed, into the ADP at about 0300, there was *Valiant* with her back broken due to the Floating Dock having snapped in two. That was the noise we heard. Searchlights were playing on the stricken ship and for a while it appeared that both she and the dock would sink. In the event she stayed afloat, but in a parlous state, and had to be towed back to England for repairs. She was lost to our force for the rest of the war. A case of self-inflicted injury.

Leslie Vancura, after the fiasco of the letter-posting, had been re-instated after six months. Since that time he had been assiduously studying for his Petty Officer exam. There was no doubt he would pass and, on 12th August, he was informed of his success. He had played a considerable role in keeping aircraft flying. At Action Stations or Flying Stations he was usually to be found on the Flight Deck. As each aircraft landed he had to assess any damage that was visible to the naked eye and organise the replacement parts to be available in the hangar within minutes. There were six store rooms and assembling the necessary spares was often a complex and demanding job. Main planes were kept in cradles, hauled up under the hangar deck head, engines were bolted onto hangar bulkheads, flaps and rudders stored in a separate stowage space under the round-down, a cramped area narrowing to three feet high, and an alarming place to be as some of the planes thudded onto the deck inches above his head. 'Van' was one of the characters of the ship. An indefatigable worker, always cheerful, known to everyone for his great feats as the goalkeeper of our deck hockey team. He was also restless, with a low boredom threshold and so he used his spare time to fashion plastic Fleet Air Arm badges. A great swimmer, he was seen diving off the flight deck on occasion, a feat which required consummate skill and bravery or total madness.

Our next operation was to neutralise a cement works at Padang in Sumatra, in the belief that this would deny the Japanese the facility of making concrete for runways, block-houses, forts, roads—or even the repair of such facilities. It seemed an inadequate target for the immense cost and logistical build-up involved, but on 24th August we closed up at Action Stations at 0530 and shortly afterwards launched our strike aircraft. Possibly it was an indication of the value that the Japanese placed upon the target that it was so lightly defended. The Barradudas bombed almost at will and flames, smoke—not to mention cement—indicated that they were successful. Unhappily we lost a Corsair.

The force that was launched to attack a small port, shipping and shore installations found little to interest them. Two modest vessels were destroyed and damage caused to cranes, warehouses and other dock utilities.

Meanwhile a strong group of fighters went to strafe Padang airfield but found few aircraft. It was assumed that most were in the air. If they were they made no attempt either to defend their base or attack the task force.

One Squadron Commander was a Royal Marine pilot who had fought in the Battle of Britain. He flew fighter aircraft with a verve and panache that defied his langorous, detached behaviour on the ship. R. C. Hay was a neat, dapper man with a light voice and a pronounced Bertie Wooster type accent. He also had a droll sense of humour. One of his reports mentioned that having run out of military targets he sprayed a few rounds at potato pickers in a field. How did he know they were potato pickers? 'I could see the whites of their eyes!' I recall him coming to the office one day and asking, 'Do you have any lassy bends?' I looked at him blankly. He went on, 'You know, wubber wings.' I grasped that he needed some elastic bands. His foppishness, real or assumed—and I never knew—disappeared as soon as he climbed into his Corsair. At that point he became an extraordinarily skilful fighter pilot and a daring, dashing, dauntless leader of his squadron.

It was difficult to know if our strikes against the Japanese were being ignored because:

i)   they were directed at unimportant targets
ii)   the Japanese had no capable defences, or
iii)   they were lulling us into a false sense of security before launching a heavy counter-attack in the near future.

In the event the raids we conducted were akin to complex exercises. Valuable experience was gained and that was important bearing in mind the relative inexperience of many of our flight crews.

For the next two weeks we moved between Trincomalee and Colombo. The latter was a civilised run ashore with decent service clubs, restaurants and shops, plus transport to Mount Lavinia beach where the surf surged in and created great fun and excitement. It was also very dangerous with a wicked under-tow. One evening a pile of clothes was found on the beach and two days later the body of one of our Marines was recovered. There were no life-guards, of course, or even warning flags. I eventually managed to get a Notice put up outside the Regulating Office where crew members checked before going ashore.

Drink onboard could be a problem too. Officially the rum ration was the only legal alcoholic beverage for the men. The officers had their own bars, with gin and whisky at 2d a measure. Some of the crew had well-placed friends or 'wingers' from whom they could cadge an extra beverage. Petty Officer Frank Short recalls his friendship with a senior Wine Steward. 'Many's the night when I slipped along to see my mate and enjoyed a few nips of decent Scotch—for which I have harboured a liking to this day.' Others resorted to ill-conceived and dangerous measures to have a drink to celebrate an occasion—or even to wallow in maudlin grumbling. A case came before the Commander where surgical alcohol had been stolen from the Sick Bay. This had been placed in a galvanised bucket, together with some ethylglycol and raisins(?), and covered with a piece of cloth. During the days it was hidden for fermentation it was accidentally discovered. When the cloth was removed to examine the contents of the bucket it was found that the galvanising from the inside was floating on the surface of the brew! A few more days and it would have penetrated the bucket itself.

126

HMS *Victorious*

Battleship Duke of York, *forcastle awash after shipping a huge sea whilst escorting* Victorious *on a Russian convoy.*

A huge Arctic Sea wave, 50 feet high, thunders over Victorious' *bows.*

All hands to shovelling snow and ice from the flight deck.

Victorious was encrusted with ice in the Arctic Sea as she guarded the southern flank of a convoy bound for Murmansk.

The Victorious, Indomitable *and* Eagle *steaming into the Mediterranean on the convoy Pedastal which relieved Malta from starvation and virtual collapse.*

Eagle, her hull ripped apart by four U-Boat torpedoes, lists over as she began to sink in less than ten minutes.

Victorious edging slowly through a set of locks on the Panama Canal. There were only inches to spare on either side.

Captain Lachlan D McIntosh welcomes onboard the US Naval Commander-in-Chief, Admiral Chester W Nimitz, at Pearl Harbour.

HM King George VI strolling the flight deck with Admiral Fraser and Captain Denny on 11th May, 1944.

The victorious Victorious deck hockey team with Training-Instructor Bennett.
The team: Holmes, Vancura, Anstis, Plant, Barker (author), Miller and Holland.

Twins, celebrating their 21st birthday, got so drunk on illicit brew that one died ashore in hospital and the other was left at Colombo and discharged the ship. Although the principle of having a totally 'dry' ship like the US Navy, was not well supported, the lower deck generally disliked the range and unlimited alcohol allowed to officers whilst they had to be content with a tot of rum—not a spirit universally enjoyed outside naval circles, nor by all in it. This depth of feeling was recognised when *Victorious* ran out of rum for some time. The bars in the wardrooms were closed in 'sympathy'. My own view was that ships should have been completely dry in wartime or that alcohol should only be available in port or harbour.

Everyone smoked. Cigarettes were so cheap, 3d for 20, that it was churlish not to appear manly with either pipe clenched firmly between white teeth or cigarette drooping casually—a la Bogart—from the corner of the mouth. Sometimes we would receive parcels from schools where all the pupils had paid coppers into a welfare fund. A parcel was given to me whilst we were in Trincomalee. It was sent from a school in the Yorkshire Dales—Leyburn in fact. Amazingly it was the school my father attended and I was able to recall many of the stories he had told me about Mr. Hartshorn the schoolmaster. I wrote to the pupils and told them where their parcel had actually arrived and all about my father's time at their school. Some weeks later I had a letter from every pupil, photographs, paintings, drawings and even proposals of marriage from sailor-struck nine and ten year olds. Somehow these incidents made Britain seem closer. The feeling of those who had been a long time in Trinco was that like the 14th Army in Burma the Eastern Fleet had become 'forgotten'. This was understandable, the war at home was much more immediate and Germany the principal foe. The Far East was a long way away and events were not well reported.

Our next operation commenced on 14th September when, in company with *Indomitable, Howe, Cumberland* and five destroyers we steamed once again for Sumatra. I stood in the ADP and looked at *Cumberland*, recalling my visit onboard at Chatham when I was training. That visit had triggered off my desire to go to sea rather than serve ashore, a decision I had never regretted.

Action Stations was called for 0500 and about an hour later we flew off Barracudas and Corsairs. *Indomitable* launched Barracudas and Hellcats. It was not an auspicious start to the operation, three of our usually reliable Corsairs had to return. Les Vancura was busy as the fighters came back, all reporting differing problems. Aircraft mechanics, unsung heroes who worked in the Hangar in miserable conditions of heat, smells of gasoline, oil, dope (surface paint), were at full stretch getting the aircraft serviceable again.

When the strike force returned it was obvious that little had been achieved. The faces were glum, some even appeared embarrassed. It transpired that the attack had been indisciplined, ineffective—despite little or no opposition—and in a word, futile. It was no secret that aircrews disliked the Barrcuda. This airplane had a most unpleasant habit of not pulling out of a dive, with the tail breaking off before the plane hit the ground or sea. Such incidents had occurred in training as well as in action. Those who knew the Avenger—from our 1943 days—were of the opinion that the Barracuda was not in the same league. Shortly after we arrived back in Trincomalee the spares for our Barracudas were unloaded and the aircraft themselves flew off as we voyaged around the bottom of the island to Colombo. Just over 30 hours later we left Ceylon and steamed north, with Catalinas carrying out anti-submarine patrols ahead of us. Captain Denny told us we were bound for Bombay where Dry Docking was to take place. The ship's hull would be scraped clear of weed and barnacles which inhibited speed. We would be about seven days in Bombay during which time at least half the ship's company would be sent on leave, R & R, rest and recuperation. There were those who had other memories of Bombay and its delights and I envisaged Atma Singh was going to be busy once again. Tommy wore a sublime smile at the thought of his Eurasian companion—the 'lady' he wished to marry and take to East Lancashire. I could never see her settled in a mill town. Time would tell.

On 30th September we entered the Dry Dock. One of the attractions of Bombay was the cinema, the opportunity to engage in a little fantasy and glamour. We did have films onboard, shown in the Hangar on odd nights. Sometimes the film remained unchanged for weeks. One such film, 'Sergeant York', starring Gary Cooper, was shown so many times that many of the ship's company knew the entire script by heart. There were those who went to see it only to stand up shouting out the words with Gary Cooper to the immense delight of their shipmates. When Cooper's friend in the film said, 'Yer Ma wants yer Alvin,' everyone, but everyone shouted the line. I swear Cooper looked slightly more perplexed each time the film was screened.

Bombay boasted a Fleet Club at Beach Candy, a Sports Club, the Neville Club, Minden Club and beautiful beaches, especially Juhu lapped by the warm Indian Ocean. Walking one evening along Marine Drive, looking for a quiet spot to watch the fiery reddish golden sunset, I bumped literally into a cousin. Tommy Chandler, from Middlesborough, my mother's home town, was in the Air Force and was as amazed as me that we should meet in Bombay. He told me that another cousin of mine had been lost on HMS *Dorsetshire*, and gave me news of other family members who seemed very remote. We had dinner, parted, and it was four years before I saw him again.

We sailed for Colombo on 6th October and it was en route to Trincomalee, some days later, that we had a mock attack by Spitfires. We launched our Corsairs to defend us and they performed exceedingly well. Although some fighters could turn inside the Corsair, its speed, rapid climbing power and heavy armament made it more than a match for any adversary. Added to which it was heavy and strong and could absorb a lot of punishment which would have destroyed lighter aircraft such as the Seafire. Our fighter pilots were delighted with it and longed for plane to plane combat with the Japanese.

Part of my duties were concerned with the remittance of pay from the crew to their families, mother, wives, sweethearts, a Savings Bank or even a well known tailor to pay for a No. 1 dress uniform! It was remarkable how little cash some of the men retained for themselves, very often too little to allow them to enjoy the attractions of ports like Bombay, Colombo, Pearl Harbour and the like. There was always a visit to the office when a promotion had just been achieved. The Pay Book had to be amended and, usually, the allotment. I see from Les Vancura's notes that on 14th October he came to see me and increased the weekly payment to his wife, of just one year, by 13/6d to £3.

Payment onboard was usually made in sterling and, in foreign ports, exchange facilities were arranged onboard. For lengthy periods in one area, such as Ceylon, then we paid Rupees. The ship had a massive safe, keys normally held by the Paymaster Commander; there were smaller safes in the Ship's Office and Captain's Office. Ledgers were completed quarterly, a fair copy of each one was hand written and these copies were sent to Admiralty, Bath for central accounting control. The fair ledgers we despatched from the Panama Canal over a year previously were now declared officially 'lost at sea' and we spent days and nights writing up new ones. Similarly we had a problem in the Bay of Bengal. The office had a Porthole and, in very hot climes, a 'scuttle' was inserted to catch whatever wind there might be and direct it into the office. A freak wave was also caught one day. At least 100 gallons of seawater was shipped straight into the office—everywhere was saturated and every ledger sodden and mainly illegible. The entire staff stayed onboard during one period at Trincomalee to re-write the ledgers as best we could. Paymaster Commander Tucker was not best pleased.

On 15th October we put to sea with *Indomitable, Renown, London, Suffolk, Cumberland, Phoebe* and 11 destroyers. Our mission was to attack the Nicobar Islands. This scattered group lay directly eastwards from Trinco and formed part of a chain of small island clusters running south from Rangoon to the northern tip of Sumatra.

I recall that I had the middle watch, midnight until 0400, on cypher duty before going to Action Stations at dawn. It was obvious that the force was trying to attract attention to itself; speculation was that we were endeavouring to entice the Japanese fleet units out of Singapore. In truth, as we learned from cypher traffic, the Americans were attacking the Philippine Islands and our objective was to create a diversion, or even give the impression that some sort of invasion was afoot.

Despite earlier indications, we had not yet exchanged our Barracudas for Avengers, and on this operation we had 21 of the torpedo bombers plus 36 Corsairs. Fifty-seven aircraft strained the parking, stowage, spares, ammunition facilities to the limit. *Victorious* was originally designed to carry 36 aircraft so the handling and servicing of 60% more required extraordinary discipline and efficiency.

Our attacks on the islands commenced just after dawn on 17th October and went on for three days. Fighters and bombers strafed and blasted all types of Japanese military targets, the *Renown* went inshore to within 12 miles and bombarded the islands with her 14 inch guns. After the initial surprise the Japanese anti-aircraft guns began to react quite effectively and two of our

Corsairs were shot down. A Barracuda was lost, reportedly failing to pull out of a dive—a wretched failing.

The second day we were again at Action Stations at 0530 but the rain was like a pale grey curtain. I huddled in my small shelter in the ADP watching the sweep pointer on the small screen. It was totally clear; we were not flying, there was no sign of the Japanese and even the birds seemed to have sought refuge. We headed south to the Nicobars nearest to Sumatra and on the 19th we launched another strike force to attack shipping—if any could be found. In truth there was little about, the Nicobar Islands had a low priority with the Japanese. Our aircraft losses were not commensurate with the damage inflicted on the enemy. Two of our Corsairs, both damaged by gunfire, made it back to the ship but crashed over the side of the flight deck when landing. Both pilots were rescued from the sea.

We remained at Action Stations for almost 16 hours. At last, the Japanese now irritated by our continued presence and well aware of our exact location, sent out a dozen fighters. Nine were flying at about 6000 feet, three more were providing cover or maintaining a watching brief at a much higher altitude. It was a tactic of the Japanese to monitor the performance of their attack planes; those who failed to press home their strike with conviction and aggression were not lightly treated on return to base.

Lt. Martiensen again directed our Corsairs onto the enemy. I could just discern the mixing of friends and bandits on the outer limit of my small radar, they were about 13 or 14 miles away. We endeavoured to pick them up with binoculars without success. Our guns crews were looking forward to a possible confrontation. In the event it resolved into a bitterly fought air battle, over half an hour, during which two of our Corsairs were shot down and four of the enemy 'splashed'. *Indomitable's* fighters caught up with the enemy high level watchers and shot them all down.

In logistical terms we had lost as many aircraft as the Japanese and the damage inflicted on shore was undoubtedly of little significance. The operation had, however, pitted our fighters against theirs and the balance of that conflict was in our favour. Both the Corsair and the Hellcat had proved a match for the Oscar, a Japanese army fighter second only to the Zero, and our pilots had good reason to be proud of their performance. Ever since Pearl Harbour, the subsequent mighty carrier battles at Midway and Coral Sea, the sinking of the *Prince Of Wales* and *Repulse*, an aura of infallibility had begun to be attributed to the Japanese fighting airman. Skilful, brave, well-trained, with excellent aircraft, he presented a formidable opponent—yet our aircrews were a match. In this respect at least the operations off Nicobar were encouraging.

It was the first time we had remained within a few miles of enemy territory for three consecutive days. Lessons had also been learned from that experience, especially in the utilisation of crew at constant action stations and the rapid arming, bombing-up and preparation of aircraft for attack and defensive purposes.

Returning to Trincomalee the weather was perfect, the sea like glass, visibility 'for ever' as the song says. Despite this a destroyer struck a mine, had to reduce speed to eight knots and be escorted back by another destroyer and *London*. I thought again of the men at Scapa singing 'Ask the *London* to help you, the *London* will carry you through.'

Victorious was not without mechanical problems. The most serious of which related to the centre screw (propeller) and the rudder. The former meant that from time to time we had to steam with only two screws, reducing both speed and manoeuvreability. The rudder failure was alarming. It was a defect which rendered the ship almost inoperable. When a command to turn had been given the rudder might jam so that the ship went around in a continuous circle until a manual corrective procedure was effected. On the Nicobar operations we had gone 'out of control' on more than one occasion. The appropriate signal would be hoisted, the mournful siren would sound and the rest of the Fleet scurry for safety as 35,000 tons of ship careered clock-wise out of control.

Tony and I had produced the first two of our radio programmes. In view of our 'dickey rudder' we had chosen 'Traffic Jam' by Artie Shaw and his Orchestra as our signature tune. The half-hours were an unqualified success and repeats were requested. It was not possible to do this—there was no method whereby the programmes could be recorded and doing them 'live' twice over was not practicable.

Tony wrote a poem about Sabang and Nicobar, with some incidents, like the Corsair unable to take off, the gun turret which remained elevated, the rudder, and prolonged Action Stations denying the men their rum, all featured in rhyme. This is what he wrote and broadcast:

NICOBAR NIGHT or SAFARI TO SABANG

Oh, East is East and West is West, and
    never the twain shall meet
Till Alexander's ships come out to join the
    Eastern fleet,
Then Hirohito's Navy will know the final
    test,
And the sun that sets on Tokyo is rising in
    the West.

The Admiral's out with fifteen ships,
    Renown has left her berth,
The experts say, 'Another op.', the mess-
    deck 'buzz' says, 'Perth';
Out through the boom they steam in line,
    "Attention on the deck,"
Face starboard, port, face for'ard, aft—until
    you crick your neck.

The guard spring to attention, unfaltering,
    fearless, brave,
The band swing out in jive time 'A Life on
    the Ocean Wave',
The fleet forms up in order, destroyers
    chase about,
Flags fly in wild abandon—'Sea Dutymen
    fall out'.

They steam toward the sunrise, they're out
    in search of fun,
It's nothing really startling, just one more
    'club bore run';
The land has hardly disappeared, the
    boom is still in sight,
When 4.5's are trained to bear, and aircraft
    are in flight.

For practices are ordered, and they look
    mighty fine,
With aircraft diving, twisting—and
    plunging in the brine,
For though you lose a number, and
    damage many more,
And you've only eighteen serviceable from
    more than fifty-four—

It's been a great experience for crews and
    A.H.P.—
And when we've whittled down our
    strength, they call a halt for tea.
The night draws in, the tropic night—the
    magic of the East
Is lost upon the stokers, 'browned off', to
    say the least.

Portholes closed tight, and hatches down,
    yet almost every night,
You'll hear some other tell-tale ship—
    Victorious showing light;
Oh, what a panic then to see the people
    flying round,
And watches falling in (and out) until the
    gleam is found.

In Jap-infested waters—with not a Jap in
    sight,
To risk the safety of the fleet by the
    showing of a light;
But all is still, the fleet sails on beneath the
    Southern Star,
Until we sight the final goal—The Isle of
    NICOBAR.

You've never heard of this great base, what
    ignorance sublime,
Where were you educated, man, where
    have you spent your time?
This blessed isle, this shark-ringed bay,
    renowned by famous men:
Take out the biggest map you have—and
    you won't find it then.

But if there be some sceptics left who say
    there's no such place,
Just answer, 'I have been there, chum, and
    left without a trace';
For up and down and in between, we
    played the whole day through,
And shells fell thick and heavy, while men
    admired the view.

But just when we were starting the day's
    activity,
The speed went up, the *Vic* spun round—
    and three times round went she.
The Admiral was hairless, destroyers took
    to flight,
But those who knew the rudder, said
    'Everything's all right'.

And so it was, we found our course, we
    steamed into the wind,
We lurched about from side to side, just
    like a man struck blind.
The aircraft stood in perfect line, the Japs
    approaching fast,
And the atmosphere in the ADR was like a
    furnace blast.

'Scramble, scramble,' came the shout, but
    not a plane took off,
The leading Corsair choked to death—with
    a splutter and a cough.
'Tis said by men who know the ropes, the
    starter would not fit,
But did the Air Mechanic know—no, not a
    bit of it!

Another group was forming fast, just off
    the starboard bow,
And all the engines started—and wasn't
    there a row!
Commander Flying waved his flag, the
    Captain lost his frown—
But what new obstacle is this? the turret
    won't lie down.

'Communication numbers' ears were
    shattered by the blast,
'Depress that blasted turret, and do it
    bloody fast';
The turret slowly came to rest, the deck
    was clear once more,
When through the ship we heard the pipe,
    'The position is rather obscure'.

Three nights and days we kept it up,
    around the coral bays,
We trailed our coats before the Jap—or so
    the pressman says.
The Jap did not attack us, he knew the
    master race,
Of course, the bounder's yellow—you can
    see it in his face.

But in the midst of this success, with
    recommends galore,
There's one sad fact stands out supreme—I
    trust I'm not a bore,
The wily Nip, God rot his soul, will never
    be my chum,
For why? I tell the awful truth—he made
    us miss our rum.

And should he be in Singapore, or bound
    for Mandalay,
We made an oath, we'd take revenge before
    the final day;
Let him beat and bomb and blast us, we
    worry not a jot,
But he really does upset us when he robs
    us of our tot.

Oh, East is East, and West is West, and never the twain shall meet,
Till Alexander's ships come out, to join the Eastern fleet;
Then Hirohito's Navy will know the final test,
And the sun that sets on Tokyo is rising in the west.

After arrival back in Trincomalee on 21st October we moved between there and Colombo until 12th November when we sailed again to Bombay. We all knew the Pacific was beckoning although many of us believed the Americans were not anxious to have us. They were not convinced that we were self-sufficient for sustained operations at sea. Time would tell. Meanwhile our priority was to sort out the two major mechanical problems.

The weather was extremely warm and at least one of the aircraft lifts remained down at Hangar level to provide some primitive ventilation. During our previous visit to Bombay a few rats had managed to get onboard, despite many precautions, and the occasional inquisitive vermin face would be seen looking out of the ventilation trunking that ran throughout the ship. There was also an outbreak of dysentery onboard at the end of October, ascribed to reckless eating ashore in Colombo. Almost any eating ashore in Ceylon presented danger but the demand for Banana Fritters never diminished.

A crowd of us went to Orlando Cove, just outside Trinco, for a swimming party. A large cardboard box, filled with Spam sandwiches, apples, bottles of Lime Juice and a few bars of 'nutty' (chocolate) was carried. That day at least we avoided the dreaded dysentery.

On our way to Bombay we learned that *Tirpitz* had been sunk. Three direct hits with five ton bombs, plus a number of near misses, had caused her to turn turtle and sink. There was a loud cheer at the news; not only had the RAF destroyed our old foe but had cleared the way for other units of the Home Fleet to sail East and join us against Japan.

Indomitable was already in Bombay when we arrived. This time the whole crew was being sent, in separate parties, to the R & R Centre at Deolali. I went on 20th November, leaving the ship in the early afternoon and taking the train to the camp some 90 miles to the North East of Bombay.

For those of us who had not previously experienced Indial rail travel it was a profound culture shock. For a start, if we thought that *Victorious* was over-crowded we suddenly realised we lived in tranquil spaciousness. From the moment we left Ballard Pier, arriving at our destination some five hours later, it was a journey of astonishment and amazement. Our carriages were reserved, but that was of little consequence. Before long we had mothers clutching infants, hanging precariously from the side of the train as they begged. The youth and beauty of many of them was a delight yet disturbing. Some of the children were under-nourished and sick, a few deformed. The soulful pleading dark eyes of their mothers peeled away layer after layer of indifference until one felt emotionally drained at their plight. Hands reached out for two annas, the equivalent of a half-penny. The train proceeded so slowly that the successful beggars stepped off and new ones jumped on seemingly impervious to any danger. Young men swarmed around and past them offering fruit, drink, tea and nuts. We had been warned not to buy. As we progressed wearily into the foothills the number of beggars dwindled but the passengers were as numerous as ever. On the roof, on the running board, clutching onto window bars, festooning the locomotive. It was a railway tableau of the life of the Indian poor.

Deolali was one of the main centres to which exhausted servicemen were sent to rest and relax. There were many from Burma and Assam, mentally scarred by bloody hand-to-hand fighting against the Japanese, others unhinged by Jungle life or physically low from malaria and dysentery. I had heard of people being 'Deolali'—slightly mad, I was now seeing them at close hand.

There was no régime at the Camp. Everyone was allowed to get up when they wanted, eat if they wished, come and go as they pleased. A small town nearby, Nasik, attracted many with its restaurants, shops, street vendors, and the inevitable bazaar of stalls and pavement sales pitches.

Everyone slept under canvas, and under mosquito nets. Wildlife was present in the form of various snakes as well as scorpions—one of which I found in my shoe one morning. Great emphasis was placed on participation sport—four legged races, cricket, hockey, netball, chariot racing, football, soft-ball.

The only rule was the compulsory wearing of long trousers and sleeved shirts after 1900 as added protection against the dreaded 'mossies'. All of us noticed how yellow the soldiers were who had been taking mepacrin tablets over a sustained period.

The camp boasted a concert party, quite as bad as that which I used to watch on Redcar sands as a schoolboy in the late 1920's. The lack of talent was compensated by sheer enthusiasm and hilarious spontaniety; I felt that some were using the stage as therapy for their simple mental disorder. Additionally the Indians came and performed feats of acrobatics, juggling, snake charming and traditional dancing.

In the morning the most welcome cry was that of the 'Char Wallah'—the tea man—with a huge urn on his back, filled with strong, steaming hot tea, wonderful. That first morning cup in the camp remains one of my abiding war-time memories—a tropical nectar comparable to our Arctic 'kai'. The Dhobey-man would take our shorts and shirts in the evening and deliver them, snow white and pristine, the following morning.

It was a restorative four days. Only once was the war directly referred to and that was when we attended a lecture on 'The Psychology of the Japanese fighting man'. Events were to prove they didn't know the half of it.

There was no question that the short stay at Deolali was a morale booster and a welcome change. The train journey back was quite as chaotic as the outward. I was surprised how quickly I had come to accept those things which had so shocked me a few days earlier. Some things never changed though. Four of our crew boarded the train laden with food and refreshment. By the time we reached Bombay they had eaten 35 oranges, 24 egg sandwiches, several cakes and lashings of tea. 'Big Eats' indeed—did any other servicemen eat like 'Jack'?

We arrived back at Colombo on 16th December, stayed three days before slipping round to Trinco. The *KGV* and *Indefatigable* had arrived; our fleet was slowly building up into a purposeful force. During the next few days we exercised off eastern Ceylon, extensive gunnery and flying trials to sharpen both our offensive and defensive capabilities for what lay ahead. Four carriers were now assembled, and though by American forces standards it was a comparatively small group, the ships were modern, well equipped and fully operational. We were undoubtedly at our strongest since the war began and there was an anxiety amongst the men to get into the Pacific and participate in the main event rather than dwelling on the side-lines sniping at the fringes of Japanese territory.

There was a strong belief that the Americans didn't really want us with their forces. They seemed to regard the war with Japan as something exclusively between themselves and the Japs. The fact that we had lost Singapore, Malaya, Burma, Borneo, Hong Kong, plus battleships, an aircraft carrier, cruisers and destroyers, as well as countless fighting men on land didn't seem to register highly. To Americans the indignities of Pearl Harbour and the Philippines made the conflict a head-to-head fight and our involvement almost an intrusion into a personal matter.

It wasn't just a question of our sailing around Australia and up to the battle zones; that was relatively simple. What complicated the situation was the logistical problems of supplying a large fleet (by our standards) with spares, ammunition, bombs, fuel, aviation spirit, food, relief personnel and even mail. The ships which performed these functions were collectively called the Fleet Train. By now the Americans had perfected their logistical systems and methods to a fine art. Their army, island hopping, their fleet constantly occupying new anchorages, the air force building airfields almost on a daily basis. The west coast of America, a power-house of production and supplies, was so much nearer to their forces. To have a 'lame duck' force join them, a group of warships which might require their logistical help, was not a pleasing prospect or one which they actively sought.

Signals flashed to and from and Admiral Fraser spent some time in London pressing for every available supply ship to be transferred to the Far East so that his Battle Group could operate effectively at long range and for long periods.

We knew nothing of the details but those of us with cypher duties saw enough to realise that the question of our immediate future deployment was a very delicate one. Our gut feeling was that the Pacific was our goal, especially as we had been nominated British Pacific Fleet although based in the Indian Ocean.

As it moved nearer Christmas Tony and I wrote a Pantomime which was an amalgam of Mother Goose, Red Riding Hood, Aladdin, Cinderella and Jack and the Beanstalk. We wanted to involve as many of the ship's company as practicable and eventually managed a cast of about 50. It was almost evenly split between officers and men, all of whom were expected to assemble or make the costumes appropriate to their part. The extravangaza was produced by Peter Lorne and the lighting and mechanical effects assembled by Warrant Officer Jock Gibson. The full Royal Marine Dance Band provided the music. It was, in truth, an incredible endeavour.

The performances were quite remarkable and whilst it is unfair to single out any of them I must mention Lt. Marks (a very ugly sister), Petty Officer James Jobling (the Wicked Baron), Stoker Petty Officer Groves (Red Riding Hood), Lt. Bill Banning (a delectable Fairy Queen), Leading Telegraphist Robert Dey (Hitler) and, of course, Tony himself as Simple Simon.

We had onboard, as a Fighter Direction Officer, Kenneth More, subsequently to become a world famous film and stage star, but he declined to take part—it could have been the making of him!

The show was an enormous success and we were obliged to run it two consecutive nights so that everyone could see it twice! As I read my monologue I could see Captain Denny laughing and nudging his companions in the front row.

Christmas Day was spent in 'Trinco'. To mark the occasion we broadcast a special edition of Dungeon Dust Time and Tony wrote an appropriate poem called the 'Isle of Lost Ships'. This is it:

THE ISLE OF LOST SHIPS

There's a place of dull damnation far
　beyond the setting sun,
Where the ships come home to haven,
　when their fighting days are done;
Sloop, corvette, and ancient frigate, all the
　ships you ever knew,
　With the depot ships a-swinging at their
　buoy,
And the submarine repair ships, with an
　old and ancient crew,
　Some of whom were there before the
　siege of Troy.

Far beyond the blue horizon lies this host
　of phantom ships,
Far beyond the realm of India, despair of
　Stafford Cripps;
You can see them in the harbour by the
　phosphorescent sea,
　With the sharks a-playing leap-frog in
　the foam,
It's a name that's filled with terror,
　mispronounced TRINCOMALEE—
　And about five thousand miles away
　from home.

Set amidst the tropic splendour—and the
　smell of rotting bones,
The original headquarters of a man called
　Davy Jones;
A paradise for lizards, but sheer purgatory
　for 'Jack',
　With the sun a-beating down throughout
　the day,
Where the iron chains are rusting and the
　blackened timbers crack—
　And we all get sixpence each—'climatic
　pay'.

This far-flung post of Empire, that they
　flung a bit too far,
With yellow men for neighbours, on the
　isle of Nicobar;
Drake and Hawkins, Nelson, Beatty, they
　all knew this blessed spot,
　Came a-sailing in the wooden ships of
　old,
But they left again as quickly, for they
　found it stinking hot—
　And it didn't seem a likely place for
　gold.

It's here the ships are coming from all
　quarters of the world,
They're sailing out from England, all the
　awnings are unfurled,
Their hearts are filled with longing, and
　their sleep is bright with dreams,
They're a-thinking that it's just a
　pleasure cruise,
With dusky maidens dancing 'neath the
　tropic moonlight beams,
　And nothing but an endless round of
　booze.

Oh, there's beer and booze in plenty, if
　you've only got the tickets,
And 'The RHYTHM OF THE ISLANDS' is
　provided by the crickets,
You may ride around in rickshaws in a
　most superior way,
With the 'wog' a-pulling harder than a
　horse,
And being truly British, you'll admit he
　earns his pay,
　'A sentiment I heartily endorse).

This land of dead and dying, this malarial
   retreat,
This long-forgotten haven of the phantom
   Eastern fleet,
Will vanish like a nightmare when we take
   back Singapore;
   And we hope it won't be long before we
   do,
For they say there's not the slightest
   chance of going home before,
   An outlook that is apt to make us
   blue.

There are hailstones big as apples, and as
   hard as 'pussers peas',
There are cinder tracks called 'football
   fields'—and dreadful on the knees;
Electric storms and lightning and the most
   torrential rains
   Come a-teeming from the sky, a solid
   sheet,
There is damp, disease, and drabness, and
   the constant smell of drains,
   And we sometimes have our doubts
   about the meat.

Oh! it's there I'm spending Christmas, and it's not the place for me;
In Hull or Hell or Halifax—but not Trincomalee;
Though they give me garnished turkey, and a roasted sucking hog,
   Nuts and raisins, Christmas crackers and the rest,
I'd be a damn sight happier wading into cold 'corned dog'
   In that little island homeland of the West.

As always it was a special day with extra seasonal provisions and a great deal of larking about. Christmas Eve had seen us send a motor launch around the Harbour with the crew lustily singing carols in the starlit, balmy night. As their voices echoed across the water it was a very emotional experience for those of us listening on the flight deck. Their lantern flickered like a firefly on the surface of the sea, the carols seemed to surge and fade in the light breeze. As the launch approached nearby ships their crew joined in the singing and a wave of deep male vocal harmony rolled from ship to ship.

One custom on Christmas Day was to visit other ships to offer seasonal greetings and pay respect to the Officer of the Day who could often be found at the top of the ship's gangway. Our launch, with a pirate crew, went visiting. The crew swarmed up the gangway of *KGV*, saluted the officer, wished him and all onboard a Merry Christmas, and promptly threw him in the water. As he realised what was about to happen he removed his cap to prevent it getting wet—he was allowed to do so because it was thrown in after him! Meanwhile we had a bunch of stalwarts at the foot of our gangway ready to repel boarders. A vengeful and motley crew from *KGV* tried mightily to get aboard but failed to do so. We had raided the battleship again, threw the same officer in the water, and some of our party marched round their quarter-deck blowing a bugle and shouting in praise of *Victorious* and some dubious comments about *KGV*.

When the Christmas festivities were over we got down to the serious business of Gunnery and Flying exercises. *Victorious* had done little in the past two months and it was time for us to 'work up' again to an effective state of operational readiness. As we exercised with *Indomitable* and *Indefatigable* it was obvious that a heavy strike was planned to take place soon. The usual buzzes and speculation went around the ship like wildfire; all had one feature in common. It was forecast that we were bound for the Pacific, via Australia, and would carry out an attack en route. Where? We knew where it would not be— Nicobars, Sabang, the dreary, almost shipless harbours of north Sumatra. No, it had to be something worthwhile.

A friend of mine, Herbert Diss, was a peace-time employee of Shell Oil. We were discussing likely targets and he said, 'I believe we will have a go at Palembang where we have a refinery.'

'What makes you think that?' I asked.

'It's certain the Japs must be getting desperately short of oil and petrol. They have no oil resources in Japan and Palembang has been a major source of fuel for their navy and air forces. If we can cripple the refinery then we will have dealt them a worthwhile blow at last.

'And what about Shell, your employer. It must seem strange for you to be forecasting the possible destruction of a major asset of the company that pays your peace-time wages.'

'I've thought about that. If we do bomb the place, and get good photographs, I will ask permission to mail some copies back to the UK HQ.'

'You can't be serious,' I said. 'They won't let you do that Herbert.'

'I think they might. After all the Japanese will know what we will have done so it would hardly be a secret would it?'

'Well we don't know for sure. In a way I hope you are right. I just hope we don't go thumping the life out of strategically meaningless coral islands and losing good men in doing so.'

He looked reflective for a moment and a hint of sadness crossed his features. His work was in the administrative office of the Fleet Air Arm squadrons onboard and casualties had to be dealt with by him, often involving the preparation of letters to next of kin.

'Yes, you're right. I hope that lives are not put at risk for targets not worthy of the men themselves. I also hope it will be over soon.'

'Amen to that.'

When we did leave Trinco on New Years Day, 1945, at 1000, there were four big carriers together at last. As we steamed east we ran into the outer edge of a typhoon and the smaller ships took a heavy battering. There were a few green faces onboard *Victorious* too, after all we had not been to sea seriously for some time.

The fleet looked very impressive, the four fast, modern carriers, cruisers *Suffolk*, *Phoebe*, *Ceylon* and *Black Prince* plus eight destroyers.

On the second day *Illustrious* turned back. We were never told why; there was a quick exchange of signals and she headed west as we pushed quickly eastwards towards Sumatra. By now we knew the target was not to be Palembang but Pangkalan Brandan where two smaller and less important refineries were located. Their position, on the eastern side of Sumatra necessitated the bombers flying across the width of that country and over a small mountain range with peaks above 10,500 feet. The operation was named LENTIL—we sometimes wondered if an Admiralty clerk with a scrabble board chose the names—and we now had Admiral Philip Vian, formerly a dashing destroyer commander of great verve and elan, with his flag on *Indomitable*. The destroyers and two smaller cruisers oiled on day three, leading us to believe that the operation might be a sustained attack.

We went to Action Stations at 0540 on 4th January. By now the weather was perfect. Calm sea, extraordinary visibility and pleasantly warm. It was not long after 0600 when eight out of our 28 Corsairs took off to attack any aircraft found on the ground at airfields near the refinery. I always enjoyed the flight deck action, possibly because I wasn't directly involved. The heavy roar of the huge radial engines of the Corsairs, the sturdy aggressive strength of these fighters as they rolled slowly forward after 'chocks away', gathering speed for take off into the pale dawn light, heralding another day of strafing and bombing in one of nature's most beautiful areas of the world.

It was comparatively peaceful for the next two hours. The flight deck was a hive of efficient, well ordered activity, bombing up the Avengers, carrying out last minute checks. All done with a calm and practised ease that came only from training and dedicated men—at least that's what they boasted to the rest of the crew.

One great advantage of the Corsair was its ability to stay airborne for up to five hours, it gave its pilot that feeling of security and relief from constant fuel gauge monitoring which was so necessary with the Martlet and Seafire.

Indefatigable carried over 70 aircraft, as against our 49, but over 30 were Seafires, much smaller than our aircraft, and 12 were Fairey Fireflies. As we had heard in Trinco these latter were equipped with rockets, an asset we had not previously enjoyed in the Fleet Air Arm.

The strike force of bombers and escorting fighters was launched just before 0800 and we watched the aircraft from the three carriers form up before flying eastwards into the sun. I was always impressed by the organisational skill and disciplined flying that went into the form up. What appeared initially to be a large number of planes milling around the sky suddenly became a cohesive unit with every plane in its appropriate place and ready for the task ahead. Our intelligence was not always good as far as Japanese dispositions were concerned. There was not much prior reconnaissance and it came as no surprise to find the odd harbour empty, airfield deserted or heavy defensive weaponry where little was expected.

The worst part of any operation, for us at least, was the unreal silence and calm that befell the ship once the aircraft had left. Flight deck deserted, handling crews sitting in groups by the island or the crash barriers. The fire-fighters, half clad in their asbestos suits taking a breather before the planes returned. All guns crews alert, look-outs scanning the low horizon, whilst down in the Operations Room the radar screens were being assiduously scanned for signs of aerial activity. Many of us wore flash masks, an asbestos type of balaclava to protect us from flash burns. They were extremely uncomfortable and, when topped by a steel helmet, very unbecoming! We tried to pick up scraps of news that might have filtered back from the strike force. Little ever reached as far as our small group, high above the bridge.

As always the first clues, at least for us, were the faces of the returning air crews. The first fighters off at about 0600 had had a good time. They were on a 'Ramrod' strike, the code-name given to a fighter sweep against enemy targets and so-called after the 'Ramrod' of the great cattle drives who rode ahead and secured the territory for the following herd. It transpired that our Corsairs and *Indomitable*'s Hellcats had found the Japanese totally unprepared for attack and so destroyed a number of aircraft on the ground as well as shooting down two others.

A force of Japanese fighters had been mustered to attack the bomber strike and were very severely dealt with by the protecting fighters; half of a squadron of 12 was shot down or badly damaged.

Here it must be recalled that our fighters had scarcely seen a Japanese fighter airborne since we had been in the Indian Ocean. A few had been spotted on the ground but the nearest most pilots had been to an Oscar, Jake or Zero was an aircraft recognition board. You can imagine the sudden flow of adrenalin, the accelerated heart-beat and tightened stomach muscles when there they were finally in combat for which they had been trained. Although our fighters were remarkably successful there were complaints—so we heard—from the Avenger pilots who suddenly found themselves flying unprotected to the target as every fighter dashed off to join in the fray. It seemed that every Corsair wanted to get into the act and make a kill. There were recriminations when everyone was back onboard, most of them good-natured, but the Avenger crews could have become possible easy pickings for any further Jap aircraft had any of them found the bomber force.

We secured from Action Stations at 1900, and in the de-briefing room Commander (F) had been busy analysing his aircrews reports and Captain Denny had advised Admiral Vian of his conclusions. Whatever these were the immediate result was for us to have an exercise on the return to Trinco. *Indefatigable* and the cruisers left us and the following day her force was regarded as the enemy whilst ourselves and *Indomitable* launched a dummy attack. The purpose was to instil better air discipline and R/T conduct by both attacking and defending groups. It appeared to work well.

That night I had the middle watch on Cypher duties and the messages came in thick and fast, one of which advised that Lord Louis Mountbatten would be coming onboard in Trinco.

It was 0900 on 7th January when we anchored. A lot of the crew went off to Dutch Bay for a swim. This was a favourite pastime (in fact the only one) in Trinco. A beautiful sandy beach, sloping gently into the almost emerald green waters, this spot was a haven from the heat and enervating humidity of the small town. 'Elephant House' was the popular eating spot and their Banana Fritters were regarded by our gourmets as the best east of Suez.

Four days later, after frantic re-storing and making way for an increase in our

Corsair complement, possibly as fighter-bombers, Lord Louis came onboard to address the ship's company. A deal of tidying up had been carried out, paint lashed on here and there, gun turrets cleaned, gangways scrubbed. The Port After Gangway was polished until the brass-work shone and the blancoed ropes whiteness was positively dazzling. It was an inauspicious start when he arrived and tied up on the Starboard side!

His address was very 'Gung-ho' and, to me, somewhat arrogant but he impressed the men immensely. 'The war out here has been going on far too long and I've been sent out to get it over. The Japanese Fleet has left Singapore to defend its homeland. You are going to follow into the Pacific and help destroy it. Meanwhile I will ensure that all the Japs are kicked out of Burma, Malaya, Thailand and Singapore; believe me I am the man to get this done.'

Like Admiral Vian, Lord Louis had been a destroyer Captain. These men were regarded by some of the 'big ship' officers as the near 'cowboys' of the Navy—dropping depth charges, firing guns, launching torpedoes, ramming submarines or even submarine pens. Aggression and risk was their forte. Now we had two of them—Lord Louis and Rear Admiral Vian.

Most of the crew were aroused and excited by Mountbatten, he imbued them with some of his own enthusiasm and arrogance—a sense of infallibility. Doubtless this was to counter the image of the Jap fighting man who had been accorded the status of 'super-man'. He was cheered to the echo and his enjoyment of the adulation was plain for all to see.

The following night Tony and I put on a Dungeon Dust half-hour. A special poem had been penned in recognition of the great man's visit. This is it:

THE SAILOR'S FAREWELL

Just a taste of the glory we left him,
    Just for a ribbon to stick in our coats,
Banished, for space that was urgently
    needed
    By landing-craft, barges, and other small
    boats.

'Give me the boats,' was the cry of Lord
    Louis,
    'All you big ships, get to hell out of here,
We don't want to lose you, but glad you
    are going,
    To ease the congestion and shortage of
    beer.'

When they said that the leader was
    coming to see us,
    Confusion and painting began in some
    haste,
The hands set to work on the top, sides,
    and bottom,
    And sponged out the guns with some
    'clean' oily waste.

This passage was blocked, and that
    gangway was lifted,
Grey paint and red oxide all over the
    place,
Till going from mess to the flight deck for
    'freshers'
Resembled a course in an obstacle race.

Cockroaches fled in alarm and
  amazement,
    Yes, even the weevils crawled back into
    bed,
And waking one morn when the panic
  was over,
    Discovered that they were embalmed in
    the bread.

Hands set to work on the port after
  gangway,
    From sunrise to evening, they laboured
    with pride
To make an impression upon this great
  leader—
    But the only 'snag' was—he arrived
    starboard side.

The day came at last, and the ship shone
  in sunshine,
    And men were selected to shake by the
    hand,
The man who had started the early
  Commandos,
    And now reigned Supreme, South East
    Asia Command.

Men with long service and badges in
  plenty,
    Those who had seen the ship built on
    the stocks,
Men who had witnessed the flame of the
  battle—
    And seen the inside of a number of
    docks.

Youths, full of keenness and lofty
  endeavour
    Were also presented, to vary the scene,
By freshness, and unshaven innocent
  features,
    They made a nice change—if you know
    what I mean.

'Hostilities Only,' some just due for
  pension,
    And many who still had a long way to
    go,
And those who had been decorated for
  valour
    Added colour and tone to this very brave
    show.

The men on the flight deck stood stiff to
  attention,
    The lift shed its small select body of
    men,
RPO's twenty feet in advance of the
  Leader,
    While the 'jaunty', according to orders,
    was ten.

The men on provisions, devoid of all
  glamour,
    Were threatened with 'jankers' if they
    should be seen,
And as a precaution, an officer detailed,
    To see, if they came, that at least they
    came clean.

No 'pep' talk, but wisdom and words of
  good omen,
    While rumours of home were squashed
    flat on the head,
Not urging us merely to seek out the
  enemy,
    But telling us bluntly to sink him
    instead.

So he wished us good cheer, best of luck,
  and 'good hunting',
    And just as an afterthought, bade us
    'Good-bye',
The cheeks of the sailors were wet with
  emotion—
    Not even the paint on the 'island' was
    dry.

No longer the sight of the sun on Sumatra,
  No more the delights of dear
  Trincomalee,
Farewell for ever to 'dobey' and 'chah
  wallah'—
Follow the fleet to the great China Sea.

Follow the Jap fleet far into the sunrise,
  Chase them and catch them wherever
  they are,
Show the Americans how you struck terror
  Into all the Jap forces on Car Nicobar.

Make haste to the Eastward, the land of
  Mikado,
    Arrive while the Japs have some ships
    left to sink,
For according to news and American
  comment,
    The Japanese Navy are all in the 'drink'.

It won't be long now, just another two
  years,
    Before we are feeling the splash of the
    foam,
The wind from the West blowing cool in
  our faces,
    The glorious sight of the land that is
    home.

A couple of days and nights of exercise followed his visit. One new tactic was that of oiling at sea with the tanker ahead of us and trailing the fuelling hose. Oiling with the tanker alongside was tricky, especially when steaming at 16 knots and performing the obligatory zig-zag. It seemed to work quite well but it was decided to reserve final judgement until we were on actual operational duties.

We finally sailed at 1500 on 16th January. The buzz on the mess decks was that the carriers were bound for Brisbane and the battleships for Sydney. Some of us knew better, or at least differently.

There was a general moan that we had not received any mail for a few days. It transpired that the train from Colombo to Trincomalee was too heavy for the locomotive to pull. Two trucks were detached—and these contained the Fleet mail. The cruiser *Ceylon*, appropriately enough, was detailed to remain in Trinco, pick up the mail and bring it on to the Fleet as soon as possible. My friend Les Vancura wrote in his diary notes for the 17th Jan., 'I have not received any mail, not a single birthday card and it may be three weeks before I get any!' A note of irritation and frustration from a man regarded as one of the chirpiest souls on the ship. Oh the trials and tribulations of Trincomalee.

Of course we were saying farewell to this blessed spot. It had not been a comfortable anchorage. It was safe and secure but the heat was a trial and despite the various injections quite a number of the crew fell victim to various tropical diseases. The most common was dysentery. Men lost up to two stones in weight—we could ill afford that—became extremely debilitated and weak. Some were transferred to hospital ashore, a few others remained onboard either in the Sick Bay or as very regular 'out-patients'.

Australia would be a different place, but how long would we be there? Where would we be? Did it matter, it was only a transit stop en route to the waters off Japan.

There was still a job to be done before Australia. It was to be Palembang, probably the most daunting task to date for the Fleet Air Arm. Our previous sorties had really been no more than operational brushes with the Japanese to gain experience for this very important strike. It was vital that the two sets of refineries near Palembang be destroyed or severely damaged. An attempt had already been made by high level bombers of the US but it seemed that their accuracy was of a low order and only minimal disruption was caused to the oil flow.

For carrier based aircraft, operating from the Indian Ocean rather than the Straits of Malacca or the Java Sea, it was a hazardous journey over a mountain range and then across a plain containing several enemy airfields. It would have been impracticable to take the fleet into the Java Sea and the difficulties of operating in the Straits of Malacca, with Sumatra to the west and Malaya to the east, would have jeopardised the carriers to an unacceptable level. The Japanese had already proved the effectiveness of high level bombing on ships in confined or restricted waters—the *Prince Of Wales* and *Repulse* were tragic evidence of that.

The force now sailing towards Sumatra was the strongest assembled by the Royal Navy for a naval air assault on any target. The carriers between them could muster almost 250 aircraft, a mixed armada of five types of bomber, fighter-bomber and fighter, plus two Walrus air-sea rescue amphibian aircraft. *Victorious* carried these and would deploy them for the first time. The Walrus was an elderly airplane, two wings above a stubby fuselage, which could be landed on water—or with wheels down on land. The single engine was a 'pusher' with the propeller at the back of the engine rather than the front. Top speed was about 90 miles an hour, although this was regarded as an exaggeration! The wings folded back but even so it was a space-hungry plane. There was sometimes a problem when landing back onboard. If *Victorious* was steaming at 28 knots into a stiff wind it was difficult for the Walrus to catch up with the ship. We would almost collapse with laughter as we looked astern and watched this ungainly craft, on full throttle, seemingly suspended at a set distance behind us. Eventually it would make it and two members of the air handling party would dash out, hands onto the lower wing and haul it down onto the deck. These two aircraft and their brave crews were to perform some great deeds in the days to come.

Admiral Vian had his flag on *Indomitable*, also in company with the carriers was *KGV*, four cruisers and 10 destroyers. On 18th we crossed the Equator, steaming steadily east toward the southern tip of Sumatra. Two oilers, in company with *Ceylon* and a destroyer, fuelled up the other destroyers; we were going to be at sea for some time. The weather was appalling, squalls, heavy seas, poor visibility—conditions utterly against launching our strike forces. For two days we circled around waiting for an improvement before proceeding to the launch area. Finally the Met Officers, after releasing their balloons, checking wind gauges—and, I suspect, wetting a finger and holding it out in the breeze—advised the Admiral that the forecast was good.

At 0530 we went to Action Stations and watched the now familiar routine on the Flight Deck below the ADP. 'Guns' said to me, 'I think we are going to need that little radar set in your "caboose" before the next two days are over. Tell the look-outs to keep a keen watch low down if we hear that Japanese aircraft are approaching.'

He looked serious today. There were usually lights of laughter, almost mischief, in his eyes and his mouth appeared to be permanently on the verge of a smile. But not today. I wondered if he had a presentiment or had suffered a bad night. He was a very open man and it was easy to tell that he was 'keyed up'. I hoped he was his normal, calm, unflappable self.

Although we had transferred some of our Corsairs to *Indomitable* we were still very full. In Ceylon we had taken onboard an enormous amount of aircraft stores and spares. In consequence part of the hangar was being utilised as storage space. The knock-on effect of this was that some aircraft had to be parked permanently on the Flight deck. The weather of the previous 48 hours, rain and especially the humidity, was unfriendly to exposed aircraft and it was no surprise when we suffered some problems at launch time.

It was not long after 0600 that the 'start up' order was given and within 15 minutes the aircraft began to roll. *Victorious* was to provide a 'Ramrod' airfield sweep of 12 Corsairs, a Combat Air Patrol of Corsairs as well as 12 Avengers on bombing duty. The launch was untidy, one of the Avengers refused to start—possibly due to weather exposure—and another took off, requested immediate permission to land and was back on deck within minutes. The result of these incidents and other misfortunes on the other carriers was an interminable 'form up' before departure for the target. In fact it was almost an hour later when the group finally headed east and began the climb to an altitude to clear the mountains, the highest of which, Dempo, was over 10,300 feet.

Again the strangely quiet hiatus until the first of the aircraft appeared about three hours later. The first thing I noticed was that several of the Avengers were damaged, with bullet holes in fuselage and wings. The crews were smiling wearily with relief, it was obvious that this had not been an easy run.

As the news of the attack spread from the de-briefing it emerged that mistakes had been made yet again, the principal of which was that the 'Ramrod' sweep and attack on the defending airfields had not taken place in advance of the bombing of the refinery but almost simultaneously. This meant that the Japs had been able to put a considerable fighter force into the air before the Corsairs attacked their bases.

There were a number of dog-fights between opposing fighters as the Avengers droned on to the target. A surprise awaited them, the Japanese were deploying that very British invention, the Barrage Balloon. These were smaller than ours and ascended very quickly; in some instances the balloons were not released until the enemy saw the attack altitude of the Avengers.

Despite the hazards, fighters, balloons and intense, fairly accurate anti-aircraft fire, the bombers pressed on to the target and scored a number of direct hits which resulted in huge columns of black smoke and bright red flames rising into the air. The subsequent photographs provided evidence of the damage caused, it was a disciplined accurate bombing.

The usual aircraft count was made to check our losses. The original force of 110 planes had suffered a 10% loss, two pilots had been rescued from the sea near to the fleet. Similarly the Japs had lost 11 planes but many more had been destroyed on the ground in diversion attacks on airfields. The principal objective of the enterprise had been realised, a heavy, if not devastating, blow at enemy oil production.

As we retreated westwards towards our oiling force we anxiously awaited the Japanese counter attack. Like many, I was certain it would come, but apart from unsubstantiated reports of 'Bogies' our patrolling aircraft were unable to establish contact and the day ended peacefully.

That evening we received a message from Admiral Vian. He said an enemy radio bulletin had stated that 75 of our aircraft had been shot down by anti-aircraft fire!! and a further 13 by Japanese Army fighters. They admitted losing 12 which was one more than we had believed.

During the next two days we rendezvoused with the tankers and after the destroyers, cruisers and *KGV* had been fuelled, we took on 1600 tons of oil—the tanker trailing the hose from ahead of us as had been practised. There were still those who shook their heads in disbelief as they watched us steaming just 50 yards astern of the tanker.

It was part of the operational plan to attack the other refining plant at Palembang, which was why we spent two days out of the launch area oiling, repairing damaged aircraft, and above all learning from the lessons of the first attack. There was evidence of poor R/T discipline between aircraft over the target, the initial launch had been badly co-ordinated and methods had to be devised to counter the balloon defences.

The 29th saw us back at the launch position, 30 odd miles off the coast. We went to Action Stations at 0545 and I could not believe the weather. Yet again heavy rain and low cloud, completely contrary to what I had read in books on the area. Mind you the books were purchased in Colombo and printed in India. This was supposed to be the 'clear' season, free of monsoons and cloud, yet here we were getting aboslutely drenched in the ADP. At least the rain was warm.

'Your forebodings were misplaced for the last operation,' I said to 'Guns'.

He looked at me with his customary smile.

'Yes indeed, but today's another day. This time I am certain they will come after us.'

'Do you have a special intelligence source?' I questioned jokingly.

'No, but the Japs will now have one about us. Don't forget we know they captured some airmen in the last raid and they have probably been able to extract information from them that we intend to launch another attack. This time they should be prepared to strike back.'

'We can cope sir,' I said with unfelt enthusiasm.

'Very likely. Trouble is we haven't had them reach the fleet before and we know from their record of naval bombing successes that they present a more formidable threat than the Germans.'

'But we have plenty of defensive fighter cover and if they do get close we are now armed to the teeth.'

'We will see. I don't much care for all this low cloud. It's a radar day today then possibly close range weapons.'

He stood in the rain, his brown, lined face streaked with water. I wondered about his age, I suppose he must have been in his early 40's, about 20 years my senior yet with an awesome responsibility on his shoulders. Over 100 guns of varying calibres were under his command—he was our defender if the enemy broke through our air cover. Yet today he looked less concerned than four days earlier when he seemed a very worried man.

The take-off eventually got under way during a brief interlude of clear sky which soon became blanketted with cloud yet again. By now the fighters and bombers were airborne and searching for their appropriate group before departure to Palembang. Over 100 aircraft were stooging around in wretched visibility and we watched anxiously to see any signs of mid-air collision.

The Air Co-ordinator for the whole strike was now Ronnie Hay, a Major in the Royal Marines, and becoming something of a legend in Fleet Air Arm circles. His was the task to assemble the force in its proper format, get it to the target, direct certain operations in that area, as well as carry out some individual air combat which he did with his usual flair, elan and thoroughly considered airmanship. He was a consummate fighter pilot and leader.

It was some four and a half hours later when we were alerted to the return of our aircraft and, as they began to form up into their landing circuit, we could tell that they had experienced a rough time. Only five of our Avengers out of 12 were in sight and that was the number which landed back on the flight deck. Three of those quite heavily damaged so only two of our bombers were unscathed. This was a devastating blow.

Some of the returning Avengers had ditched near the Fleet, having been nursed and cajoled to near safety before flopping into the sea close to a rescue ship. These were destroyers, skilfully handled by their Captains to reach aircrew quickly once they had hit the water.

There was a sense of shock onboard, 11 of our aircrew were lost, mainly from our Avenger squadron. Some of those who landed had minor injuries; all in all it was the heaviest setback *Victorious* had suffered since commissioning in April, 1941.

On the credit side the Corsairs had done well and the 'Ramrod' attack against Jap airfields had been much more effective than four days previously.

The total losses of the four carriers amounted to some 40 aircraft from all causes, enemy fighters, balloon barrage (claiming at least two Avengers), anti-aircraft fire, and ditching because of severe damage. Some 31% of the strike force was lost, a rate of attrition which was too high to sustain over a lengthy series of operations.

The oil refineries were heavily damaged as the early photographic evidence revealed. Within hours we had pictures of towering columns of smoke and flame, bright white explosions as tanks ruptured raining burning fuel on nearly installations.

Petty Officer Diss was given permission to mail a selection of photographs to Shell so that they could assess the damage. It seemed to me that the Japanese would repair them anyway, their need to do so was imperative otherwise what was the purpose of the raid?

Some time prior to our aircraft returning to the Fleet we had detected a long range snooper. Fighters were vectored onto him but he made good his escape. We now knew that the enemy were aware of our exact location and we could expect a visit from them 'ere long.

At the end of October, 1944, there had been an immense naval battle off the Philippines, the battle of Leyte Gulf. It was probably the most devastating, bloody sea fight in the history of naval warfare. The US Navy had inflicted a grievous defeat on the Japanese Fleet, sinking four aircraft carriers, three battleships, 10 cruisers and a number of destroyers. It was at this battle, in an act of sheer desperation, that the Japs introduced their latest weapon, the Kamikaze (Divine Wind). This was an aircraft, normally a fighter, manned by a suicidal pilot and loaded with high explosive. The pilot, usually decorated for valour before take-off, and wearing items of apparel exclusive to Kamikaze airmen, had only one objective—to crash his aircraft onto an enemy ship, preferably an aircraft carrier. It was the most effective weapon yet devised in World War Two aerial warfare, a human bomb with a man's brain as its guidance system.

It was not long before noon that a small force of 'Sallys', a twin enginned bomber, were picked up on the radar. They were attacked by our Combat Air Patrol but dived down to sea level to make their approach to the Fleet.

By now the day was cloudy and grey, the water slightly choppy, with a warm wind blowing. We watched from the Air Defence Position. My small radar had picked up several 'blips' but they had disappeared from the screen at a range of about seven miles. It was all down to visual sighting now. There was a squadron of Seafires in the air and as we picked up the enemy aircraft on our port quarter some four miles away we could see the fighters wheeling and diving down onto the Sallys. It was not long before the first of them was splashed, then another. The remainder pressed on, at no more than 40 feet above the waves.

'Torpedo bombers I think,' said 'Guns', he had already given instructions to the various gunnery positions to open fire when the planes were in range.

'Do you identify them?' he asked. I looked at my recognition chart displayed alongside my radar set.

'Look like Sallys to me sir, but they could be Dinahs.' Jap aircraft, in the main, had been given male and female names by the Americans; fighters Jake, Hamp, Zeke, bombers, Betty, Sally, Dinah. There were exceptions—Tojo was a fighter, as was the Zero, possibly their best.

As the bombers got closer another was shot down by the Seafires. The remainder were making for *Illustrious* and *Indefatigable*, it was not our turn today. The anti-aircraft guns of the protecting cruisers had commenced firing as had those of the carriers themselves. The crackle, crump, thud, rattle of weaponry drifted across towards us. The Seafires were still darting down onto the Sallys, firing a long burst, climbing quickly upwards to turn and plunge down on their target again. They were now as much at risk from the anti-aircraft fire as were the enemy. A Sally now cartwheeled into the water, exploding into a pall of thick black smoke only some 250 yards from *Indefatigable*, and another was shot down astern of *Illustrious*. The protecting anti-aircraft cruiser of *Illustrious*, the *Euryalus*, was so busy firing with gun barrels depressed horizontal to sea level, that she failed to check fire when her guns traversed the carrier itself. Two shells thudded into *Illustrious*, one just below the flight deck, the other hitting the after end of the island.

We watched as the shells burst, brown and destructive, on our sister ship.

'Ye Gods,' said 'Guns', 'did you see that? What bloody fool has fired on our own ship?' He looked both furious and shocked that such an accident could occur.

'*Eurlyaus*, wasn't she on the Malta convoy with us?'

'Yes sir, with *Charybdis.*'

He lifted his binoculars to his eyes, by this time the last of the Sallys had plummeted into the sea. Seven had attacked, seven shot down. The last one fell near the *KGV* although that ship was not its intended target.

'Guns' turned around. 'That the lot then?'

'Yes sir, seven came, seven splashed.'

'There may be more to come later. They seem a very determined lot.'

An understatement I thought, the Sally pilots had appeared to be positively suicidal. It was some time later that we learned it was indeed a Kamikaze operation. The bombers were determined to crash into any of the carriers at just above sea level.

Signals received from *Illustrious* confirmed that she had suffered damage and casualties, 12 men killed and more than 30 injured. It had indeed been a traumatic day.

We turned away from Sumatra and headed north-west shadowed by the odd Jap reconnaissance plane. These persisted until early evening but no further attacks were launched at us and at 2100 we stood down from Action Stations.

For two days we took stock of the situation. The operations had been fairly successful but the price paid was high, particularly on the last strike. The aircrews onboard were distressed by the loss of so many of their friends and comrades. The sad procedure of packing up the effects of those who had been killed or declared missing was under way. Letters to next of kin, sympathetic and commendatory, were being written.

Some of us sat on the flight deck in the evening sunlight and tried to analyse the whole Padang operation. We knew, of course, that the Commanders, Captains and Admirals, in possession of all the information, would be doing the same. Their views mattered, ours were coloured by more personal considerations and gut reaction, rather than objective reasoning based on facts. Nevertheless, like all who served at whatever level, we debated the issues.

Chief Writer Rex Starling, with years of experience and naval wisdom, was never short of an opinion. He expressed the view that we were operating on a shoe string and that if we were going to the Pacific, and to be effective, we must have better support—logistically.

'Look at us now,' he went on. 'Low on oil with the tanker virtually dry, no reserve aircraft to make up our tragic losses, no amunition ship for bombs and aircraft weaponry. We could not mount another attack on Palembang and really finish off the refineries if we wanted to.'

I ventured the view that all these factors were well known to naval command and the Admiralty and that Australia would be able to provide a depth of logistical support we had not previously enjoyed.

'Only if the Americans and ourselves put the materials there in the first place. Australia will be fine for provisions and simple supplies but aircraft, munitions, oil, will need to come from the US. New aircrew, certain spares, supply ships will have to come from the UK,' responded Rex.

Three of us sat with our feet resting on the bar that stretched across the rounded front of the flight deck. The ship virtually disappeared beneath our feet and we could hear the bow waves hissing away to port and starboard as the ship cut through the royal blue sea. The sun was setting and the sky, a pale yellow with tiny dark clouds very high, looked like a desert with patches of black scrub.

Tony spoke. It was the perennial question. 'Do the Americans really want us in the Pacific? Are we in any way compatible, apart from our desire to defeat the Japs and end the war?'

'I honestly don't think they do want us,' said Rex, 'they are now strong enough to wear down the Japs without us. But for post-war image purposes in the remanants of our Empire—Singapore, Hongkong, Malaya, Borneo—it is essential that we are known to be participating in the final defeat of their new colonisers. In any case I am sure the once omnipotent white man will never have the same influence out here again.

'What you are saying then,' I said, 'is that our presence in the Pacific will be more a political factor than a military one.'

'Yes, I believe so.'

We went on talking about the role of Britain after the war. Tony, a strong Conservative, nevertheless believed we should shed our Empire as soon as possible. I think he had not liked what he saw in India and Ceylon.

The sun slipped out of sight, the sky was now a dark gold which reflected on the sea, turning it into a molten bronze. It was getting a little chilly. Tony said a short prayer for those who had been lost on the 29th. As I listened I thought what a comforting priest he would have been.

The following day we had a 'Crossing the Line' ceremony. Most of us had crossed it at least twice, but some 400 or so were deemed not to be 'truly shell-backs of Neptune' and had to be so initiated.

A large canvas pool was constructed on the flight deck. Filled with water it also housed four Royal Marines, standing waist deep. Above them and across the pool was a platform on which was balanced a 'barber's chair'. The 'barber', in a long white robe and anti-flash helmet, wielded an enormous wooden 'razor', his assistant had a huge container of 'lather'. Each hapless victim was put in the chair, 'shaved', tipped into the water below and seized upon by 'Davy Jones assistants'. They immersed their charge three or four times, chanting homage to Neptunus Rex, and dumped him out onto the flight deck.

Several of the officers were punished for offences against Neptune, even though they were 'shell-backs' and Captain Denny was arrested just near the Bridge and brought down to be shaved and ducked. I had the impression they were a little over-enthusiastic with the Skipper and wondered if his sharp eyes and mind were noting a few names or even considering a work period instead of a 'make and mend'!

On 3rd February we were caught on the fringe of a cyclone and we pitched, tossed and rolled heavily, the smaller ships suffering minor damage. What was the purpose of paying our respects to Neptunus Rex if he immediately punished us for our trouble? Despite being slowed by the weather we reached Fremantle at 0700 on the 4th.

Commander Tucker had told me the previous evening to be ready to go ashore in the morning with a Royal Marine bodyguard. We took a Jeep and drove to a Bank where I filled two standard naval green suitcases with the equivalent of £75,000 in Australian pounds. As soon as I arrived back onboard we arranged a payment to the crew and also exchanged sterling for Australian currency. Some had saved cash in Trinco and so would be going ashore 'rich' in a Europeanised environment.

Meanwhile some benevolent soul sent a ton of grapes to the ship and a large number of Christmas parcels arrived from the Australian Comfort Fund. Les ate over one and a half pounds of grapes at one sitting.

The other three carriers, two cruisers and six destroyers sailed immediately after oiling; we departed the following morning at 1130. A Royal Australian Army Captain was onboard and he gave us a talk on Sydney; its history, amenities, attractions, possible problems, clubs, theatres, cinemas etc. It all sounded very promising.

CHAPTER ELEVEN

To the Bitter End

For those who have not experienced the sensation of sailing through Sydney heads and onwards into the harbour at 0730 on a glorious summer day, you have missed one of the most staggeringly beautiful scenic sights the world has to offer.

We assembled on deck, above deck, on the island, ADP—wherever—and marvelled at the breathtaking cliffs, coves, beaches, lush vegetation which heralds the seaborne visitor to Sydney. It was dazzingly spectacular and quite the most lovely harbour I had ever seen.

As we progressed slowly towards the city the small steamers, ferries and yachts acknowledged us by whistle, flag, siren, with people waving welcome from their decks.

We tied up alongside the Zoological Gardens and had Landing Craft to shuttle us ashore on the other side of the harbour. I looked at the famous Bridge, determined to walk across it, because my father, a steel-working machinist at Dorman Long, Middlesborough, had planed many of the plates and girders forming part of that remarkable structure.

The next few days were spent savouring civilisation. Walking in Hyde Park, watching the locals playing 'two-up' with pennies, sitting in the peace and tranquility of St. Mary's Cathedral, strolling down Elizabeth Street, into David Jones the large departmental store, or taking a bus to one of the many beaches.

Clothes were rationed but we were given 15 coupons a man, and with a little judicious bribery, Tony and I managed to obtain a few more. After spending hours in David Jones, marvelling at the range and variety of the merchandise on offer, we both purchased Sports Jackets and casual trousers as well as lumber-jack style shirts and brown shoes.

The Australians were as hospitable as the Americans and we were frequently stopped on the street, or on the steps of a Services Club, and invited to meals and homes. Many of course were 'Poms' and anxious, nostalgically so, to establish links with someone from 'home'.

Seventeen days were to elapse before we left Sydney on 28th February. We had been waiting for stores and spares—another example of our tenuous position so far from UK—and the final two days before departure northwards were frantic with activity, loading ammunition, bombs and masses of provisions.

Now we were on our way to Manus Island, one of the Admiralty Island group situated in the North Bismarck Sea to the north of New Guinea.

On 4th March we were in the exact position that we had been on 2nd July, 1943, we had therefore circumnavigated the world, by sea, traversing both the Panama and Suez Canals. The climate was cripplingly hot. The light winds from astern offered no respite and the temperature below decks was a constant 100° with a high level of humidity. The vast flight deck, 7500 square yards, absorbed and retained the heat of the sun. It became almost too hot to walk on with thin soled shoes or sandals. The heat penetrated into and through the Hangar roof, and the hangar itself became an enormous sweatbox with noxious aircraft fumes thrown in. The engine rooms and galleys also generated heat and this rose, from the lower reaches of the ship, upwards to meet that from above. The result was an enervating, energy sapping humidity that made every task an effort and concentration very difficult. The drinking water fountains splashed out warm water, the showers—on cold—were like taking a semi-hot bath; one sweated as you soaped and rinsed, drying with a towel was a waste of time and effort.

Manus Island anchorage was a test of endurance and morale for the ship's company. The fleet had now assembled, along with store and supply vessels, and was awaiting instructions for the next operation. We carried out the usual exercises and worked up the aircraft squadrons to operational status. It all seemed purposeless and the mood onboard was one of depression. This was not improved when, on 16th February, a member of the crew of the Captain's motor launch was drowned.

For all ranks, below officer level, who died or were killed, their 'effects'— possessions in other words—were sold to other members of the ship's company. This procedure was called 'Sale of Effects' and took place on the Flight Deck. A table would be rigged and the effects of the dead sailor carefully laid out. The Master-at-Arms, Lt. Peter Lorne and myself, would form the team carrying out the sale, taking cash or promissory notes and ensuring that a dignified procedure was followed. The object was to raise as much money as possible for the next of kin, usually the mother or wife. The Master would auction the item, I would take the cash or register a promise to pay by means of a pay deduction, and give the money to Peter Lorne who placed it in a conveniently sized metal box.

Everything was sold, from a bar of chocolate, matches, unused razor blades, notepaper, pen, cigarettes, as well as all the uniform clothing. The amounts bid depended upon the circumstances, and before the sale commenced I would advise all prospective bidders of the next-of-kin status and that we wanted a maximum display of generosity. Master-at-Arms would then auction. I saw a 2p bar of chocolate sell for £3, a half-spent box of matches for £5. Some would buy and then return the item immediately for re-sale. On this occasion, in sweaty, tropical, humid, stifling Manus, we raised £365. That was almost two years average wages, or enough to buy a small house. Sailors were generous to their own, and some of the sales were very emotional.

We sailed on 18th for Ulithi Atoll in the Caroline Islands, arriving two days later. This 'sublime' spot, a coral atoll about 16 miles by four miles, was the most remarkable anchorage I had ever seen. It was an almost circular barrier of coral, with small sandy bays and palms, and had been captured from the Japanese about eight months earlier. Its uniqueness was in the amount of shipping accommodated there when we arrived. Standing on deck I counted 30 aircraft carriers, a dozen battleships, cruisers, destroyers, tankers and supply ships by the score. It was an amazing armada, a display of naval force and strength unlikely to be witnessed ever again. Launches and small boats criss-crossed the harbour as they conveyed Captains and Commanders to meetings with Admirals, store ships and tenders nosed alongside the fighting vessels to top them up for battle, aldis lamps flickered signals from ship to ship. I wondered if anyone really knew what was going on and what we were all to do in the immediate future. Could anyone devise a viable plan for such a conglomerate force?

I need not have worried. On 23rd March, not long after dawn, the British Pacific Fleet weighed anchor and steamed, seemingly unnoticed, out of Ulithi. As we passed the serried ranks of ships of almost every kind it seemed as though we were sneaking off to wage a private vendetta gainst the Japs. We were not to be absorbed into the US Fleet, a mighty part of which had left two days earlier. We were soon told that we were now Task Force 57, attached to the US Fifth Fleet. I knew from cypher work that the US Fleet was either the 5th or 3rd dependent upon whether Admiral Spruance or Admiral Halsey was in Flag Command. We barely qualified as a Task Force—at least by American standards—as we were relatively modestly equipped in aircraft and armament, but TF 57 we became and headed north in the Western pacific towards Formosa and Japan.

After two days we met up with our Fleet Train and the cruisers and destroyers were oiled. We were comprised of two battleships, four aircraft carriers, five cruisers and 11 destroyers, one of which, the *Queensborough* had been adopted by my home town Lytham St. Annes—which considered itself, somewhat arrogantly, to be the Queen of Boroughs. As we proceeded to the target area we conducted gunnery exercises on drogues towed by US twin engined bombers. We despatched four drogues, quite quickly, all by close range weaponry, as the weather was unsuited to use the 4.5, 5.25 or 6 inch guns.

Captain Denny announced that our task was to neutralise a number of airfields in Sakishima Gunto, a section of a group of islands known collectively as Riyuku. These islands, located between Formosa and Japan, were the staging posts for aircraft flying from Formosa to Okinawa. The latter was under direct attack by US forces and if we could prevent re-inforcement of Jap air strength from Formosa we would be performing a useful function.

Intelligence was sketchy. We now had the latest Type 'X' machines in the cypher office. These were like a large typewriter and provided a decyphered tape after the machine had been pre-set to a given code on a series of circular discs rather like a brief case combination lock. It was much more complicated of course, but once the machine had been set-up decyphering was very fast. We still had the old one-time pads as well as some unusual boards into which one slotted row after row of mixed letters, printed on cardboard strips, and then used a vertical line to read the decyphered message downwards. Apparently these were mobile cypher systems used by US forces onshore and without access to more sophisticated means of secret communication. Despite all these innovations, including a 24 hour clock—where 12 was at the bottom and 24 at the top (instead of 12), we knew little of what was actually based at the airfields we were to attack.

Cynics onboard said the islands would be as empty of Japs as the Nicobars, otherwise the Americans would not want us to go there. The feeling that our Allies did not want us with them still persisted, so it was natural that our being apparently 'side-tracked' to a minimal target area reinforced that view.

On 26th March, we closed up at Action Stations at 0545, the fleet being about 90 miles from the islands we were to attack.

As a result of the low level attack on us by the Japanese Sallys after the Palembang attack we now employed the American tactic of positioning two destroyers between the coast and the main force so that they could give warning of any low-flying aircraft. The destroyers, known as 'picket' boats, would use both their radar and look-outs to detect intruders.

First to fly off not long after 0600 was a Ramrod sweep of Corsairs, to be followed later by a bombing force of Avengers, escorted by fighters. The airfields scheduled for attack were to be put out of action if practicable—hangars destroyed, fuel dumps blown up, runways cratered, and any aircraft seen to be shot up. Secondary targets were also listed, a barracks and a radio station.

For two days we launched a series of bombing raids and rocket and machine gun attacks on enemy positions. The results were unimpressive. There were few Jap aircraft about, the airfields were often constructed of steam-rollered coral, of which the islands were virtually made, and any damage inflicted was repaired within hours. The anti-aircraft defences were competent and after 48 hours of attacking we had lost 19 aircraft. These included that of the Commander of 1836 Squadron, Lt. Cdr. Tomkinson. He was seen to bale out and successfully take to the water but our air-sea rescue Walrus could find no trace of him shortly afterwards. A thorough gentleman, a very capable and much respected leader, his loss was very keenly felt by all who knew him but most of all by his squadron who held him in such high regard.

Whilst we were bombing and strafing by day we had reason to believe that the Japs were moving aircraft through the airfields at night. During the night of 26/27th we were called to Action Stations at 0245, I was just about three quarters way through a Cypher Watch so was delighted to dash up to the ADP. There was intermittent moonlight, clouds scudding across every now and then

—reminded me of Alfred Noyes' lines—'the moon was a ghostly galleon tossed upon cloudy seas'. Somewhere, we were informed, a 'bogey' was lurking. *Indomitable* launched a Hellcat, a rare exercise indeed in semi-darkness, and the enemy aircraft withdrew. We stood down at 0400, only to close up again at 0550 to launch more daylight attacks.

At this time the Fleet enjoyed the protection of a constant 16 aircraft Combat Air Patrol, with a further 32 on standby on the four carriers.

The pilots of our aircraft were provided with a survival kit for use in the event of a crash landing on-shore; water purifying tablets, first aid kit, compass and other sundry items. Many were also given gold sovereigns with which to trade or bribe for food, information, or even for their lives.

We carried hundreds of sovereigns onboard, all kept in the main safe. At about this time Commander Tucker said to me, 'Barker, I think we had better devise a plan to take care of HM sovereigns in the event of our having to abandon ship.'

'Of course sir, what did you have in mind?'

'You and I will take all the gold, plus the dollars, with us onto our rescue boat or float.'

'How are we going to carry the sovereigns and the currency sir?'

'I have stored two hold-all bags in the bottom of the safe, come with me and see if they are adequate for the task.'

We went to the safe which was located very near to his cabin. He was a tall man, very thin, grey hair and spectacles perched almost on the end of his nose. He bent over the safe, worked the combination and pulled back the heavy steel door. We took the two hold-alls, opened them up and started loading the bundles of notes and bags of sovereigns. When we had finished, Commander Tucker said to me, 'Let's walk with them to the end of the flat and up the first gangway.' He closed the safe door and we moved away. The bags were heavy and the Commander was breathing hard when we reached the top of the gangway.

'That's no good,' he wheezed. 'Maybe if we have to do this in a real situation you will take the heavier bag.'

'Of course sir.' We descended the stairs and walked back to the safe. I waited until the cash and gold was stored back then made to leave.

'Don't forget now Barker. I will be relying on you to help me safeguard HM's property.'

'I will be here sir and ready to carry the heavier bag.'

He smiled and looked benignly over his glasses at me.

'You're a good fellow. I like the way you deal with people at the office. I also like that irreverent radio programme you do with that friend of yours. Any more in the pipeline?'

'Yes, sir, as soon as we are out of the battle area for a few days.'

'Good, let me know when the broadcast is to be. Have you ever considered making a career in the Navy? You should consider taking a commission. I will give you a good recommendation.'

'I haven't really thought about it sir, maybe when the war is over.'

'Yes, everything will be much clearer when peace comes.' He smiled again, pulled back his cabin door and went inside. As I made my way to the Ship's Office I hoped Abandon Ship would never be piped. I didn't fancy my chances with a weighty hold-all, hanging onto the ropes on a Carley float.

By now the Fleet had retired to the Fleet Train, about 200 miles back from the launch position. Two Escort carriers, *Striker* and *Speaker,* were waiting with replenishment aircraft. We took three Corsairs, and also tried to oil and take 'Avgas' but it was a painful, tedious, disorganised affair. We were not able to fuel like the US carriers, from alongside, but from the trailing hose ahead of us, and we were hours connected, disconnected, as the fittings broke under the strain, It was amazing that now we had a Fleet Train on station the process of refuelling was still so poorly handled.

By now we had been informed that the Americans were landing in Okinawa on 1st April, and it was essential we should be on station and attacking Sakishimo Gunto to provide as much of a diversion as possible. Few of us believed that anything we might do would be regarded as other than of nuisance value but at least we might prevent any air re-inforcement by day from Formosa.

Remarkably, on 30th March, Good Friday, despite all the problems—heat, heaving seas and generally disruptive routine, the cooks in the galleys managed to bake some hot-cross buns. It seemed an odd Christian gesture in this heathen war of the Far East, but the buns were enjoyed and the thoughtfulness of the provisions staff much appreciated.

Maybe the Lord was responsive to this gesture for later that day, in the evening, one of our escorting destroyers decided to take a short cut on changing station and cut across our bows in the true cowboy style of many a destroyer commander. An alert Officer-of-the-Watch threw our mighty turbines into immediate full astern and *Victorious* rattled and shook violently as we shuddered to the sharp reduction in speed. Echoes of the *Punjabi* and *KGV* I thought, or even RMS *Queen Mary* and cruiser *Curacoa.* No doubt the destroyer skipper and his colleagues enjoyed their flirt with disaster, livened up two dreary days, but we heard that a few sharp words were sent their way.

Action Stations at 0600 and the first sweeps were despatched to beat up the airfields and buildings once more. Combat Air Patrols were launched throughout the day and groups of bombers flown off late morning and late afternoon to crater the airfields yet again.

We were at Action Stations all day, watching our own aircrews return and awaiting the enemy response. None was forthcoming and the airmen's faces bore witness to the fact that little had been achieved in the attacks onshore. No doubt the Japs were bracing themselves for the expected attacks on Okinawa and preserving their defensive response accordingly.

On Easter Sunday the Americans assaulted Okinawa by air, sea and land. Marines invaded and planes and heavy ships carried out a constant bombardment of Japanese positions.

We flew off our first Ramrod about half an hour after we closed up at Action Stations at 0615. As usual we had two picket vessels on station and we settled down for another routine day. It was less than an hour later that we were warned, in the ADP, that a force of enemy aircraft had been detected about 70 miles away and approaching the task force. We were now on full alert, extra fighters were flown off and some of those sent on the Ramrod sweep were recalled to help defend the Fleet. Our Corsairs were the first to sight the Jap aircraft, Lt. Martiensen proving yet again what a superb FDO he was, and an enemy fighter was shot down.

The Jap force then broke up into small units of two or three aircraft, continually changing height to confuse the radar and fighter direction. They were identified at altitudes varying from 19,000 to sea level. It appeared that there were more than a dozen Jap planes getting nearer and, despite the attention of our various fighters, they closed quickly on the Fleet. By 0720 we had them in sight, along with the pursuing Seafires and Corsairs.

Once again we had the problem of both friendly and enemy planes being within gunnery range. After what had happened to *Illustrious* off Sumatra it was natural that the variouꞋ gunnery teams were reluctant to open saturation fire on aircraft that could well be our own. Additionally a couple of Japanese aircraft bore some resemblance to our Seafires and Hellcats. Recognition, in a split second, was not easy as we had discovered years previously on the Malta Convoy.

A Japanese plane, now flying within the fleet area, carried out a brief machine gun attack on the *KGV*, giving rise to some comments from those sailors who now believed that battleships were the dinosaurs of naval warfare.

'That'll have got them out of their hammocks quicker than "Wakey, wakey",' I heard one 'Scouse' look-out say to his mate. But *KGV* was not the target, the battleships never were, and the Jap twisted to turn his attention to *Indefatigable*. He quickly climbed then levelled momentarily before launching into a dive on the carrier. We watched as her close-range weapons opened up, but it mattered little, he seemed impervious to gunnery and dropped, now very quickly, onto the centre of the flight deck. There was an immense explosion, and white smoke rose in a thickening cloud from alongside the bridge in an ever increasing density, reaching almost as far astern as the first arrester wires. As aircraft on deck caught fire the smoke cloud became black, quickly rising to 200 feet.

News came to us that eight men had been killed and almost 20 injured. Both crash barriers had been put out of action and the flight deck damaged, splinters from which had caused injury and other damage. Most of those killed were in the island structure. This was our first Kamikaze attack from the single-seat fighter force which had wrought destruction upon the US Navy. Our carriers were inferior in many respects to the latest of the US Fleet which were larger, faster, better armed and had greater aircraft capacity; but what they did not possess, and which was to prove to be their undoing as events unfolded, was an armoured flight deck.

Forty minutes after being struck the *Indefatigable* was landing on aircraft, an event which would have been out of the question had she been a US ship with a thin steel plate deck covered with a wooden surface. Jap carriers were of similar construction and so their attacks were based on the premise that a direct hit, especially amidships, would penetrate the flight deck, go through into the hangar putting the carrier out of action completely, destroying dozens of aircraft and killing hundreds of sailors. They were wrong with the British, and even US critics of our carriers had to admit that the *Indefatigable* would have had to be sent to Pearl Harbour had she been American.

The Kamikaze was now the principal offensive weapon of the Japanese air force. It was incredibly economical and very effective in its strike rate compared with conventional bombing. Bombers were normally much slower than our fighters, but their fighters, equipped as Kamikaze planes, were often as quick and as manoeuvrable as their opponents.

The Japanese pilots were all volunteers and there was a waiting list which exceeded the number of planes available. To them it was not suicide but a means of meeting their ancestors after having performed the ultimate act—sacrifice of life—in defence of their homeland, its traditions and codes of honour and bravery.

Their skill requirement in terms of flying ability was not the standard needed by allied airmen. After all they were to complete a single mission and what was required of them was blind, unquestioning determination blended with a fanatical bravery. These men were decorated before take-off—for what they were about to achieve—and dressed in a traditional uniform complete with silk scarf, reminiscent of First War aviators, knotted loosely round their foreheads or necks and printed with quotations and poems from time immemorial. Of course, and we did not know this at the time, many were locked in their aircraft and flew without parachute. They were destined for death one way or another, so why not a spectacular and devastating smite at the round-eyed enemy.

No sooner had the *Indefatigable* been struck, than another Kamikaze, unable to penetrate the gunfire barrage, flung itself at the destroyer *Ulster*. It didn't hit but the near miss caused such serious damage that she lost power for her engines and lay becalmed—a sitting target. The cruiser *Gambia* had to take her in tow and dragged her south to Leyte in the Phillipines. Thus one Kamikaze had taken two vessels out of our force.

We looked over to *Indefatigable*, it was only 0830 and it appeared as though nothing had happened to her. She was on our starboard beam and through binoculars I could see the flight deck party and others still tidying up parts of the deck, throwing pieces of debris overboard, but to all intents and purposes she was fully operational. It gave us some comfort that if the same was to happen to us then possibly we might escape as lightly.

The day proceeded without further incident until just before 1800. A single Kamikaze approached us at virtually sea level and away from the picket boats; it was undetected until it suddenly gained altitude after whistling over the top of our destroyer cover. It turned towards us. Information was shouted down to the Bridge that we were the target and the Japanese fighter was directly astern of us, as if completing a landing circuit. As our close range weapons opened up Captain Denny put *Victorious* into an immense starboard turn. The ship shuddered and rose up and down as she slewed violently. The Zeke, now committed to his final, funereal dive, tried desperately to turn to starboard too but he was now too near and too low to do so.

As I watched it come to us I was nudged slightly out of the way by the ship's photographer, as determined as a Hollywood pressman to get his picture.

The noise was deafening, the blast of the guns, now firing wildly, the roar of the Kamikaze. As it came level with the bridge, it was now below our position and seemed certain to hit the port side of the flight deck. *Victorious* gave another desperate heave to starboard and the Jap caught his starboard wing on the very edge of the deck, overturned and plunged into the sea alongside us. There was a huge explosion and almost immediately a column of water, well over 100 feet high rose into the air and then tons of it rained down onto the ship. Half of the Zeke's mainplane was on the flight deck which was also strewn with small fragments of the plane. There was a powerful smell of petrol and oil. When the drenching ceased, it was seconds, one could see oddments from the cockpit and pieces of the pilot's body.

A photographer on the *Illustrious*, a mile ahead of us, took a photograph at the moment of the explosion and this became a prized possession onboard.

The following day, we heard on the US Forces radio how successfully we had coped with our first Kamikaze attacks. By this time we were in the re-fuelling area, again beset by appalling weather conditions. It was difficult to locate the tankers. In the event there were only four, instead of five, and once more we took onboard less oil than we really required. Mail came up from Sydney and was received with great acclamation, it had taken roughly 28 days from UK.

At this time we took five aircraft from *Slinger*, one of the accommodation carriers, to replace losses through operational and other causes. Aircraft which returned damaged from missions and were unable to be repaired onboard were pushed over the side. Last minute checks had to be made as each plane was about to suffer the watery drop—on more than one occasion we found an air mechanic frantically endeavouring to unscrew the aircraft clock before it went to Davy Jones. Such clocks were prized souvenirs and the ship's carpenters would enclose them in a fine, polished oak frame for a consideration of three or four tots of 'neaters'—diluted rum was not acceptable. There were norms to be observed even in illicit trading.

On 6th April it was back to the islands again and action stations at 0600 as we relieved the US Task Group which had been bombing Sakishima Gunto in our absence with the Fleet Train. The names of the airfields were now becoming household words onboard—we had even included them in a 'Dungeon Dust' show awaiting to be broadcast when conditions permitted. 'We have ranged the world from Riyuku to Timbuctou, Nobara to Bombay, Hirara to Wooloomooloo, maybe Plymouth one day.'

Standing on the ADP and watching our Avenger strike take off we had an interesting diversion when, after the first in line had coughed stutteringly into silence, and was pushed away, the second Avenger headed straight for the island. We watched, horror-struck, as the bombed-up plane slewed rapidly off its straight line for take-off and thumped unceremoniously into the base of the island below, and slightly astern, of where we were standing. Several of us dropped like stones onto the ADP deck waiting for the thunderous explosion we were certain would follow. There was no noise other than that of the remaining Avengers revving up. Sheepishly we rose, not 'Guns'—he had remained upright—and looked below. The aircraft was looking decidedly sick, as were the crew who were suffering from cuts and bruises. We heard later that the starboard brake had locked, causing the plane to slew to the right.

It was a quiet day until the very late afternoon when a small force of bandits was picked up on the radar and intercepted by the combat Air patrol. Three were driven off but the fourth wriggled its way into the area of the fleet and made for *Illustrious*. Like us on April Fools Day, the carrier performed a prodigious turn to avoid the Kamikaze which scraped the outside of the island structure with its wing tip before plunging into the sea and exploding harmlessly.

The following day was the same pattern. Continuous bombing and shooting up of the airfields—some fighter pilots told us they were so short of realistic targets that they strafed the odd soldier or civilian to keep their eye in. Generally we were not happy with what we were doing. It seemed we had been side-lined. We knew that tremendous actions were under way off Okinawa, indeed we heard that Task Force 58 had that day sunk a battleship, a cruiser and four destroyers when they found part of the Japanese Fleet off northern Japan.

Intelligence also filtered through that dozens of Kamikaze attacks were being launched against US naval and supply ships involved in the attack on Okinawa. It was believed that the suicide planes were flying from Formosa and keeping well north of the islands we had been so assiduously attacking.

As we withdrew on the night of 7th April, Captain Denny told us we would be changing our operational plan and, in future, subject to agreement by CINCPAC, our target would be Formosa. There was some light cheering at the news but it was tinged with disappointment. Anything was better than Sakishima Gunto but the mess deck feeling was that we should be alongside the US naval forces to the north, which were now suffering severely from continuous suicide attacks.

The Cypher messages coming through made those of us involved in decyphering feel that our part in the grand order of beating Japan was, as yet, peripheral. Of course we were stretched, having the longest supply line of any fleet in the history of naval warfare. Almost 18,000 miles from the UK on the Suez, Australia route. Cyphers also provided news of new carriers en route to join us. The *Colossus, Vivacious, Glory, Vengeance, Venerable*, some about to leave UK, others on their way.

Sitting talking to Les Vancura, he told me that 90% of our stores, other than

161

aircraft and spares, were sent from Britain, only 10% from Australia. The US Fleet was supplied so much more quickly and liberally from San Diego and Pearl Harbour.

Saturday, 8th April, we made a rendezvous with tankers and store ships. We flew on some replacement aircraft and the cruiser *Uganda* passed over to us 50 long-range tanks for the Corsairs—even cruisers were working as supply ships. All these operations were carried out in wretched weather. I was beginning to wonder if the tales of Pacific Islands, which I had read as a youth, were in fact figments of the author's imagination. Even Ulithi had been a far cry from 'Treasure Island'.

As the war in Europe was coming to an end with the Allies advancing victoriously on all fronts there was a deep yearning among the ship's company to get it finished in the Pacific. News that the Americans were now sending 300 to 400 bombers a night from the Marianas to fire-bomb Tokyo was hailed with delight. Yet another reason for us to be at the heart of things. Morale onboard was flagging somewhat. The crowded, cramped conditions, the heat which caused skin ailments and infections, the continuing sadness as we watched the slow decimation of our aircraft squadrons. Every operational day planes would be lost. With just over 50 planes in total, many of the aircrew were well known to those of us who came into regular contact. Including Palembang we had lost almost one in three of our aircrew since 25th January, just two and a half months.

We now made our way to a position off Northern Formosa. A US Task Force was also in the vicinity but not within sight of us. Their presence was an earnest of Admiral Spruance's intention to try and stop the movement of enemy planes from Formosa to the Okinawa battle-front and so stem the losses of US seaborne forces. Naturally when we arrived on station the weather was again wretched and any flying was ruled out except in dire defensive circumstances. Doubtless the Japanese took advantage of the day's relief from attack to send more aircraft to Okinawa.

The 12th dawned reasonably clear, we were at Action Stations at 0630 as the first Combat Air Patrol took to the skies. Within half an hour they encountered a small force of enemy fighter planes, not sure if they were Kamikazes, shot one down, the remainder escaped into cloud.

The bomber force from our carriers was sent to the airfields from where it was believed the Japanese were flying to Okinawa. The sum total of the day's activities was that 16 planes were shot down, 67 claimed to be damaged. Our losses were four. The most spectacular success was reported from *Indefatigable* whose Fireflies suddenly sighted five enemy aircraft and shot down four in a short, one-sided dog fight.

By now the rescue services had been developed to a fine art. The Americans had a string of submarines, no longer needed to attack enemy shipping, neatly arranged near bombing targets. Any allied aircraft damaged so badly it was unable to return to the Fleet was instructed to ditch in the vicinity of a submarine which would surface and take the airmen onboard. There were submarines in Tokyo Bay, almost under the nose of the Japs, risking their own safety for that of their comrades. Some heroic deeds were performed.

We had the inimitable Walrus, 'Pusser's Duck' or 'Shagbat' as it was fondly known. Few knew why, and those who did kept it to themselves. Two of these remarkable and unlikely flying machines were on board *Victorious*. They flew on rescue missions, usually escorted by two or four fighters, and I saw them return, on more than one occasion, with grateful aircrew pulled out of the 'drink' after ditching. Sometimes the Walrus carried marks of the dangers it courted—bullet holes, shredded wing fabric and the like. They brought back injured airmen to whom they had to administer medical aid before arrival back to the Fleet and hopsital ship treatment. Remarkable aircraft flown by even more remarkable men, unsung heroes in a war then being forgotten in Europe as Germany collapsed into defeat and disintegration and Britain was consumed by euphoria.

For two days we pounded the nominated targets, and it was satisfying to know that our raids were regarded as more than mere irritants by the fact that several attacks were launched at the force in return. Most of these were met by our fighters and turned away, sometimes with success. It was always a joy to hear over the R/T, 'bandit splashed'. On the morning of the 13th we were attacked before daylight, a very unusual tactic. There was an urgent call 'Alarm to Arms' with the imperious bugle call broadcast throughout the ship. Men ran to their Action Stations in various stages of dress, to find that flares had been dropped over the Fleet and warships were bathed in an eerie pinkish white light. Six Japanese planes were in the vicinity but sustained gunfire from many of the ships, not *Victorious*, had the desired effect. The 'bandits' disappeared from the screens so we assumed they were not nocturnal Kamikazes.

Not every enemy plane was a suicide bomber, some were conventional high altitude bombers which had so effectively sunk naval vessels from a height of 15,000 feet or more. But a new twist in the Kamikaze story was revealing itself off Okinawa. What we later came to describe as 'Chase me Charlie' made its dramatic appearance against the Americans.

A normal bomber, say a Dinah or Betty, would approach the Fleet at a fair altitude, say 10,000 feet and, from a few miles away, would drop what appeared to be a torpedo. This was, in fact, a small rocket propelled missile with a pilot, which hurtled down at speeds of up to 600 miles an hour and tried to crash into a ship. Although extremely fast and therefore almost impervious to fighter attack or gunfire, the devices were not so manoeuvrable as a conventional suicide bomber (if conventional is the right word), a factor which came to nullify their other advantages. Frequently they splashed harmlessly into the sea.

That day, 13th April, we heard that President Roosevelt had died. It was like the loss of a friend. Many of us were hardly out of short pants when he became President of the United States, but we realised that Britain owed an immense debt of gratitude to the man who had, through political guile and far-sightedness, helped us during the crucial year and a half between the collapse

163

of France and the entry of the US into the war after Pearl Harbour.

The following day *Illustrious* left us, bound for Leyte in the Philippines.

By this time we had not had any new provisions for five weeks and stocks were getting low, another consequence of the long supply lines. The bread now had weevils in it. Men could be seen holding a slice up to the light to identify the small black dots which indicated the presence of the tiny beetle. Some would very, very, painstakingly pick each one out until the slice looked like a piece of Gruyere cheese, others just ate it philosophically whilst the macho few spoke of a 'meat sandwich' and scoffed the bread with bravado.

On the 16th, Avengers flew off to attack Formosa at 0630 and 0900. There was an immediate response from the Japanese. Three separate waves of high altitude bombers tried to close on the Fleet but were driven off by well directed fighter cover. During the late afternoon two of the 'Chase me Charley' piloted bombs were launched towards us. Probably due to lack of training and practice—how do you practice with these weapons I mused—they were released far too early and had insufficient rocket fuel to reach us, crashing harmlessly (not for the pilot) into the sea.

That evening Tony and I pondered on what kind of people we were fighting. It made no sense to us with our Western values and perceived codes of military behaviour. Surely the Japs knew that defeat was now inevitable and suicidal sacrifice pointless. Was it 'Unconditional Surrender' which they could not accept, a bleak solution which left them without face or honour? We knew that Japanese interpreters with the Fleet had contacted Kamikaze pilots on their wave-lengths and advised them to bale out, 10 miles ahead of the Fleet, at 10,000 feet, and be rescued and treated as honourable prisoners of war. But to them a prisoner of war status was not honourable, life appeared less sacrosanct to them than it did to us. I went off to middle watch cypher duties at midnight, my head far from clear to cope with the intricacies of Type X or the 'one time pad'.

The next day was business as usual, us bombing, them retaliating, us driving them off. The news from the US Fleet, to the north off Okinawa, was grim. Three carriers, four battleships and one cruiser hit by suicide bombers. As Les Vancura recorded in his diary: 'I can't make out why we are not sent further north to assist, but we are under ultimate American control and must operate where we are told.' His was the gut feeling of the ship's company. Yet again the mood was one of irritation and impatience.

When we flew off our strikes on the 20th the pilots returned to report that all four airfields were now out of action and ground resistance very light. There was little sign of Japanese airborne activity.

The Task Force then made tracks for Leyte. We were now on mainly dehydrated food, all fresh vegetables having been exhausted. Some of the ship's company mistrusted this technology and existed on weevil-ridden bread, tinned herrings and other staple, traditional naval fare.

We had been at sea for 31 days since leaving Ulithi and had steamed 12,000 miles—equivalent to half way around the world. The ship was light on stores, ammunition, spares, victuals etc., and heavy on unserviceable gear which had to be disposed of.

Leyte was reached at noon on 23rd, a 'hell-hole' if ever there was one. The Fleet anchored miles out from shore, among some of our own supply ships such as the *Unicorn*, a 'Woolworth' carrier.

It was cripplingly hot and we were too far off shore to permit leave. Quite frankly we believed it was a tactic devised to keep our ship's companies from a possible 'hell-raising' run ashore and conflict with the Americans and locals. To mollify the alcoholic desires of 'Jolly Jack', the Admiral authorised beer to be brought from shore and served to the men at noon and 1700. One and a half pints each time. This was the first occasion that alcohol, other than rum, was officially distributed. It was a beneficial supplement to the liquid intake which needed to be high to counteract the dehydrating effect of the conditions onboard.

Action-man Vancura was in his element. With a captive crew, all ship-bound, he dashed around organising a Sports Day, to be held on the Flight Deck on 27th April. He cajoled, bribed and bullied. Despite the enervating heat and weariness there was a good response. There were only two 'straight' races—the 100 yards and the relay—all the rest were comedy. When the odd, listed miscreant did not appear, Les himself stepped in, running himself—and others—to exhaustion.

Two more days passed with excruciating slowness and the longing to go to sea, with all its privations and dangers, far outweighed any desire to stay at Leyte.

We heard that Mussolini was dead, hanged from a lamp-post by Italian 'patriots', and that the Russian and US armies had linked up in Germany. The end in Europe was only days away.

We sailed just after dawn on 1st May with *Formidable* in company as *Illustrious* was experiencing intermittent engine trouble. She was surely homeward bound because the day before we left she was disposing of many of her stores.

News came of the suicide of Hitler and Goebels, and the capture of Berlin by the Russians. Events were really rushing apace near home making us feel somewhat envious that we would not be in or around Britain when the tremendous euphoria of victory would seize everyone in its joyous grip.

To add further disillusionment, the first indiction of release prospect filtered through. It was to be related to Age and Service—absolutely proper—but when Captain Denny spoke to the ship's company he made his views crystal clear.

'By the end of this year, not more than 30 men, I say again, not more than 30, will have been discharged from the service.'

This announcement was met with astonishment by many. I could see the logic of it, after all when would Japan be defeated? Within seven months? Who could say. But Jolly Jack was thinking that those fortunate enough to be in European and Mediterranean waters would be released on time, for the rest of us what was colloquially called 'A Green Rub'!

When we broadcast our radio programme, Tony included a poem, entitled

'The Release of the Slight Brigade'. This is it:

THE RELEASE OF THE SLIGHT BRIGADE

('By January, 1946, not more than 30 men will have left this ship to be demobilised. I say again—not more than 30—three zero.')

They cry in Parliament, 'Who goes home?'
They swear on the mess-deck, 'Who goes
    home?'
But there comes no answer from rigging or
    dome,
For only thirty of us go home.

You should have heard them shout,
Turning their lockers out,
What's all the noise about—lucky three
    zero;
Never a man dismayed,
Not in the least afraid,
These men had made the grade—thirty—
    three zero.

Up from the holds they came,
Crippled and blind and lame,
Staking a rightful claim—more than three
    zero;
Badges and service pay,
Oh, what a grand array,
'One hundred and ten to-day'—gallant
    three zero.

Youngsters in line as well,
Braving the shot and shell,
No, not a hope in hell—thirty—three zero;
'Some of you may be free
In the next year or three,
Maybe by '53—now only thirty.'

Only the really old,
Wizened and gnarled and bold,
Enter the sacred fold—of the three zero;
What can the others do,
Sign on for twenty-two?
Yes, and be damned to you—thirty—three
    zero.

'Snotty' and 'Admiral', who goes home?
'Hooky' and 'rooky'—well, who goes
    home?
And a voice from the turret cried,
Echoing far and wide,
'When do we get outside—with the three
    zero?'

As we steamed steadily northwards to the old familiar battle-ground, the tankers oiled the destroyers and cruisers. The weather was warm and conditions reasonable. We seldom experienced clear skies and regarded cloudy conditions as being more to the Japs advantage than ours.

Yet again Sakishima Gunto. This time the battleships and cruisers were to earn their keep by going in-shore to bombard the islands with medium and heavy calibre gunfire.

This could have been a tactical mistake. We were denuding the Force of a substantial part of its anti-aircraft fire in exchange for probable marginal damage to enemy on-shore installations. The whole purpose of our continual bombing and strafing was to create maximum damage from the Fleet Air Arm. The danger to us, and the US naval forces, came from Japanese airfields, most of which were not within range of the cruisers guns. Yet the cruisers fire-power was a crucial element in our protection, its absence could create problems.

The Avengers were launched on their first strike at 0600. By now the carriers had an escort of only eight destroyers, a move with the US Navy would not have countenanced. The Japs were expecting us and, finding that our anti-aircraft defences were critically reduced, decided to launch a series of Kamikaze attacks. Without picket boats on station to give early warning of very low flying aircraft the situation was tailored to enemy requirements.

Our bombers had returned before 0900 and confirmed they had once again cratered and heavily damaged enemy airfields. How effective this had truly

166

been was in doubt from the moment Japanese aircraft were picked up on our radar. There were several groups, all small, occasionally uniting into one formation then splintering off into segments. The whole enterprise was being controlled from a high level enemy bomber, flying well above 20,000 feet and almost impervious, at that time, to our fighters and gunfire. The Corsairs and Hellcats had their hands full coping with the Kamikaze planes at a much lower level.

My own radar screen was blank when there was a shout from a look-out on the starboard side. As we quickly shifted our gaze towards *Formidable*, a suicide fighter-bomber was in the final stages of a headlong plunge onto her deck. How did it escape detection? This was an un-nerving experience. Where had the plane come from? The immediate conclusion was a flight at 50 feet above sea level, a fast steep climb, followed by target selection and full power dive onto it.

The crackle and thump of anti-aircraft weapons, and the black, brown and grey smoke denoting exploding shells reached us just as the Kamikaze struck *Formidable* almost exactly amidships. As the initial explosion subsided, and the smoke cleared, we could see fire rampant among the deck parked airplanes. An enormous pall of black, oily smoke rose from the carrier, she quickly turned out of wind as her fire-fighting crews started to eliminate the blaze. We heard later that it appeared a bomb had been dropped almost at the moment of impact and that shards of it penetrated the flight deck and through the hangar to the decks below.

Before this news reached us, however, another undetected aircraft attacked *Indomitable*. It was like watching a news reel at the cinema, somehow the action had the quality of a spectator sport. The bombing thump of *Indom*'s heavy guns plus the chatter and clatter of the lighter armament was very distinct. Meanwhile the Kamikaze had disappeared. I turned to look at my radar set. There were now several aircraft within a range of a few miles. I had no idea whether they were friends or bandits. The Kamikaze appeared again, still intent on *Indomitable* as it powered its way at the ship. It seemed to be on fire, but indestructible, pressing the attack until it flattened out, looked as though it was performing a normal landing on the carrier, careered along the deck and over the side.

Within minutes another Kamikaze selected *Indomitable*. This time the cumulative effect of fire from the carrier and a nearby escorting destroyer caused the attacker to crash into the sea just forward of its target.

The radar blips were beginning to sort themselves out. There were still suicide planes about but our fighters were now among them and all surface units ceased fire as two Japanese were splashed. It was a very brief interlude yet a remarkable testimony to the guile, dash, determination and nerveless bravery of our foe. Five of them had managed to get within striking distance and although all had been destroyed either by their own action, or ours, they had put *Formidable* out of action and rendered useless a number of her aircraft.

In the early afternoon we had the battleships and cruisers back with us and not much later more Kamikazes approached the force. This time we picked them up at a fair range and our fighters were vectored onto them with positive results. The whole afternoon the radar plot was very active, there was a desperate persistence about the enemy that he had not revealed to us before. We had now some idea, albeit on a much reduced scale, of the continuous attacks suffered by the American Fleet to the north of us.

The evening brought no respite but a signal success was achieved when the controlling bomber was found at high altitude, over four and a half miles high, and promptly despatched. This left the Kamikazes without supervision or direction and we suffered no further attacks on the force. At the end of the day we had suffered one plane shot down plus 13 put out of action, permanently, by the suicide bombers. *Formidable* had repaired her flight deck, taken back her fighters which had been temporarily accommodated on ourselves and *Indefatigable*. More than 50 men had been killed or wounded on *Formidable* and, as we turned eastwards to join the Fleet Train, we speculated on our first few days back off the Ryuku Islands.

Where had the enemy planes come from? Formosa? Surely not the islands we were bombing and bombarding. How had the late morning strike got so close to us without detection? My own small radar display had shown nothing at all. We were very vulnerable to sea-level approach, especially if we failed to deploy the picket boats. Perhaps we should maintain a force of Seafires, marvellous at low level dog-fighting at 2 to 3000 feet and put the beefier and faster Corsairs further upstairs?

I have to say that these were probably not the considerations occupying the minds and intellects of the Senior Officers of the force—not at all. We hammered out these problems at our level, musing on a glass of iced lime-juice as we resolved the tactical issues under debate. We kept our thoughts to ourselves, we all knew 'our place' although I did mention them to 'Guns'.

'Rear Admiral Barker is it then?' he responded when I told him. 'We have 2200 plus onboard and half of them are prospective Admirals.' He was smiling.

'I think it is interesting for us to talk about these matters without having the responsibility for their ultimate solution. It reveals a lively involvement by some of us.'

'Just as well you don't have to sort out the problems. But if it stops you all thinking about being at the celebrations at home then it's doing some good.'

It was on the 6th May that we heard all the German forces in North West Europe had capitulated to Montgomery. I could see his face from the day he came onboard and imagined how he would be relishing his victory. We had a short Church Service on the Quarter Deck that morning, our Chaplain was now a sensitive, approachable and most likeable man. We prayed for those killed and injured and for an early end to the wretched war in the Pacific and Far East.

By the 8th May we were back in familiar waters, believing that even the dolphins and tuna knew us by now. We also had an attendant Albatross, gliding in our slipstream, sleeping on the wing and never, to my knowledge, moving his wings. Old sailors, in the manner of the Ancient Mariner, were convinced the huge bird was a harbinger of bad fortune. Most of us thought it was just interest in the 'Gash' (rubbish) which we ditched, periodically, providing fine fare for a scavening bird.

It was too inclement to launch air strikes but *KGV* and *Howe* slipped quietly off to indulge in a bombardment. The cruisers were left with us this time. When our first aircraft reached the islands the following day the airfields were operative—yet again—and bombs were dropped to re-crater them. The busiest people were our Avenger pilots and the airfield labourers; we were keeping them all gainfully employed.

Our Ramrod pilots had worked out a version of the 'burning newspaper in the latrine routine'. They would wait and watch for the lavatory huts to be occupied, usually shortly after breakfast, then give them a quick burst of cannon or machine gun fire. We believed that motions were passed very quickly and unanimously at these meetings. Sadly it was evidence that some of our highly trained fighter pilots were, through boredom, reduced to pranks normally attributed only to the Gladstone Dock jokers.

We had just had a can of boiling hot tea delivered to the ADP when 'bandits' were identified flying fast and very low towards the force. The same tactic as before but this time we picked them up. The Kamikazes had now worked out a series of attack options, some of which relied on being able to decoy some of the fighters away from their prey. In the gaps which opened up, as Seafires, our close defencive cover were lured away, other suicide bombers came through. They then performed the usual rapid climb prior to the death dive.

Today, 9th May, it was our turn. Did they have us on a rota I wondered, momentarily.

With the enemy planes now among us and clearly in sight the force increased speed and began a series of dramatic turns. We had an enormous rudder, 45 tons of it, and, as we knew from its various malfunctions, it could turn us almost on a sixpence. Captain Denny seemed to enjoy throwing *Victorious* about as much as one of his predecessors, Captain Bovell.

As the first Kamikaze approached us from astern the ship began a monumental slew away, and the Jap found himself approaching us directly from the beam (side). For a few seconds I imagined he was going to hit the island—which would have created severe problems for those of us confined there. Unbelievably he looked like landing across the flight deck—rather than along the length—and as he did so he touched down, skidded and began to break up. As the plane hit the forward 4.5 inch gun turret, near the lift, it exploded. At that moment three men died and 18 were injured, including my friend Lt. Bernard Jealous with whom I co-wrote our ship's newspaper in our previous Pacific foray. Bernard's legs were virtually blown off and the men killed were all under his command. A hole about two feet across was made at the edge of the flight deck plus a bulge about 10 feet overall. The ship's blacksmith and plumbers were quickly on the scene to assess the damage and arrange repairs.

The Kamikaze had been hit time and time again by our short range weapons, possibly this had prevented him pulling away from his cross deck attack. We could not believe that he was not blasted out of the sky for it was plain to us 'up top' that he was the subject of very accurate fire.

We had not properly recovered from the hit when another suicide fighter set his sights on us. This one came in from astern and once more the Captain gave the ship fierce rudder. The platform of Bofors and Oerlikons at the after end of the flight deck got an accurate fix on the enemy. It was hit repeatedly yet, like his predecessor, he pressed on though now on fire. Control was slipping away from the pilot, maybe he had lost consciousness, for his plane faltered, dropped into a flat flaming glide, caught the flight deck a fairly harmless blow and careered over the side in a ball of flame and smoke. It was spectacular. His attack was not in vain, four of our Corsairs were crippled where they were parked and their remains had to be heaved over the side later.

It was not possible to believe what we now saw. A third Kamikaze hell-bent for us. All hell let loose again, the ship shook and rattled as the guns boomed and barked, one of the 4.5 inch guns firing through a perfect smoke ring it had just created. This time the enemy changed his mind, probably judging that the *Howe* was a softer target. He was already damaged when he passed us, slowly it seemed, and crashed in a ball of fire short of the battleship.

There was no shortage of Kamikazes. The problem of them being in close was all too apparent. Seafires, keen for a kill, continued dog-fighting even within range of the ships weapons. I witnessed one of them have its tail bown off by anti-aircraft fire and cartwheel into the sea. The sky was peppered with exploding shells of all calibres and the noise quite deafening. So much was taking place that I wondered if anyone was really in control or was the ship being managed by immediate survival reflex actions of Captain Denny. All we could do was alert guns crews to bear on what we could see. It was then up to them and the quick wits and seamanship of our Captain.

Being attacked in this manner was most unpleasant. It was like playing tennis with a gaping hole in your racquet and the ball aimed at you. What on earth motivated people to terminate their lives on a slab of alien steel? It became very personal. Like many others 'up top' I had the stomach-churning discomfort of feeling that this contest was between him and me, with him holding all the advantage. For another thing, either we had belts of suspect ammunition or these men were protected by a power outside our ken. Watching the planes being hit, sometimes shuddering from the impact, but nevertheless still pointing and coming straight at you, created doubts about our infallibility and their fallibility.

Just imagine. The night before we had listened to the World Service and heard Churchill speak about the defeat of the forces of 'Narzee' evil. We had spliced the mainbrace—all the men had an extra tot of rum served and drank 'To the King—God Bless Him'. Now here we were, men dead and injured, debris and damage forward and aft, and with bodies to sew into the weighted sail-cloth to be slipped gently and sadly over the side of the quarter-deck.

There bobbing momentarily on the dark green sea before sliding down forever out of our sight but not our remembrance.

But it wasn't over. Another Kamikaze flirted with *Indomitable*, decided that *Formidable* seemed a better bet, and dived straight into the parked aircraft on the rear of the flight deck. The resultant fire was spectacular, a blazing display of pyrotechnics as Corsairs burned with the enemy they would have fought in the sky. Now they were consumed together in an inferno of smoke and flame that took over 15 minutes to bring under control. Burning petrol had seeped through into the hangar so the sprinkler system was activated, flooding a number of planes with salt water and thus rendering them totally inoperable. Almost 20 of *Formidable's* 54 bombers and fighters were the tally of a single Kamikaze on this occasion. Taking the hit a few days earlier into account, our sister ship was now down to her last 15 aircraft. The news was received with some alarm, the depletion of our assets was fast gathering pace.

As we left the operational area to find our oilers and supply ships, the artisans set about repairing our flight deck. They used timber, armour plate (a few spare always held in reserve by the island) and a very quick drying cement. It was tested by running an aircraft over it. Amazing how our 'chippies' and 'blackies' could turn their hands from trick boxes to armoured deck repairs. Our injured we transferred lengthily from us to a destroyer, then an auxiliary carrier, then the hospital ship—this latter becoming increasingly busy. Bernard Jealous had had both legs amputated by one of our surgeons in our small operating room. He was conscious and cheerful as he was transferred, remarking to one who was working the apparatus, 'What a way to get a draft chit.'

I learned later that he had died and felt deeply saddened. The war for which he had volunteered, in Europe, was at an end. There was rejoicing everywhere, no doubt joined by his parents unaware that their talented son had been maimed then died. Like so many others he had so much to which to look forward.

On my 23rd birthday, 12th May, we were back at Action Stations off the islands once again. The success of the Kamikazes had prompted an enormous amount of inter-ship radio traffic as Captains and Admirals decided on the most effective defence against the Japanese. Oddly enough, some of our earlier conclusions were adopted, unwittingly of course. Picket boats were depoyed just over ten miles distant to give us an earlier warning of low flying bandits. The fruitless bombardment of the island by the heavy ships was abandoned and an anti-aircraft destroyer assigned to protect our stern as the light cruisers had done on the Malta Convoy. Our own fighters were given clearer instructions about when to break off an engagement in the near vicinity of the fleet and so avoid the dreadful tragedy of being shot down by their own side.

These long days at Action Stations yielded a new phenomenon, 'Action Rations'. Each of us had an oblong tin, about 4" × 2", sealed with adhesive tape, to be opened if food failed to materialise from the galleys. We normally ate quite well in the ADP, enjoying some of the spare fare served to the Bridge.

The tin contained Horlicks Tablet, Glucose sweets, a mini-bar of chocolate and sundry other 'goodies' so memorable I have completely forgotten them. One had to bear in mind that this treasure trove had been despatched 18,000 miles through Capricorn and Cancer, across the Equator (twice). it's delectables were not quite as fresh as when so zealously packed at Bourneville or Slough. My friend Tony was so moved by the appearance of this 'sailor's friend' that he penned a poem—thus:

THE MAGIC TIN

Listen, my children, and you shall hear
A better story than Paul Revere;
Of oil for the lamps of China,
    But none to light Japan,
Of an accurate raid that the carriers made
    Just as the year began.

A secret oil refinery, a little less refined,
A clear-cut target area, now not so well-
    defined;
For bombs have made an awful mess,
    And caused a deal of pain,
And what was once a super plant
    Is just a sticky stain.

But leave the rest of this noble tale
To the BBC and the 'Daily Mail';
The bombers set the headlines,
    Of course, it should be so,
But the tale I tell is of floating hell,
    And a hundred and thirty—below.

Below the decks, you understand,
Among the works of the centre gland;
Where the men who make the water
    Are dying by the score,
And you think of all you wasted—
    But you won't waste any more.

These are the men who brought you here,
Stoker, and 'tiffy', and engineer;
Think of them down the boilers,
    Consider them there in the vaps—
How do you think the water
    Got in 'them goddam taps'.

They do what they can for the men down
    there,
They know the burden they have to bear;
The rolls of bread they relish,
    With sausage neatly padded,
But what is this—it can't be true—
    Yes, something has been added.

A little tin just two by one, is all the latest
    fashion,
Adorned by red adhesive tape, and
    labelled, 'Action Ration',
Containing when you open it, a most
    delicious feast,
Enough to keep a man alive—for half an
    hour at least.

You tear the ribbon, lift the lid, and what
    do you suppose,
Ten meals for every matelot within the box
    repose;
With barley sugar, beech-nut gum, and
    malted milk in cubes—
Or, up in Northern waters, they can
    substitute two Zubes

To suck throughout the livelong day, if
    things are rather black,
A definite improvement on the cocoa and
    'hard tack'.
The vitamins from A to Z are all contained
    therein,
And modern scientific minds have
    crammed them in one tin.

I wonder now if H. G. Wells, when writing
    'Things to Come'
Envisaged six-course dinners in disguise as
    beech-nut gum;
I pass the question on to you, who ate
    them all the day,
And don't forget the empty tin—return it
    to Sick Bay.

What fate awaits this treasured tin, I only
    can surmise,
Wait till next Action Stations, and get a big
    surprise,
It may not be Sumatra, there are even bets
    on SYDNEY,
But what a lark, next time to find—a pie of
    steak and kidney.

The minstrel boy to the war has gone,
He's got his father's sash on,
He has no sword, but what of that—
He has his 'Action Ration'.

It was good to promote some humour onboard *Victorious*. The routine of two days in, two days out, was wearing and exhausting, the men needed cheering to take their minds off events both at sea and at home. As 'Charlie' Merton Frise said to me one day, 'When I know Tony and your programme is coming on I find a prime position near to the mess deck speaker so I don't miss a word. Thank the Lord for a good laugh.' Sometimes we did not feel in humourous mood as we sat at our respective Action Stations, in quiet moments, and scribbled lines in pencil on scrap paper, usually old, discarded signals. We met during lulls in activity to check progress as to content and quantity of material.

There were also request programmes. During our visit to Sydney we had been able to enlarge our record library beyond the three Indian Sitar and six Arab mood music discs purchased in Bombay and Port Said respectively. The favourite female vocalist was Doreen Villiers and not Vera Lynne who was regarded, at least on *Victorious*, as a 'soldier's singer'. The sultry voiced Villiers, listened to repeatedly by Peter Lorne, would render the noisiest mess deck into nostalgic silence.

We had a 'Brains Trust' too. Questions such as 'Define the line between Genius and Madness' were indicative of the state of mind of many onboard—regarding themselves as either over-endowed in brain power or utterly insane for finding a warship as their home. An Australian born officer would take five minutes on any subject, rarely the one to which the question referred, and gave the rest of us time to collect our thoughts. I doubt we had an avid following.

The 17th May brought another tragedy. We had been carrying out all our normal Ramrod, fighter cover, bombing, strafing the previous day. Furthermore *Victorious* had established the fleet record for aircraft handling. In 12 minutes we landed and parked 30 aircraft—five every 120 seconds—we were also in possession of the Flying off, re-fuelling and re-arming records. It was in these circumstances, all the air handling party hyped up by their endeavours, that a young pilot came in to land at about 0745 that dreadful morning.

The Corsair had not long been airborne but quickly flew into landing circuit attitude to return onbaord. As the plane approached from astern, 'Guns' tapped me on the shoulder and pointed.

'Look at him, he is never going to make it coming in at that speed. Surely he is going to be waved off.'

Whether he was or not we never knew. The aircraft came over the after end of the flight deck at what must have been twice normal landing speed and seemingly too high. Dropping suddenly, and almost crazily, it picked up two wires, was dragged down onto the deck as they exerted their braking influence until they were torn from their hydraulic moorings by the sheer speed of the plane. The Corsair now careered along the deck at virtually unbroken impetus, crashed into the first and then the second crash barrier, exploded into a ball of flame and hurtled over the side to total destruction.

Meanwhile on deck a fire had started. As I watched, horror stricken, I saw one inert figure, like a disjointed puppet, another, on fire and moving feebly in its death throes. Ahead of them three aircraft lay broken and useless. Rescue teams, first aid staff, fire-fighters, were on the scene within seconds. Both the men were dead and, as I stared unbelievingly at the devastation below, I knew that they were friends.

Lieutenant 'Bill' Banning, tall, handsome, fair haired, had been the Fairy Queen in our Pantomime. He had made his own costume, including crown and a Belisha Beacon for his wand. A shy man, but superb organiser on the flight deck, it was some of his skills which enabled us to hold the various records.

Lying not far away, by the twisted main stanchion of the second crash barrier, was the torched corpse of Stoker Petty Officer Groves. Another principal in the Panto, Groves had turned out as Red Riding Hood. At six feet tall he had cut a comic figure in a short white dress, ankle socks, gym shoes, red sash and a scarlet hood draping into a mid-length cloak. We persuaded him not grow a moustache, a touch, he thought, that would add some distinction to the part.

My eyes misted with tears as the bodies were covered and then removed. We had lost a pilot too of course, a brave young man—they were all brave who flew from flat-tops—but I didn't know him. Banning and Groves were friends as well as comrades and I felt the uselessness of their deaths very deeply. Not even killed by enemy action, bitter enough, but lives ended by a cruel mischance at the hands of a shipmate.

As a result of the barrier demoliton we had to divert our planes to the other carriers. They became over-crowded and take-off and landing procedures were unduly protracted because of the physical need to shuffle aircraft around so much.

The new detection procedure seemed to be working well, or the enemy had taken a brief respite from his endeavours. There was little activity and the response to the bombing of the islands was almost a studied indifference. Possibly their Kamikaze planes had been temporarily depleted, we felt sure now that there would be no shortage of volunteer pilots.

Late in the afternoon of 17th one of our fighters was obliged to ditch not far off shore. We radioed his last known position to an Air Sea Rescue US submarine and were delighted to learn that night that the pilot had been picked up and was now safely ensconsed onboard his underwater host.

Back with the Fleet Train we undertook our first serious ammunitioning at sea. The *Robert Maersk* sent 500lb bombs over at the rate of 150 an hour, it was interesting to see the initial diffidence by both ships bomb parties until a proper level of confidence had been established. Bombs look evil, especially so when precariously balanced between two ships steaming alongside at almost 20 miles an hour.

That afternoon we sold the effects of Steward Lander and SPO Groves. Lander had been killed by the Kamikaze strike on the gun turret. The contrast could not have been more marked. Lander, a 19 year old Glaswegian, had a dependent mother. He was an Officers Steward, hard-working and diligent, a pleasant young man. I have already written about Groves, married, but his wife had left him for another man, whilst he was serving on *Victorious*. His domestic life was in a mess but he did not let his personal problems intrude into his work or friendships onboard.

Those who gathered on the flight deck to attend the Sales were informed of the differing circumstances of their two dead shipmates and asked to exercise their judgement in bidding accordingly.

Lander's effects realised just short of £400, a record for such a simple collection of clothes and possessions. He had barely more than the minimum uniform requirements and, to my recollection, few personal items of value. The bidding was, at once, generous and willing.

SPO Groves' effects, with almost twice as much gear of all sorts, barely reached £10. There was no question of his colleagues sending cash to the woman who had deserted him. Thus was a rough justice applied to these cases. However valuable an article might be, or however desirable, if the cash realised was not in a good cause then there was a resolute resistance to buy. Some articles were not sold at all and we had them confiscated. It was a sad closing chapter to a story full of promise years earlier when Groves had joined *Victorious*.

The Fleet's capability for self-inflicted injury was catastrophically demonstrated onboard the luckless *Formidable* on 18th May. Whilst we were ammunitioning, and far removed from enemy strikes, our sister ship suddenly seemed to be on fire. At first we thought it was a problem with her re-fuelling which she was undertaking at the time. It was much more serious. A member of the maintenance staff, possibly an Air Mechanic, accidentally triggered off the guns of a Corsair in the hangar. An Avenger, just in front, promptly exploded, cascading fuel onto other aircraft and all over the hangar deck. The sprinkler system had to be activated and, by the time the fire was fully extinguished, a total of 28 planes had become useless. The cost in terms of cash exceeded one million pounds, a staggering sum for the chance pressing of a gun button. Warnings were immediately posted in our hangar about the dire consequences of such utter carelessness.

As we oiled on the 19th we heard that *Illustrious* was now homeward bound. The shaft of her centre engine was U/S and to all intent and purpose her war was over. There were shouts of 'Lucky Bastard' and other sympathetic, kindly comments when the news was conveyed over the ship's radio system. There was not a little envy in the manner of its expression.

Already the Captain had warned us against 'Getting soft' now that the European war was at an end. He recommended we write home no more than once a week and concentrate on applying ourselves to the 'task ahead'. The admiration for his courage and seamanship, leadership and conviction, was unbounded, but the men cared less for his brusque, almost arrogant manner. A stern disciplinarian, like many short men he made up for his lack of height by aggression and heavy punishment against wrong-doers. Had the question been posed 'Tomorrow we go through the Gates of Hell, who do you wish to lead us?', the answer would have been a loud and clear affirmative for Captain

Denny, but he was not regarded as a compassionate, understanding man. Perhaps at these times we needed the former. The incident onboard *Formidable* would have had some draconian consequences on *Victorious*.

Action Stations was at 0600 on 20th May but when it was reported that thick cloud obscured the target areas we stood down and went about our normal duties. To those of us who had to administer the ship the work waited to be done; pay and allowances had to be worked out, Discharged Dead procedures completed for those who had lost their lives. Records to be sent to the Admiralty at Bath. Everything seemed so mundane compared with what was happening above decks, and added to all this was the constant round of Cypher watch-keeping. Eventually I found it was easy to cope with three and a half hours to four hours sleep a day.

It seemed that destroyers had a penchant for steel to steel confrontation with capital ships, and *Quilliam* was no exception. In conditions somewhat similar to the *KGV/Punjabi* incident, a thick sea fog, this destroyer rammed *Indomitable* and severely damaged its own bows. *Black Prince*, the cruiser, immediately, but cautiously, went to assist and earned itself the task of towing the destroyer from the scene at five knots.

Bad weather continued to dog our efforts to maintain the pressure on the Japs. If it wasn't fog, it was strong, almost gale force winds or the targets were obscured. Action Stations at 0545 was too often followed by 'securing' at 0800. Frustration became the order of the day although there must have been an element of relief among the aircrews that another day of survival had been achieved. The strain was showing on some of them, especially those—not all of course—who had survived the longest in their respective squadrons. Statistics and odds were bandied about, but the unknown factor was luck and no-one could train in that commodity. Then there was the superb airman, like Ronnie Hay, whose 'situation awareness' almost guaranteed his survival.

It was 21st May when Captain Denny informed us that we would be soon leaving the operational area for Manus and then to Sydney for more permanent repairs to the damage we had sustained earlier in the month. The news was greeted with excitement on the Mess Decks. I had heard look-outs talking of their 'Sheilas', in the usual graphic details. They had not changed from those I had listened to on the train three and a half years earlier. There was chat of 'homers'—a term to describe the residence of a grippo (host) who had invited the sailor to enjoy the benefits of life with an Australian family. Spirits rose again, it was the resurrection of 'Jolly Jack' the Casanova, the Maiden's Dream, the Restauranteur's Delight, the Baron of the Bars.

A wave of enemy fighters approached us on the 24th but the new detection and protection systems worked well. They were driven off by the Combat Air Patrol before they even sighted the Fleet. Our strike force found that land-based bombers, from the newly occupied airfields in Okinawa, were also attacking the Ryuku Islands. It seemed like a case of over-kill as we had found very little there.

After a further day of pounding Sakishima Gunto we left and headed south.

Commander (Flying) the much liked leader of the ship's naval air arm, advised the air crews that these were to be last attacks before the delights of Sydney were sampled once again. That night there was a wild party, a boisterous, roisterous affair. The smallest aircrew member in the wardroom was designated as a rugby ball and was passed from semi-inebriated man to man in wild charges. One appeared as Tarzan, whooping and jungle-calling which the release of pent-up emotions had triggered off.

Now that we were en route to fresh provisions a rather expensive dinner was laid on—roast chicken and all the trimmings—and be damned to the consequences, likely to be further doses of dehydrated potato, egg and onion.

By now a newspaper was being printed in Sydney, once a week, for the ships of the British Pacific Fleet. We received copies when we arrived at Manus in the Admiralty Islands. All broadcasting in Manus was put out by the Americans, in their inimitable style. Manus, for example, was Station WGBH 'The Voice of the Admiralties'.

Our administrative lives in the Navy were governed by Kings Regulations and Admiralty Instructions, known as K.R. & A.I. For our 'Dungeon Dust Time' broadcast in Manus we announced ourselves as 'Station K.R. & A.I., the voice of the Admiralty'. We thought it amusing. The following morning, Paymaster Commander Tucker stopped me and said, "Very droll, Barker, very droll. I have made a note of it to use as a private joke on the appropriate occasion."

Manus was an anchorage which lacked any appeal. The heat and humidity were enervating, the sheer boredom of the place depressing. We arrived at 0800 on 30th May to find *Implacable* at anchor, so a frantic unloading of spares took place. Supplies were so tight that the inter-ship swapping and transfers were the only means of ensuring that the ships about to go into action had sufficient equipment to make good the inevitable losses.

Thankfully we weighed anchor at 1300 the following day and set course for Sydney. The Captain announced that we may be there 21 days, having our temporary repairs made permanent by the dockyard workers. He also told the ship's company that everyone would be given four days leave to recharge mental and physical batteries before going back to the battle area which would now be off the Japanese mainland.

Two days from Manus we caught the edge of a typhoon and all the ships had a torrid time. Although we had experienced mountainous seas in the Atlantic and Arctic, there seemed to be an added ingredient in a typhoon—sheer, unrestrained fury. It was as though the ocean was not just violently disturbed but had acquired a destructive malevolence, a life-threatening power. Much further north, where the storm was concentrated, the US Fleet suffered horrendously. Forty-one ships were damaged. Four destroyers listed from side to side through an increasing arc until they turned turtle and sank with almost complete loss of life. The US carrier *Hornet* had the forward end of her flight deck rolled back as though it was a sardine can being opened with a turn-key. Although I never saw the signals exchanged it is alleged that our force

177

received a message from the US fleet enquiring, 'How did you fare in the typhoon?', to which the reply was, 'What typhoon?' True or not, I did see a message from The Lords of the Admiralty enquiring whether we might make use of a vehicle, amphibious, known as a DUKW or 'Duck'. A signal was sent, reading, 'My Lords, we would love a Duck!'

By this time the men were turning their thoughts to the shopping delights of Sydney, a veritable Aladdin's Cave for 'rabbits' (presents) to take home, eventually.

Looking at Les Vancura's diary for the 1st June, he writes, 'I must get a new bracelet and strap for Beth's watch. I intend to buy two sheepskins and give one to Kit as a present. Most importantly I will try to get some Pyrex dishes, cups and saucers for our new home at No. 7.' Among all his laconic notes of naval events appears the thoughts for those at home, the thread linking him with his loved ones some 12,000 miles away.

It was 5th June when we passed through the 'Gate' to Sydney Harbour at 0930, anchored in mid-stream waiting for the *KGV* to come in—she was due to berth ahead of us. Eventually we docked at 1600, after a frustrating, nail-biting few hours for both the matelots and those frantic to renew, or even rekindle, the passions of the weeks in February. Leave was given from 1700 and there was a concerted rush ashore—described by one—as akin to 'the Kentucky Derby'. Of course pockets were filled with cash, hearts and bodies brimming over with love and passion—there was going to be a spending spree of gigantic proportions.

One of the problems was the licensing hours. The bars closed at 1800 and from that time on the streets were filled with inebriated sailors who, between getting ashore at 4 p.m. had poured into themselves as much beer as any reasonable human frame could withstand. Bearing in mind that some of the sailors had existed, in alcoholic terms, on a daily watered down measure of rum for some months, the rush to remedy the drink starvation brought many to their knees, some to their backs. Many would make for Hyde Park to lie on the benches, or grass, semi-comatose, raging drunk, stupidly inebriated or just fast asleep, until the Naval Patrol happened across them.

Others, slightly merry, cheekily and boldly so, would wander down to Kings Cross, there to find temporary solace and frequently ill-remembered physical release in the arms of one of the 'ladies' of the area. I wondered if the American approach, as at Honolulu, might not have been preferable. There the official brothels catered for hundreds of men daily. I recall seeing a queue of servicemen, some chatting, some reading comics or papers, shuffling slowly along the pavement towards a set of double doors. Curiosity drew me to them and when I enquired what they were waiting in line for, the laughter could have been heard in San Diego. It transpired that most of them were hoping for an assignation with Mamie Stover, legendary prostitute heroine, who ran 'The Bull Ring' and disposed of men in a few blinding seconds of exquisite pleasure which remained in their consciousness for weeks to come. In Sydney, it was as tawdry as Plymouth, Portsmouth or London.

The dockyard at Wooloomooloo was now an impressive sight. Four aircraft carriers plus the *KGV* and smaller ships all berthed alongside each other.

On the second day we commenced storing. Commander Tucker came into the office and spoke to me about the pay arrangements for the two separate leave parties. At the same time he said, 'We are taking on 96 days of provisions in the next 48 hours Barker, what does that tell you?'

'That when we leave here we won't be back until Japan surrenders,' I replied.

'That's right,' he went on, and stooping lower to my desk, added, 'Make sure you have a good leave here, it may well be a long time before you have any more.' He stood upright, nodding as if to confirm what he had just told me, slid the door back and left.

Rex Starling called out, 'He can be an old Jonah you know, he has no more idea than you or I when we will be back. After all most of us see the same cyphers.'

Great excitement reigned in Sydney when, on 9th June, Gracie Fields arrived from Brisbane to give two concerts for the forces in the new Hyde Park British Centre, due to be opened officially by the Duke of Gloucester on, or about, 25th June.

It was well and truly initiated by 'Our Gracie'. She turned in a performance of such energy, wit, sentimentality, bawdy humour, that the audience stood and cheered for minutes on end. Gracie Fields epitomised all that was British at the level of the sailor, soldier and airman. A sturdy character of great resolution, grit, loyalty, endurance and humour. It is difficult to over-emphasise how much such a concert did for morale, how it alleviated homesickness by making men weep openly about it, how the laughter released tensions and soothed sadness over lost friends.

On 17th June, Tony, myself and another colleague, Jimmy Carbines, left Sydney by bus for a small village on the Hawkesbury River where we had arranged to stay at a farm for four days. During the afternoon there was torrential rain and the road conditions became increasingly difficult. It was late when we halted in a little town, stopping outside the Police Station. At this juncture the driver advised all onboard, four of us, that he could not continue as the road to the village was bound to be flooded. He suggested we seek help from the local police. The three of us went in and waited in front of an old desk. In a few moments a sergeant appeared.

'Well lads,' he said, 'I'm Sergeant Jorgensen, what can I do for three handsome naval men wandering loose in a place like this?'

We explained that we were on our way for a holiday at a farm some miles away but had been abandoned by our bus driver because of the state of the roads.

'I'm not surprised,' he opined. 'I doubt if anyone will get through before morning.' He paused, looking at us closely, then went on, 'Even if the rain stops now. Have you lads been fighting the little yellow Nip, little yellow bastards?'

'Yes,' we replied in unison. 'Good on yer boys, good on yer.' He was smiling now, the thought of his saffron faced, slant eyed pet hates being bombed and strafed gave him a pleasurable feeling. 'You will need somewhere to sleep tonight I suppose.'

'Yes please,' I replied. 'A small guest house or lodgings would be ideal.'

He laughed out loud, we had clearly put him in a good mood.

'There's only one establishment here offering any accommodation and you're standing right inside it!'

'You mean the gaol?'

'Too right, my cobbers, my Nip-beating friends, here is where the accommodation is.'

We didn't immediately grasp his meaning, so he went on to explain.

'I have two cells, both empty at the minute. Very clean, fresh bedding. You can use them and I promise not to lock the doors.' He was enjoying this. As we stood and thought among ourselves he was muttering, 'Beating the hell out of those little yellow Nips, I hope to hell those bastards are feeling real crook.'

We looked at each other. We had no options—it was outside, somewhere in the sodden main street of this one-horse town, or the inviting warmth of the 'station'. There was an all-pervading smell of polish and disinfectant but we were used to odours less acceptable than those.

'If it's alright with you Sergeant we will be happy to be your guests.'

'Good men. All true Poms are you?' We nodded. 'Thought so, I'm from Swedish stock myself.'

There was no doubting it. Piercing blue eyes, a steely cornflower colour, hair thick and pale, almost paradoxically, silvery gold. He appeared to be in his late thirties.

Have you men eaten?'

'No,' replied Tony. 'We were actually due to be given our evening meal at the farm.'

'I'll see what tucker I can organise. Sit yourselves down in that room over there. You're lucky there's three chairs and a table—it's our 'grilling' room among other things.' He went out still smiling and saying quietly, 'Little Nips, yellow bastards.'

We made ourselves comfortable. I looked out of the window, barred of course. The rain was still slanting down in what seemed to be a series of curtains drawn across the road, each one about two inches from the other. It was as intense as a monsoon and the water hit the ground so fiercely that it bounced back up about three inches. The road was now obscured, not by flooding, but by the silvery grey double intensity of water forming a dancing, bubbling carpet.

'Looks as though we made the right decision,' said Jimmy. He was the quiet one, with a permanent smile waiting to crease into an open grin. Jimmy didn't say too much but his utterances were usually pithy and to the point, an economy of conversation that concentrated on the essentials.

'Too right cobber,' responded Tony in his best Aussie accent. 'I reckon this is fair dinkum.' He was a fine mimic and had a flair for picking up local dialects.

180

When we were in Ceylon he continually spoke like a local. It was always kindly imitation, especially if in a country where cricket was played. Tony was an excellent batsman. Elegant style, sharp-eyed with effortless stroke-play, his presence at the crease always presaged a display of the grace in pure, text-book batsmanship.

Sergeant Jorgensen came in with two large dinner plates, heaped with eggs, bacon and beans, and put them on the table.

'I'll be along with the other plate and eating irons in a minute.' He was too and we set about the food, to which had been added almost half a loaf of crusty bread, with hungry abandon.

The sergeant sat with us as we ate. He told us that Australia was the land of the fair, opportunity, good life and beautiful women. We felt he was biased but enjoyed his company and hospitality which, in many ways, resembled that which we had experienced in America. Australian friendliness was a giant remove from the reserve of the British. As so many of the people were of UK stock we concluded, that once free of class consciousness, the British could be as warm as our 'colonial' hosts.

The small town was quiet that night, no doubt due to the weather, although the sergeant informed us it was a fairly trouble free spot. We sat and talked for hours and, before we knew it, it was ten o'clock. At this point the sergeant was relieved by a constable who was to remain in charge of the station until 8 a.m. the following morning.

He was introduced to us as 'Mac', an enormous man, at least 6'2" with the physique of a weight-lifter. We began to realise why the town was so quiet. 'Mac' reminded me of the father of one of my schoolfriends, a Detective Sergeant, who looked forward to the Orange Day Parade in Liverpool when he usually found an excuse for banging a few heads together.

We slept like dogs—there was a warm fire—and Mac woke us at 0700 and informed us that breakfast would be at 0730. When he brought it I truly believed he had mistaken the time of day. On each plate was a Gammon steak that barely left room for the two eggs and quarters of tomato.

'Is this normal gaol fare?' asked Tony.

'Well let's say it's a slight improvement in your honour. Not every day we have Pommie guests, especially those who have been Kamikazied. I reckon we owe you some decent hospitality.'

We were embarrassed. There seemed no limit to the generosity of Australians.

Just after nine Sergeant Jorgensen reappeared. 'The floods have subsided sufficient for the roads to be passable. There's a small bus leaving at ten, it will drop you three at the place you are staying if you tell the driver—it's just a slight diversion for him.'

'Fine,' I said, 'we really are most grateful for the time and trouble you have taken, but most of all for your hospitality and kindness. We have been most comfortable, fed like royalty, and enjoyed the company of Mac and yourself. We don't know how to thank you.'

181

'You don't have to. You have a good time in Australia and take care of yourselves when you go back to finish off those little, yellow Nips.'

The time had come to go. We shook hands, trying hard not to flinch in the bone-crushing grips of our hosts. As we waited a few minutes for the bus I reflected on what had happened to us. Fed and cared for by men nearly old enough to be my father, mothered, by two policemen, 12,000 miles from home. The square-bashing days of Chatham four years earlier seemed light years away, and yet they were the opening chapter in a book which would have been considered a fantasy at that time.

By now a wintry sun was shining and the town took on a pale yellow morning glow. It had so many of the characteristics of a Western Film set. Clapboard buildings, boardwalks offering shade and shelter, shops full of 'country' equipment for farmers, miners, hunters, fishermen.

It was late morning when we arrived at the farm-stead ranch. A large bungalow-type house, with many out-buildings and stables, set amidst trees which I could not identify, it looked a pleasing prospect.

We were welcomed by the owner's wife whose name I have long since forgotten. Maybe the ensuing events eradicated it from my memory. She was a good-looking woman, mid-thirties, dark, with a figure accentuated by a dress that seemed unusually urban for a farmer's wife. As she looked at us whilst the introductions were made, I sensed she thought Tony was the handsome, sophisticate she might have read about in romantic novels. She was right—he was handsome and sophisticated, Jimmy and I were inarticulate peasants in his company—a man who had rubbed shoulders with prominent folk in the 'acting profession'.

As we went indoors, and were shown to our rooms, I knew she was flirting with him—even worse he was responding with that charming, slightly twisted smile of his. He was a natural gentleman, with impeccable manners, a cultured accent and oozed charm. When Tony was shown his room, with a double bed, and Jimmy and I were given a twin bedded room some two doors away, I had a feeling of dread, a foreboding that the elements which had delayed our arrival were to be replaced by other factors which might prejudice our stay.

Lunch was a cold meats and salad arrangement. Supper at seven was to be the main meal—delayed an hour in our honour. The afternoon was to be spent horse-riding.

Horses were allocated according to our riding ability and experience. As I had never even sat on a horse, even a rocking horse, I was given an allegedly docile, elderly mare. Tony, of course, claiming to be an accomplished horseman, had a fine, shiny animal. Jimmy, a diffident rider found himself astride a large, but fairly quiet horse.

I was given a few elementary instructions by the farmer/rancher. He had appeared at lunch-time. A modest man, both in physique and conversation, he seemed not to notice the looks his wife was according Tony. He chatted about his life as a farmer, his pride in his land and animals, his regret at having no children. Every now and then his wife would raise her dark eyes

182

heavenwards as if to signify her boredom with the same old story.

I listened carefully to his 'do's and don'ts', the horse neighed a couple of times and nodded its head firmly up and down, apparently in agreement.

When we were finally deemed fit and ready to go we were given directions about the ride into the canyon, liberally shaded by eucalyptus trees and the home of various fairly exotic animals and birds.

The expedition started well enough. Tony led the way, looking for all the world like Errol Flynn with two reluctant and novice musketeers in his wake. He seemed to ride effortlessly with full control of his horse. Mine was only too clearly aware that I was a desperate equestrian coward. But it was tolerant, awaiting an opportunity to show who was riding who. It didn't have long to wait.

About three quarters of a mile from the farm we entered the Canyon—more of a steep valley really—the sun was screened by the trees and the light faded rapidly. A Kookaburra—or laughing jackass—suddenly screeched into maniacal mirth. Possibly at the sight of me riding a horse with which it was familiar. I am certain now that this horse had encountered the bird before, but it reacted as though it had been confronted by a battle-tank. It reared slightly, not enough to unseat me, turned, pinned back its ears and headed back to the ranch.

What was probably a modest trot seemed like a headlong gallop to me. I was beginning to slide off the saddle and whilst I was not losing control—not having enjoyed any—I was, to coin an immortal phrase—hanging on for dear life.

The horse knew the score precisely. It was enjoying my fear-enriched discomfort, making for home having had what it regarded as sufficient exercise, and felt so comfortable that it stopped, nonchalantly chewed a few leaves, then resumed it's journey. As we neared the ranch it was overcome by home-sickness. It quickened its pace and we came into the last stretch at a quick canter. Not stopping, it literally bolted into its stable. Had I not, by this time, been as much off as on the horse, I might well have been decapitated.

I slid off its back and sat, trembling, in the straw. Looking at the gently heaving side of the beast made me realise that the joint forces of Nazi Germany and Imperial Japan had not imbued in me such a sense of abject terror.

By now the farmer had arrived. We had already christened him 'Tim the Ostler'. He surveyed the scene.

'Decided to come back then did she?' he enquired. I noted that he did not refer to the possibility of my having decided to return.

'Yes, she was frightened by a kookaburra and immediately turned for home.'

He laughed. 'She's no more frightened of one of those birds than she is of me. She just wanted to come back, probably fed up with the same ride down the canyon. But she's harmless enough and quite gentle. Didn't gallop home did she?'

I had to confess that it was not what Buffalo Bill would have regarded as a gallop, but to me it was like riding in a short version of the Derby at Epsom.

183

Tim was smiling. I was growing to like him and felt unhappy at what was a likely scenario later that day. He already knew, for he said:

'Handsome fella that friend of yours, Tony.'

'Yes, he is. In civilian life he is an actor. Most actors are attractive and know how to make themselves even more so. It's their manner, use of the language, gestures, body movement.'

'I don't know about all that but I can tell when a bloke's attractive because my wife takes a fancy to him.'

I didn't know what to say. The meaningful glances had not gone unnoticed by Tim. I thought I should warn Tony.

He and Jimmy returned at that point—despite Tony's apparent equestrian skill his horse, and Jimmy's, had also decided to amble back to the stables. Not at quite the frantic trot of my mount, but at a more sedate, controlled quick walk. Despite their enforced return, both of my friends looked thoroughly comfortable, balanced and proud as two Conquistadores in Peru.

'What happened to you then?' asked Tony. 'Felt you'd had enough and turned back?'

He knew full well what the score was.

'You could say that,' I replied, 'especially if you were speaking to the horse.'

He laughed. 'We had intended to ride on towards the end of the canyon but the horses were slightly reluctant.' This was his actor's way of describing how the horses had taken charge.

He turned to Tim. 'A fine horse, a real pleasure to ride.'

'Yes, he's my favourite too, a spirited horse with a strong personality.'

And mine, I wondered? A docile, drudge incapable of a single, independent thought? I resolved it would be a long time before I rode again; indeed it was not until Christmas 1971 when 10 of us, imbued with Glenfiddich courage, cantered alcoholically in Hyde Park.

We all walked out into the open. There were still dark clouds, small, scudding across the sky but the sun shone intermittenly and quite warmly. It was a delightful place—a million miles from Sakishima Gunto.

Supper was a plain but gargantuan meal. We did justice to it, appetites sharpened by the fresh, clean air and in my case, a blessed sense of survival. Beer was the beverage, not the favourite drink of any of us three but we managed to cope with the foaming 'schooners', replenished even before they were emptied.

A log fire blazed in the sitting room, its embers crackling and the flames weaving their yellow and orange mystic patterns. There was a smell of apple-wood. The warmth, the flickering fire, the alcohol, were all sleep inducing. It was difficult to keep one's eyes open.

Regaining consciousness, after a short drift into semi-awareness of the droning conversation, I heard chat about London, England, Honolulu, America—it was a naval travelogue in which I was not appearing. Rousing myself I announced that I was turning in. Jimmy quickly confirmed his intention to do so, leaving Tim, his wife, and Tony, still sitting around the glowing log grate.

I fell asleep as I climbed into the sheets. I recall their cool crispness and slightly soapy smell, 'Fairy' soap that my mother used. The last words I heard were of Jimmy murmuring 'Goodnight'. I believe I failed to reply.

The commotion woke me. Voices raised, running footsteps on the floor-boards, doors banging. Turning on the light I saw it was about 2 a.m. Sitting up and listening intently I could now hear whispering. Not the conspiratorial kind but harsh voices modulated to prevent over-hearing. Then silence.

It was after seven when Jimmy shook me. Gathering my scattered wits, still dulled by over-indulgence in food and alcohol, I began to recollect the early morning rumpus. Jimmy knew nothing of it, blithely and probably wisely, having slept undisturbed for almost nine hours. As I told him of what I heard he quickly concluded that Tim had frustrated an attempt either by Tony to fulfil a tryst or his wife from visiting our friend.

Breakfast was a quiet, almost sullen affair. Tim's wife hardly appeared, being confined to the kitchen from where Tim brought our food. He had a thoughtful, almost distant look and spoke only to bid us 'Good morning' and check our breakfast needs. Tony had not yet given his version of the early morning happenings.

Eating finished we walked towards the river which, very swollen, was rushing headlong and conveying branches, logs, drowned sheep and other sundry flotsam in its light brown surging water.

Tony outlined the night's events. Around 0200 he was awakened by the door knob of his bedroom door being turned slowly, but squeakily. As the door was being pushed open he could see, in the semi-darkness, the figure of Tim's wife about to enter his room. He confessed he was both delighted and guilt-ridden at the prospect of entertaining his hostess in the astutely provided double bed. But fate, in the form of Tim, was to intervene. The door was almost wide open when he grasped his wife by the shoulder and pulled her back into the corridor. She ran a few steps, was caught, then ensued the conversation I had heard, but not clearly enough to determine what was said. Soon, an unknown hand, presumably that of Tim, closed Tony' door with a bang, the triumphant slam of a victor over the vanquished. Then the bang of Tim's door concluded the nocturnal escapade.

'Would you have had her in your bed?' asked Jimmy.

Tony put on his Shakespearean voice and paraphrasing 'Macbeth' said in villanous tones:

'Is this a woman I see before me, her bosoms toward my hand. Come let me clutch thee. I have thee not, but yet I see thee still.'

'That's what happened—I had her not but yet I see her still, faintly, framed in the doorway, eager for the pleasures of my bed.'

'You're all talk,' challenged Jimmy. 'I wager you would have chickened out. In any case I know you are a religious man. I bet you were pleased when Tim rescued you.'

'Gad, foiled again, by thunder,' hammed Tony. 'Jimmy, I almost certainly would have told her to go back to her bed. This was a time when "every prospect pleaseth" but, with the wife of a host, however precarious their relationship might be, I could not, would not have been seduced by her.'

'Yes, but Tim doesn't know that does he? You could have cut the atmosphere with the butter knife this morning,' I said. 'I don't think we can stay here any longer. Imagine sitting around after supper tonight—what a prospective explosive situation. I think we should leave.'

'I leave it to you two,' replied Tony, the tone of his voice revealing his lack of enthusiasm for remaining at the farm.

'We'll leave,' said Jimmy, 'let's get back to Sydney.'

So it was agreed. We returned to the house, packed and sought out Tim. He was not there but his wife was—looking slightly chastened but still with a flicker of invitation in her eyes. She took the news without comment, just telling us that there was a bus at noon.

After settling our bill we bade her farewell and asked her to express our thanks and say goodbye to Tim. She nodded and, as we walked away, called out 'Tony.' He looked back. 'I shan't forget you.' He just waved.

We stayed two nights in Sydney, seeing John Van Druten's 'Voice of the Turtle' at the theatre and 'Lost Week-end' at the cinema. By day we went sight-seeing or shopping. Each one of us still had a small supply of clothing coupons. Tony and I bought identical brown sports jackets, shook hands and made a solemn oath that we would meet again, after the war, wearing our jackets.

David Jones was a splendid store and to us, at least, was like Aladdin's Cave. Organised members of the ship's company, like Les Vancura, had shopping lists detailing items required to take home—one day. Such things as knitting wools, dress materials, suitings, even knitting needles. He was a voracious shopper, but always with a purpose and plan. Many of us just frittered our resources away.

I knew my mother needed some new gloves, black leather, soft kid if possible. David Jones was the answer.

As I browsed at the Glove Counter, the selection was immense and confusing, a voice asked 'Do you require any help, sir?"

Looking up I found myself confronted by a stunningly beautiful ash blonde with hazel eyes, perfect features, full mouth widening into a dazzling smile. I had not spent years in Tony's company without learning some of his sophisticated behaviour toward the female gender.

'I should be most grateful if you would help me choose a pair of suitable gloves for my mother,' I replied. 'I am a little uncertain as to the size but my first concern is to find a good quality pair.'

'I will show you our best ones then we can deal with the question of size, sir.'

Soon there was a good selection spread across a dark teak counter top. She put a pair on her own hands, to show me how they looked when worn. Four or five other pairs followed in quick succession. I was beginning to become more interested in the wearer than the gloves.

The last pair looked luxuriously elegant.

'May I feel how soft they are?' I asked. On impulse she held out her hand and I enclosed it in one of mine. Even through the thin, soft leather I could feel a slight shock, like static electricity. I looked at her and we stood gazing for a few seconds, me still holding her hand. She blushed, disentangled her fingers from mine and asked what I thought of the gloves. I really didn't know what to say, I had lost interest in them.

'If you think these are the best then I will buy them, the size for my mother will be about the size of your hands.'

'You're sure?'

'Yes. They will do fine.' They were soon neatly wrapped, in gift type paper, and I paid for them. I stood at the counter not really wanting to move.

'Will there be anything else sir? We have some really attractive scarves a little further down the display counter.'

'No thank you. You've been most kind and helpful. Thank you so much.'

With that we looked at one another again. I could feel a butterfly sensation in my stomach, my heart beat quickened. My mind was working overtime, trying to think of an excuse to prolong our meeting.

'If I think of anything else I need I will return to ask your advice. Thanks again.' I felt I had left the way open to see her once more, to ask her about anything in the store.

'Please do. naturally I know all that we sell in the store and where it can be found. I'll be happy to help.'

There was nothing more to say, except 'Good-bye', and I moved off. As I walked away I thought how stilted and formal our conversation had been, as though we were both deliberately trying not to let familiarity intrude.

That night I told Tony what had happened.

'Raymond,' he said, 'you are a married man. It is alright for me to enjoy a brief flirtatious relationship—even with a married woman—but not you.' I didn't exactly follow his reasoning.

'But I only want her company. Like all of us I am starved of female association. I just need to walk out with, and talk to, an attractive woman. I am both too shy and moral to get into a relationship other than something purely platonic.'

He smiled. 'Famous last words, Raymond.' He put on a Cockney voice. 'Yer 'onour I only intended . . .'

I laughed, and said, 'It won't be like that.'

'Oh no, take advice from an older, wiser, more experienced man—don't see her again.'

Needless to say I didn't take his counsel. The following day I was back at David Jones, at the Glove counter too. I couldn't see her anywhere. Another assistant asked if she could help.

'Well, yesterday I bought a pair of gloves from a young lady on this counter. I would like to speak to her again, if I may.'

'What did she look like?'

I couldn't really say what I felt—ravishingly beautiful—so I answered 'Tallish, about 5'8", ash blonde . . .'

She interrupted. 'Oh that would have been Frances. She is having a tea break at the moment and will be back in about 10 minutes. In the meantime if I can help?'

'No thanks. I'll come back shortly. It's about something we discussed yesterday.' I walked away to the perfume counter then wandered on, aimlessly passing the time. After 15 minutes I made my way to a position from which I could see the Glove counter. She was back, and looking no less lovely than the day before. It was with an assumed nonchalance that I returned to the gloves and scarves. She saw me coming and, with that dazzling smile said, 'Hello again. I wondered if it would be you, my colleague told me a handsome naval man had been asking after me.' Did that mean she thought I was handsome I wondered.

'I have decided to buy a scarf, also for my mother,' I added hastily. 'Could you show me some which are fairly discreet. My mother is about 48 and rather conservative in taste although she does like blues.'

We walked to the scarves, dozens of them. Silk, cotton, woollen, in a variety of colours and shapes.

'I understand you name is Frances,' I said. 'I had a sister named Frances, who died when she was four. I also have an aunt of that name who is a Brigadier in the Salvation Army.'

'Obviously a popular name in your family,' she replied. 'What is yours?'

'Raymond. Raymond Barker. I come from Lytham St. Annes in Lancashire although I am now onboard HMS *Victorious* which has been my home for more than three and a half years.'

'My surname is Horner, you know like Jack who sat in the corner. I live in a suburb of Sydney, at home with my parents.'

I chose a scarf, a royal blue square with a maroon line running about one inch inside each edge. It was plain but neat. Mum would be pleased.

As I paid for the scarf I asked, as calmly as I could, 'May I see you after you have finished work. Perhaps I could walk you home?'

'That would be a problem. I live at North Wolstencraft across the Bridge and travel home by train. But you can walk me to the station.'

'What time do you finish?'

'A quarter past five, it will be almost half past before I am out of the store. I will walk to the main entrance and meet you there.'

She smiled, I smiled, we parted.

Barker, I said to myself, what are you doing. Married, with a loyal and devoted wife at home, consciously seeking the company of a beautiful woman. For what purpose? A platonic friendship, company not born of being incarcerated in the same massive steel boat. My naval friends were special to me, very special, but I needed space, above all to widen my conversational boundaries by meeting and talking with new people.

When Frances appeared she looked stunning although, with high heels, some half an inch taller than me. A bright, heart melting smile, a slightly nervous 'hello' and we were together.

'The station's not far away,' she said, 'but I must catch a train not later than six o'clock or my parents will worry about me.'

'Are you an only child?'

'Yes, and I sometimes wonder if the disadvantages outweigh the advantages. What about you?'

We were now walking slowly down the very busy street, workers from shops and offices rushing to get home. It was uncomfortable holding a conversation in such circumstances. But the station was not far away, maybe we could sit for a few minutes.

'I had two sisters, Frances and Nina, both died when they were four. I can just remember them, especially Nina who was a scamp and teased me greatly.'

'That's sad to have lost a family so young.'

'Yes, my father who had a torrid time in the First World War, wounded three times, and who doted on his little daughters, has never really got over losing them.'

Silence fell between us as we struggled to keep together in the commuters headlong rush to Wynyard station. When we arrived we sat on a bench.

'I will have to catch a train in fifteen minutes, my evening meal will be ready. We are not on the telephone so I cannot tell my mother I will be late. You don't mind, do you?'

'Of course not. I am so happy to be with you, even for such a short time. Maybe another evening we could go out to dinner, you having warned your mother in advance.'

'I'd love to. Why don't we fix a date now and I can arrange matters at home?'

'Today is the 22nd, I am on cypher duties tomorrow over the dog watches (4—8 p.m.) we are going to sail on the 25th, so it must be the day after tomorrow, my only chance before returning to Japanese waters.'

She looked disappointed. 'You are going so soon?'

'Yes, and I think we will be up there until the war ends. That seems to be the general impression. Anyway, what about the day after tomorrow. Can I meet you same time, same place and you can choose the restaurant?'

'Alright,' she put her hand in mine. 'Until then. Goodbye.' I felt my hand being squeezed and could feel the warmth of her through the white gloves she was wearing. We stood up and she walked quickly away, turning briefly to wave.

It was difficult to get her out of my mind the following day. The ship was still being over-run by dockyard workers and stores suppliers. Our 20mm guns, the Oerlikons, were being replaced by the much heavier 40mm, the Bofors. Recent experience had shown that the strike rate and effectiveness of the 20mm against Kamikaze attacks was very limited. The Japanese seemed to fly right through the most dense barrage whereas the US Navy reported that the 40mm, with mixed armour piercing and tracer ammunition, was very effective—despite their horrendous losses. Ingredients for making Blaze Bombs were also shipped onboard. A lethal combination of powder and fluid which, when mixed on impact, became incredibly inflammable over a wide area. Extra long-range tanks for the Corsairs indicated that they might be flying on deep penetration missions or on protracted protective roles. The urgency of all this activity was very apparent.

I met Frances, 'same time, same place' as agreed. She had gone to great lengths to appear smart in a conservative way. A two piece suit, dark blue, plain white blouse, matching shoes and handbag. She put her arm into mine and we walked into Hyde Park. The new British Centre had been opened a few days earlier by the Duke of Gloucester, who had also visited *Victorious* in dock. With 500 beds, lounges, restaurant, bars, concert hall, the Centre was a superb enterprise. The Park was busy with servicemen, regrettably some already drunk.

The weather was not warm, but comfortable, and we sat on a park bench among the beautiful trees and watched the Australian world go by. The 'two up' players, tossing coins and gambling, the early inebriated meandering hazily across the grass, the lovers, arms around waists, female head on male shoulder, walking tenderly and dreamily, oblivious of others. We talked about everything under the sun (except my marital status). Frances was a bright, articulate woman, some three years my senior, and I was surprised that she worked on a counter in a departmental store.

Time came for us to dine. It was early eating in Sydney, 6.30 p.m. and the restaurants were busy. The cuisine was typically Australian, huge portions of well-cooked food, eaten in a noisy environment of chatter and constant movement. I already felt I had known Frances for years and was relaxed and comfortable in her company.

She questioned me about my ambitions after the war and I told her I had not thought that far ahead. Even the prospect of the war finishing still seemed uncertain. How could you defeat a people like the Japanese with their penchant for suicidal death before surrender? Hadn't they thrown themselves off cliffs on a Pacific Island rather than be taken prisoner by the Americans.

The meal over, we walked into the Park again, this time strolling round, just content to be together. Then to the station; it was only 9 o'clock but Frances was anxious not to be late home. As we stood in Wynyard I reminded her that I would be sailing the next day. She promised she would pray for my safety and write to me in the hope that I would return to Sydney to see her again.

We stood close, holding hands, I kissed her cheek. She looked at me, eyes beginning to brim with tears and said, 'Goodbye Raymond, take good care of yourself and come back to me.' With that she went.

As I watched her go, tall, slim, lovely figure, neatly elegant, I asked myself, 'What have you done Barker, what of the harmless and simple pleasure of being with an attractive woman. Is it turning into something more fundamental?'

I was pre-occupied when I returned to the ship which was now fully stored, patched up and again ready for action—if one discounted our rudder problem. Tony came to the office to see me that evening to learn the latest news.

The German battleship Tirpitz, in her Norwegian fjord hide-away, reeling under the explosions of bombs dropped by Victorious' bombers.

Christmas 1944. Some of the cast of the Pantomime written by Tony Sagar and the author. Some of the 'girls' were never seen in quite the same light again when they re-appeared as stokers, seamen and engineers!

The oil refinery at Palembang well and truly ablaze after the raid in January, 1945.

*Two Kamikaze torpedo bombers ablaze in the sea after succumbing to anti-aircraft fire.
A third can be seen at just above sea-level approaching* Illustrious. *It was also destroyed.
Defending fighter planes wheel above the scene.*

A Kamikaze blazes, along with four Corsairs, after hitting Victorious *on 9th May, 1945.*

The wreckage of a Japanese suicide bomber on Victorious' deck entangled with that of his enemy, the Corsair fighter.

The effects of Steward Lander, killed by a Kamikaze, are auctioned to raise money for his family. At the table, the author, Peter Lorne and Joseph Deegan.

Lt. Cdr Charlton, known as Fearless Freddie, with his Corsair on fire after landing. His exploits during the war were legion. He was shot down four times, credited with eight enemy aircraft. He eventually died aged 72 in January, 1990.

An injured pilot is carefully lifted out of a Walrus rescue amphibian after landing back on Victorious. He was picked up under the noses of the Japanese after his aircraft had been shot down.

Victorious arrives in Sydney Harbour in late August, 1945; the first of the front-line carriers to return to Australia following the defeat of the Japanese.

He listened carefully as I told him that I thought Frances was very fond of me and that I was attracted to her.

'Just as well we are sailing tomorrow. We may never come back to Sydney, so if I were you I would just regard what has happened as a pleasant, unexpected interlude. Now it's time we did another 'Dungeon Dust Time', you start on the ads for the intro and the ending and I will do the usual poem. Then we can write the rest together. It will take your mind off Sydney and give the chaps something to laugh at as we head for the hell-hole yet again.'

'OK AJ,'—(he was Anthony James and I often called him 'AJ')—'thanks for the advice. Let's concentrate on important matters, like the war and "Dungeon Dust".'

We sailed at 1145 on 25th June, in company with our destroyers, embarked our squadrons and anchored in Jervis Bay for the night. At 0700 the following day we steamed north to Manus, carrying out flying exercises on the way. By now we had many new aircrew, some of whom had not had experience of operational conditions. They needed, and were given, rigorous practice.

Our designation had been changed from Task Force 57 to Task Force 37—we were now part of the Third Fleet. In truth it was exactly the same. Under Admiral Spruance it was the Fifth, under Admiral Halsey it became the Third. Halsey enjoyed a reputation of being a hard man, gung-ho, macho, all American tough guy. His nick-name was 'Bull' and he had just promised that when Japan was defeated he would ride through Tokyo on the Emperor's white horse. He sounded very interesting!

We rendezvoused with *Formidable*, exercising our aircraft together, still en route to Manus. The *KGV* and *Indefatigable* were still in Sydney, the ship's company were moaning that we had been 'last in, first out'. It was getting much warmer as we reached the Coral Sea, now joined by *Implacable*. The Captain informed us that we would probably be required to attack the Japanese mainland in what was hoped would be the final assault on the Japs. He warned, once more, that all out effort was required, we should not be thinking of when we would be out of the Navy but must concentrate on defeating the enemy. Again we were counselled not to waste time writing home, we must all perfect our separate skills to defend the ship and end the war. Of course it needed to be said, if only to relieve the boredom and give flagging spirits something to complain about as we approached the Admiralty Islands, the dull sweat-box of Manus.

News reached us that the US carrier *Bunker Hill* had been hit by two Kamikaze aircraft—383 killed, 247 injured. What a catastrophe despite the banks of 40mm's. Reading Les Vancura's diary for that day, 2nd July, he writes, 'They may carry more planes than us, but give me our armoured flight deck every time.'

We passed New Guinea on 3rd, it was raining steadily throughout the day. It made little difference, even the exercise walks on deck in the late evening, when the day's flying was over, went on as normal in the rain. Men, stripped to the waist, often in bare feet, padded the length of the flight deck eight times to cover a mile. Soaked by the warm rain they found escape from the steamy caverns and corridors below decks.

Cyphers revealed that our scheduled oiling rendezvous, on operations, would be exactly in line with Tokyo—no doubt as to our ultimate destination. We anchored in Manus the next day. Since our last visit the black out had been lifted and the harbour was now almost empty of shipping. Manus had now out-lived its usefulness, the stores anchorages were now much further north. We already had two month's of stores onboard. Few of the crew went ashore. It took almost an hour in the ship's pinnace and there was little to do anyway. To ease the boredom the Captain allowed beer to be brought aboard again and one bottle was issued to each man. It was sweated out in less than half-an-hour.

The force departed on 6th July, crossing the line later that day. We had already lost count of how many times we had crossed and re-crossed the Equator.

One of the new Blaze Bombs was tested. I am somewhat amused by Les's description, 'It blazed *merrily* away,' it seemed far from merry to me. All the attempts to put it out with water or foam failed, the chemical had the property of generating its own oxygen.

The *KGV* and attendant destroyers appeared on the scene, Task Force 37 was now at full strength.

The radio news gave details of the tremendous bombing campaign on Japan by Flying Fortresses. It prompted the question of what our role was to be, with such limited offensive resources, compared with the land-based bombers operating almost round the clock. Some of us concluded that the immense show of force, both airborne and naval, was bound to affect Japanese morale and reveal the hopelessness of their military situation.

BBC World Services announced that *Victorious* (twice), *Indefatigable* (once) and *Formidable* (twice) had been hit by suicide bombers in early May, with some 70 killed and over 40 injured. Presumably this was released at that time because the next-of-kin would have been informed and mail would have reached home from Australia from those of us unaffected by the bombings. By and large the men were happy; some came to ask advice on how to let their relatives know that they were OK. I told them that they were not to worry, if they had written home from Sydney then relatives would know they were safe.

By the 16th we were fully integrated into the attacking US naval forces. I witnessed five US carriers oiling a few miles away and learned that 10 more were within 50 miles of us. At last we were central to the action. This boosted morale as the men felt Admiral Halsey was placing a proper value on our capabilities and strength.

Yet again the weather was poor, even though it was Japanese mid-summer and we had almost 16 hours of daylight. On the 17th we were in an area just 70 miles off the coast and 120 miles from Tokyo itself. It was Action Stations at dawn and we despatched fighter-bombers to attack airfields, the battleships went inshore to bombard Hitachi. There were no enemy reprisals and only four Jap aircraft had been sighted airborne since our arrival in the area.

The weather caused us to seek other targets where conditions might be better. On 20th we oiled and received mail, there were two letters from Frances, addressed to 'My Dearest' and 'My Darling'. I experienced a strange feeling of mixed dread and joy. I truly wanted her to like me but was fearful of her doing so. The sight of two blue envelopes, addressed in a bold, but feminine hand, and post-marked Sydney brought ribald remarks from colleagues. I prayed we would not return to Sydney but secretly hoped we would.

As we steamed southwards to avoid a typhoon, Captain Denny informed us we had been allocated targets on the Inland Sea of Japan, and especially Kobe. The seas became quite rough and it was fortunate that we had embarked fresh provisions from a store ship the previous day.

It was 0500 when we closed up at Action Stations on 24th July and we launched strikes of fighters and bombers. The Avengers were briefed to attack an airfield but, as little aerial activity had been observed, they were advised to seek out shipping targets on the Inland Sea. Despite the deplorable weather—it seemed the Japs were able to influence it—the Avengers sighted and successfully bombed an Escort Carrier of the Japanese Navy. It was severely damaged. Perversely the weather improved at night and we remained at Action Stations most of the hours of darkness, the fleet bathed in the pale, silvery light of a full moon, shining like a huge, glossy pearl.

We had two hours rest before returning to Action Stations at 0505. Strikes were despatched to find the damage carrier and, after a thorough pounding from planes from all our carriers, it was sunk. Happiness all round as the aircrews returned safely. At 1615 the Fleet was approached by eight 'Beacon Guided Torpedo Bombers', a variant on the manned suicide type. Seven were shot down long before they came within range of our guns. Again I spent most of the night in the ADP as we steamed under a cloudless sky. The sea had a silver sheen and the occasional dolphin leapt clear of the water in a friendly frolic. It was so peaceful and the great armada made a stirring sight ploughing resolutely and silently through the vast Pacific.

On 27th July we heard from the BBC that a Labour Government had been elected with a majority of over 200. There were cheers on the mess decks, frowns in the Ward Rooms. It was the first time that over two thirds of those onboard had been old enough to be involved in voting—although we had not done so. Tony remarked to me that we would all be sorry, I merely thought how delighted my father would be.

Reading the cyphers that night I learned that *Glory, Vengeance, Venerable* and *Colossus*, all light carriers, were now in Manus with battleships *Duke Of York* and *Anson*. All the wolves were now gathering for the final kill.

As we went to Action Stations, again at 0500, I wondered how many more weeks we would be doing so. Information pouring in from many US sources indicated the parlous state of Japan and plans were now well advanced for seaborne landings on Honshu itself. I felt sure that these would create a new high in casualty rates on both sides. Perhaps Japan would succumb to the non-stop fire-bombing and punishing bombardment from naval air and sea forces.

Today there was some anti-aircraft fire from the batteries around the Inland Sea. Two of our planes were hit but ditched near to the fleet and the crews were picked up.

By now we were running short of bombs, and strikes were still scheduled for as far ahead as 10th August, but on 1st we met up with the Fleet Train and fuelled with both oil and avgas as well as bombing-up. The following day we tried to take on provisions but the seas were rough and we ran dangerously close to the supply ship before abandoning the attempt.

Due to the next proximity of a typhoon our movements were amended and re-scheduled almost by the hour. Reports were received that the Japs were conserving their air strength and massing planes for a possible do-or-die airborne invasion of Okinawa. There were rumours galore and indeed on 5th August a small force of Jap bombers sank one US warship and damaged another.

Our own strikes were then postponed until after 8th August. No explanation was given for this and the force retired from the operational area to rejoin the Fleet Train. Mercifully the supply ships were able to come alongside and we embarked potatoes, cabbages and apples. We had been spared by one day the doubtful privilege of dehydrated vegetables—an acquired taste, like senna pods.

The news of the dropping of the first Atomic Bomb on Japan was broadcast on the ship's radio on 8th August. We found it difficult to comprehend that a device, weighing not much more than the bombs carried by our own Avengers, should have such devastating and cataclysmic results. Twenty thousand tons of TNT, an explosive power 80,000 times greater than our 500lb bomb, packed into a single missile seemed unbelievable. We were not told of civilian casualties but informed that four square miles of the city centre of Hiroshima had been totally destroyed. I tried to put it into a perspective I could understand. It meant that such a bomb, dropped on Preston, where I went to College, would wipe out the entire town.

Everyone was wildly speculating as to the likely response by the Japanese. Would they now surrender, especially as the Russians, as opportunist as ever to extend their territorial influence, had declared war on Japan and marched into Manchuria. They could well have done so the day after hostilities ceased in Europe.

The second bomb fell on Nagasaki on the 9th and the following day the Japanese accepted most of the peace demands of the Allies but they wished to retain their Emperor and were reluctant about 'Unconditional Surrender'.

Meanwhile the war went on. We were back off the coast and launched strikes against any targets available. Shipping was bombed and strafed, as were airfields. It was business as usual until the Japanese capitulated totally.

On Saturday, 11th August, we withdrew, yet again, to our replenishment area for fuel and stores. The weather was still creating difficulties and we seemed to be forever on the periphery of a typhoon. The conditions prevented our return to resume strikes on the 12th and, in the early afternoon, Captain

Denny spoke to us over the radio. He said that the Japs had provisionally accepted the Allied demands and that our Task Force, except the *KGV*, two cruisers and several destroyers, would be departing for Manus. There was a loud cheer. A signal received from 'Bull' Halsey read: 'Armistice in operation, from now on all Japanese aircraft are to be shot down in a friendly manner!'

Steaming south to Manus, through a vicious typhoon, with some of the smaller vessels performing aquatic acrobatics which their Naval Architects could never have imagined, we pondered on the situation.

Despite the cheer which greeted Captain Denny's announcement, a few of us felt deprived. A prize had been won, with blood, sweat and tears, and we were not being allowed to attend the ceremony. The *KGV* was to represent the Royal Navy but surely it should have been a carrier, the work-horse of Task Force 37/57 and, as we had been the only carrier involved in all the operations of the Eastern Fleet, it ought to have been *Victorious*.

One might have thought that our one desire would be to get out of the area, to peace and civilisation. But the adrenalin was still flowing; we were on a high because victory had been won at last even though the immediate fruits would not benefit us. Ships become communities and *Victorious* was a remarkably strongly bonded one. Many of the crew had been onboard for four years, especially the lower deck members. The sense of belonging was real, we all depended on one another and none of us had ever been let down. The display of togetherness I had witnessed in Scapa from members of the *Punjabi* and *London* was no less real on *Victorious*; the ship was like a village with all the inhabitants inter-related. It was Cosa Nostra—our family—a pride in the ship keeping the members close.

There was disappointment at the thought of steaming away into oblivion. This view was not canvassed or generated by activists, it found expression simultaneously, a huge swell of united opinion among the ship's company. The current feeling was that we had a right to be steaming into Tokyo Bay as a symbol of the Royal Navy's carrier endeavour, to represent those ships which had suffered the casualties and borne the brunt of the Japanese suicidal defence of their homeland.

It was 15th August when we heard that the war was officially at an end. Captain Denny spoke to us just after 0900. His brief announcement was loudly cheered.

As the weather became calmer and warmer the order came to 'Splice the Mainbrace', an extra tot of rum was issued to each man to celebrate peace. Admiral Vian flew onboard and thanked us for all that we had done, our effort, he said, was exemplary in every way.

The day before we reached Manus a medical team assembled to certify men as fit to be discharged back into civilian life as their release date approached. There was some hilarity; one usually got discharged for being unfit, would lack of fitness now mean extended service?

The temperature had risen to over 100°. Again conditions below deck were almost intolerable. The decks were so hot to the feet that sweating bodies moved nimbly on the tips of their toes to avoid burning, and water from the showers rose up in a dense cloud of steam making breathing difficult.

We arrived in Manus on 18th August after 43 days at sea. Our Pacific War was now at an end, a bitter end, a strange, shabby, almost anonymous end.

CHAPTER THIRTEEN

Super Trooper

We lingered in Manus a bare 24 hours, a day too long for most of us. The time was spent unloading unserviceable gear, divesting the ship of stores now surplus to requirements. What were our requirements? As far as the crew was concerned the prime one was to go back to the UK. Many of them would qualify for immediate demobilisation and, now that the war was over, they believed the sooner the better.

En route to Sydney we heard that American Lend Lease had stopped. The generous system of aid which had allowed a bankrupt Britain to sustain its lonely fight until Pearl Harbour had ended. There would be continued rationing at home for some time yet.

For some reason the entire ship's company was innoculated against Typhoid. The batch must have been past its 'sell by' date as crew members went down like nine-pins. Everywhere was depleted of men as many were unable to leave their hammocks or camp beds. Information had been coming in that the carriers, with their vast hangars cleared of aircraft, would be used as accommodation vessels for returning prisoners of war. Probably some of these might be suffering from Typhoid, hence the innoculations.

It became cooler as we proceeded south, and on 23rd our squadrons flew off and we anchored in Moreton Bay off Brisbane. The news was that Captain Denny was leaving *Victorious* when we arrived in Sydney so it was a stirring farewell as our aircraft departed.

Our arrival in Sydney was quite remarkable. It was late afternoon when we passed through the 'Heads' and into the great and magnificent harbour. Almost every vessel, merchantmen, small warships, ferries,yachts, motor boats, sounded sirens and hooters or fired flares. Planes flew overhead and dipped their wings in salute. Many of our crew, lining both sides of the flight deck and dressed in smart gear, for a change, had tears running down their cheeks at the warmth of our reception. Be damned to Tokyo Bay—the Japs wouldn't have welcomed us like this.

On Saturday morning I went ashore and made for David Jones. As I approached the Glove and Scarf counter Frances saw me and gave a heart-melting smile of welcome. She had heard on the radio of our arrival and was hopeful I would be able to get ashore immediately. We met later, walked and talked. She was anxious to know what was to happen to me. I didn't know except that we would be in Sydney for some time. Oddly there was nothing romantic about our being together but I did experience a great warmth and pleasure in her company.

The Sunday morning brought a Church Parade and Divisions on the flight deck. Captain Denny, now promoted Rear Admiral, spoke to the assembled officers and men. His dry, clipped, yet soft voice was carried by the light morning breeze over the 2000 who stood before him. Oddly enough he still seemed somewhat withdrawn, possibly sad, despite the well-earned promotion. I thought at one point as he spoke that he may have been affected by the occasion but, upon reflection, concluded this could not be. His strength was his dedication and single-mindedness, there was no room for sentiment and he expressed none.

When he finished speaking, 2000 voices were raised in a cheer of such volume that it rang and echoed round the dockyard. All the pent up feelings of relief at the War's ending were expressed in that loud and continuous hurrah. It also carried heartfelt thanks for the skill and resolution our Captain had displayed in keeping the ship safe, especially during our first Kamikaze attack. For a moment he smiled, then broke into an impish grin, saluted us all and stepped down and out of our lives. The cheering continued until he left the flight deck.

His successor was John Campbell Annesley, a greater contrast one could not imagine. Friendly, chatty, personable, his tall figure moved around the ship with a nod and smile for almost everyone he encountered. An example is related by Petty Officer 'Charlie' Frise.

'Shortly after Captain Annesley's appointment I was summoned to the Compass Platform to rectify a problem with the "Clear View Screens". These revolved mechanically to throw off water and give a clear sighting ahead, but were not operating efficiently. When I spoke to the Captain he recognised my heavy Devonshire accent and asked: "Are you a 'Janner'?" (A Janner being a true Devonian.) "Yes sir," I replied. "I come from a village near Ivybridge." "Good Lord Frise," he said, "not Cornwood?" "No sir, but I know that village very well." We talked all the time I worked on the screen. When I had finished and was about to leave he said, "Come on and have a drink Petty Officer," and took me to his day cabin where he poured a stiff Scotch, handing it to me with the words, "Let us toast the men of Devon, true sons of the sea." And we did.'

Charlie's experience was not an everyday occurrence but I could not imagine any of our previous three Captains indulging in such fraternisation. Maybe the euphoria of peace was the reason.

We remained in Sydney until 25th September. In the meantime a great deal had happened.

On Friday, 31st August, there was a Victory Parade and contingents from *Victorious*, *Implacable*, *Formidable*, *Black Prince* and one of our destroyers took part. I was nominated to represent the Administrative Staff. It was a stirring occasion. As we marched proudly down the main streets, young women broke from the crowd, embraced and kissed us. Shredded paper and streamers thrown from the higher windows covered us in giant confetti. The bands played with vigour and the marchers strode forward with all the carefree relief that this was a celebration of joy and happiness.

The Salute was taken by the Lord Mayor on the steps of the Town Hall, he beamed mightily as we inclined our heads towards him. He was truly enjoying the occasion. As we dispersed, pieces of coloured paper clinging to our uniforms and faces stained with lipstick traces, the people of the city offered meals, trips, visits to the theatre, hospitality. It was overwhelming.

Victorious was undergoing profound changes. The Hangar was being made into a massive dormitory with partitions in appropriate places to offer some privacy. A Canteen was also constructed at one end so that those in the hangar had some facilities apart from the ship's company. Our journey home was to be that of a troopship plus a deck cargo of planes, spares etc.

The Captain gave us all four days leave. Tony and I had chatted about a visit to the Blue Mountains but with winter not yet over in Australia we were unsure. Frances, who I had been seeing twice a week for a meal, a walk and a talk, asked me if I would like to stay at her home for the leave period. Her parents would make me very welcome and, in any event, were anxious to meet me. Tony advised against it, but I succumbed. She managed to obtain three days leave from David Jones so we would be able to visit some of the sights together.

After meeting her from work one evening we caught the train across the Bridge to North Wolstonecraft and walked down Berry Road. No. 26, like all the properties, was a bungalow, brightly painted, small front garden, typical Australian suburbia.

I was greeted warmly by her parents who said they had heard 'a lot about me'. We went into the sitting room and immediately Frances' mother dropped to her knees, followed quickly by her husband and daughter. I felt obliged to do likewise. There followed a long prayer, thanking the Lord for my deliverance, the successful ending of the war, a request for the remission of our sins, and so forth. As I knelt, and the voice droned on, I wondered what kind of people Frances' parents were. Upon rising, Mrs. Horner led the way into the dining room. The evening meal was preceeded by a prayer, quite long. I glanced up as I listened. Frances, eyes tightly closed, was concentrating intently, although it was now obvious to me that she must have heard it many times before. Or had she? Was this devout demonstration just for my benefit? It was not.

The meal was eaten in semi-silence, broken only when I complimented Mrs. Horner on her cooking. I felt embarrassed, almost an intruder, for here was a family very different from my own. My mother, a talker, would liven up meal-times by regaling my father and me with gossip, some of it bordering on the scandalous. Father would talk about his work-mates, the day's happenings, football, cricket, almost anything.

Mr. Horner was a small man, Frances being at least two inches taller. Although only in his early fifties he had a lined, care-worn face. Grey hair aged him too. By contrast his wife, tall as her daughter, was well built, running to stoutness. A large, round face, ruddy complexion, pale hazel eyes, prominent nose, hair a mousey brown. She had a dominant bearing and her husband recognised this.

Meal over, we retired to the sitting room, the radiogram was switched on and Tchaikowsky's 'Pathetique' played softly in the background. Against this sad, almost sombre music, a discussion was launched by Mrs. Horner on the power of prayer and religion. As a first time guest I did not wish to take issue on some of the views expressed. The discussion became almost a monologue, neither Frances, nor her father, wishing or daring to disagree with her mother. Eventually Frances suggested we go for a walk, it was almost dark and her father said words to the effect that it should be neither too far or too long.

Outside she clutched my arm and squeezed it.

'I'm sorry about all that. Mother's a zealous member of the Plymouth Brethren and father goes along with her. He is not as devout as her but is a believer nonetheless.'

'What about you?' I asked. 'You seemed to agree with all your mother said and I noticed how seriously you observed the prayers.'

'Yes, I am religious in a very simplistic way. I don't need elaborate rituals or vestments to convince me of Christ's life on earth or the existence of God. And you, you said very little and when you spoke it was non-commital.'

'That's because I'm an agnostic. I've seen enough during these past years to shake my original beliefs which began at Sunday School and endured until I joined the navy. Now I am unsure.'

'But prayer and Faith defeated the Japanese.'

'I don't think so. American industrial strength was the true victor, prayer and faith in the right of our cause may have helped.'

'Raymond, I prayed for you every day you were in Japanese waters and you returned safely.'

I didn't want to continue the discussion because I knew she would only become upset and it would be insensitive to challenge her beliefs which were sincere and deeply held. We walked in silence then I asked, 'What shall we do for the next three days?'

'I've been thinking about that. We can take a few trips. Botany Bay. Bondi Beach. Cronulla. The Zoo. Watson's Point. Oh there's so much for us to see together.'

We turned back to Berry Road. There was a wintry moon and it was quite chilly. I hoped the next three days would be fun. That was all I wanted really, fun in the company of an attractive woman.

The days were fun. We travelled on trains, buses, trams; we walked miles in quite beautiful surroundings. Watched the surfers hurtle headlong on the crests of huge Pacific rollers before they tumbled under the curling lip of the wave and disappeared in a crashing, thunderous maelstrom of foam and froth.

We walked across the Bridge and I told Frances of my father's work on it—and how he had called his first daughter Frances.

The nights were difficult. I felt uneasy with her mother, possibly a guilt complex because I had not revealed I was married, but as I had no designs on her daughter I didn't think it was relevant. Religion was always uppermost in the conversation, not as an element of discussion but as a behavioural factor—prayers, church music, bible readings. I was always urged to 'have a good night's rest'—a euphemism for 'Please go to bed soon so that we can go and you are not left alone with our daughter'. At the same time the hospitality was generous and kind. I was told I could drop all my laundry in and have it 'thoroughly washed and ironed'. It did cross my mind, fleetingly, that this may have been a comment on the whiteness of my shirts.

Back onboard the changes were gathering pace and on 18th September, 400 men from *Formidable* and *Indefatigable* were embarked for passage home. Some others were ex Prisoners-of-War and their pathetic condition was difficult to accept. If some of us had felt badly done by, when out of fresh food or on Action Rations for a couple of days, then it all paled into its proper perspective as these 'stick men' made their way slowly and cautiously around the ship.

Captain Annesley told us we would be sailing for home on 25th. This announcement caused a hasty shopping spree and Les Vancura wrote: 'I went ashore and bought a juice extractor, vegetable shredder, raisins, sultanas and sundry groceries.' A few days earlier he recorded a nocturnal event at the small hotel in Sydney where he spent his four days leave.

'Last night, or rather this morning, at 0130, a woman came into my room and started to undress. She was slightly "oiled" and said she had mistaken my room for another. Her name, she said, was Maisie, and asked if I was Johnny. On being assured that I was not, she left.' I could think of dozens on *Victorious* who would have willingly been 'Johnny' for a while.

Victorious was looking less like a warship and more like a floating hotel. It was almost under seige from visitors, hundreds of whom were shown around each day. It was not unusual to have the office door flung back on its runners and a voice announce, 'This is the Ship's Office, from which we all get paid.' Half a dozen faces would look in, impressed by the dark brown desks, diligent workers, heads bent over ledgers and documents. There was much to do, all those taking passage had to be put on the ship's books, payments made and records prepared for the Admiralty. Many ex-prisoners had no documentation, not even the 'dog tags' normally worn around the neck giving name, serial number and religion.

It was 1030 on the morning of the 25th September as we were pulled away from the Jetty by tugs. Hundreds had assembled to wish us farewell. The Marine Band played 'Now is the Hour' on the flight deck. Cheering, waving, crying, friends, a few distant relatives, newly found sweethearts with tears streaming, all combined to create a scene of deep emotion. Streamers were thrown, everlasting love declared, as *Victorious*, rust stained and war weary, moved slowly into the Harbour to begin the long voyage home. A few fainted

201

on the dockside, overcome by the surge of combined sadness and excitement. Onboard, some sailors thanked their lucky stars that when they eventually disembarked, some 12,000 miles would separate them from that tearful 'Sheila' at Wooloomooloo. The first turn of the screw had indeed paid a lot of debts.

The Australian Bight served up its usual mix of wind and high sea. The flight deck was declared out of bounds as the Captain was worried that those taking passage might be at risk on the violently pitching platform.

At 1000 on October 1st, we entered the harbour at Fremantle; and anchored in the roads. We now had just over 1000 taking passage, and the prime requirement was to embark as much fresh food as practicable in order to victual some 3000 people three times daily.

There were two letters from Sydney, in light blue envelopes, slightly perfumed and each bearing an acronym on the sealed down flap. One, I recall, was H.O.L.L.A.N.D. The letters had been delivered to the office, where they were the subject of some mirth and not a little teasing. The 'Oohs' and 'Aahs' were punctuated by feeble and sometimes crude attempts to decode the acronym. I had no idea what it signified, and do not to this day. I wrote a warm, farewell letter in reply.

The following day we sailed for Colombo and, within 24 hours, received a signal from the Admiralty to increase our speed by five knots and so hasten our arrival in the UK. Good news all round, especially for those poor souls taking passage, some of whom had not seen Britain for four years.

Tony and I decided to arrange a Variety Concert and planned for it to take place when *Victorious* was in the Red Sea, where the weather would be warm and the sea calm. It would take place on the flight deck, with a stage rigged and full lighting arranged. Volunteers came forward from among our passengers, one of whom had been a soloist singer in an English Cathedral. Kenneth More teamed up with Doctor Rogerson and the pair did a very creditable 'take off' of the Western Brothers—two languid satirists who sang at the piano. The Marine Band produced a Jazz Quintet, there was a conjuror, a Barber Shop quartet. Tony and I wrote a melodrama, in true Victorian style, of a virginal maid left alone whilst Jack, an intrepid sailor went to sea to defend his country. Meanwhile, the village squire, Jasper (who else) had designs on the forlorn Mary. Naturally, as Mary was about to be deflowered, against her will of course, Jack returned. Without removing his kit-bag from his shoulder, he administered a thorough thrashing to the dastardly Jasper. Tony was Jasper, and hammed his way through outrageously to the delight of our enormous audience. Booed and hissed, he snarled back at the jeering crowd who cheered lustily when Jack appeared, bronzed and brave, to protect Mary's honour.

There was also a Fancy Dress competition with Betty Grable look-alikes from the most unlikely mess decks. Until that night I had never noticed a single stoker who resembled Betty Grable, except for having two legs—now there were three!

Amidst all the fun and frolic there was sadness. Petty Officer Herbert Diss, who had requested the photographs of Palembang, died from acute leukemia.

I sat with him, in the Sick Bay, from time to time. A daughter had been born to his wife not long after he had left the UK, a girl he was never to see. We buried him at sea, after a funeral ceremony on the quarter deck on 16th October. It was a very moving experience, committing a colleague to the sea, and I always found myself emotionally disturbed for some time afterwards.

By the 18th we had reached Port Suez after experiencing an inferno for almost three days. No wind, the sea shimmering crystal, a searingly hot sun made conditions below deck hellish. As we entered the Canal a breeze, warm but welcome, came off the desert, ruffling our Ensign and creating a treasured draught on the hangar deck. It was late evening when we anchored off Port Said and began to oil. The entrance to the Canal was a spectacular sight with serried lines of troopships, men of war, tankers, stores vessels, tugs, bum-boats. The Egyptian traders were alongside as soon as we anchored, selling souvenirs, figs, dates, post-cards. Baskets were lowered from the decks, the goods hauled up and inspected. If they passed muster the money was then sent down in the basket. 'Gully-Gully' men performed sleight of hand with chickens and eggs, middle eastern instruments were played non-stop to demonstrate their musical appeal. The bazaar was water-borne, replete with sounds and smells. There was good humoured banter with the Egyptians displaying a remarkable knowledge of crude Anglo-Saxon, doubtless acquired from previous encounters with British mariners.

When we sailed into the Mediterranean on 20th October, the weather became much cooler. Freed from the enervating humidity the ship's company began to show signs of excitement and anticipation of getting home. The next day we had a Harvest Festival service in the small church. Tropical fruits and vegetables decorated the altar and, whilst it was hardly rural England, the ambience was a potent reminder of the shores of home—drawing nearer each day.

We were traversing the Straits between Sicily and Tunisia and I went up to the ADP for the first time in more than two months. The look-outs swivel chairs were empty, the seats stained and worn. The binocular housings covered by grey-brown tarpaulin. My radar 'shack' was dusty, the glass display panel above the small, primitive set, still bearing the chinagraph pencil crosses and symbols denoting 'bandits' at 'Angels' seven. The headphones hung loose, the voice-pipe lid was closed—no more to carry the urgent orders from 'Guns' to the D/F's and guns crews. Could it be more than three years since I watched *Indomitable* hidden in brown smoke and towering bomb-made fountains, or *Eagle* sinking so swiftly with her throbbing innards ripped out by a salvo of torpedoes. The laughing destroyer Captain with his Rugby football club shirt or, as seemed more likely, his public school team top. I sat on a look-out chair and gazed at the blue-green water, its choppy surface disturbed by our surging bow wave, and felt great sadness. A hundred fathoms down lay battered, broken ships, now being fossilised to house marine life among twisted metal and shattered timbers. How many fractured, torn airplanes lay on the seabed, their national markings now an irrelevance. I heard a step, a voice disturbed

203

my reverie.

'What are you doing up here?' asked 'Guns'.

'I might ask the same of you sir,' I replied. He looked at me intently, his brown, heavily lined face in a reflective pose.

'Thinking back are we? Memories of August 1942?'

'Yes, they are still vivid. I was only just 20 then and it had a profound effect on me. I suppose as the years go by the memories will dim.'

'I don't think so. Was your father in the First World War?'

I nodded.

'Ask him when you get home if he remembers events of almost 30 years ago. I think you'll find he does. It is both a benefit and a burden that we recall the pleasure and pain in our lives.' His tone changed, briskly he continued, 'Let's stop being morbid and look forward to Portsmouth in five days time. I am leaving the ship. You will probably be drafted too. How long have you been onboard now?'

'Almost four years. It will feel strange onshore.'

'It always does. Every commission I've ever done has left me feeling slightly lost when I've returned to Portsmouth. You are Devonport Division?'

'Yes, but I was only there a few weeks and then based in a school. I know Chatham much better.'

We stood in silence for a while, relishing the fresh air and the breeze.

'You know the ship is going to return to Australia as quickly as possible. There are so many to be repatriated from the Far East and Australisia that every carrier is likely to be pressed into troop carrying service.'

'I had heard rumours but no-one has been taking them too seriously because we will all be ashore.'

'Not everyone,' said 'Guns'. 'Some will remain, at least for one round trip, to maintain continuity.'

I began to have slight misgivings about my own situation. My release date was some time away. Many of my colleagues and friends were due for almost immediate discharge—Tony among them. Maybe I would be lucky.

'Guns' walked round the ADP, paused at the top of the gangway leading down to the rear of the Compass Platform.

'Cheerio,' he said. 'I don't suppose we will meet again, certainly not up here. Thanks for all your help. I wish you well.'

I walked over to him and we shook hands. He turned and went quickly down below. A few moments later I followed.

At 1000 on 24th we anchored in the Bay of Gibraltar, and a stores unit was sent ashore for fresh produce. A short distance away lay Algeciras, from which daily intelligence reports were gathered by the Germans on the movement of ships in and out of Gibraltar. It was no longer of any consequence. There was no shore leave, a disappointment to many who had hoped to top up their stock of 'rabbits' to take home.

The Bay of Biscay served up its reputed gales and high seas and many worried that we would be delayed. Telegrams by the dozen had been sent ashore at Gibraltar forecasting our arrival in Portsmouth at 1000 on 27th.

The Channel too was rough and we heard that a number of ships, including the *Queen Mary*, were standing off the Isle of Wight, unable to proceed further to Southampton or Portsmouth.

The fates were kind, *Victorious* pressed on, like a dog running home, and it was precisely 1000 when we made fast. The main Southern Railway jetty was crowded with cheering, shouting, crying relatives and friends. There was confusion created by those onboard who could see their loved ones onshore but were not recognised in return—and vice versa. Names were shouted, but lost in the general din. I noticed how many of the women wore hats in marked contrast to those in Australia, and how dull and dowdy they seemed to be.

The first to leave were the ex Prisoners-of-war, some of the reunions on the jetty were as emotional for those of us watching as for those brought together after years of doubt and despair. When all those taking passage had been disembarked, and all the squadrons, a few of the ship's company left us but the majority remained onboard.

Our 'commission' ended at Devonport when, on 1st November, we proceeded into the basin and tied up opposite HMS *Terrible*, a new carrier launched as the war ended. Even though we were a 'Devonport' ship this was the first time *Victorious* had been in its home port.

We flew our decommissioning pennant, a ribbon from the mainmast, its length determined by the months and years the ship had been crewed by a largely unchanged ship's company. Our pennant was over 200 feet long! It fluttered bravely in the breeze for about 150 feet but the sheer weight of it brought the last segment down to almost flight deck level.

Again the crowds were present, this time mostly confined to relatives and friends of the crew. Joyous reunions, dads seeing children for the first time, sweethearts with the wedding banns in their handbags, tearful mothers, proud fathers and a sprinkling of old colleagues, discharged earlier from *Victorious*, now appearing to welcome shipmates safely home. Bands played, hooters and sirens wailed and shrieked. Dockyard 'mateys' stood around as nonchalant and unconcerned as ever. Customs and Excise Officers sharpened their pencils and dusted off their Ready Reckoners and Percentage Tables manuals. *Victorious* was 'home', six years and two months after being launched.

Within days the crew was either on leave or drafted to HMS *Drake*—Devonport Barracks—a 'stone frigate' in 'stripey's' parlance. My friends and colleagues left the ship in dribs and drabs. Rex Starling, Les Vancura, Peter Lorne, Bill Waggett, Charlie Frise, Tony Sagar, Geoff Haylett. James Jobling, who was now to pursue a full time career in the Navy had left us in Australia. Losing Tony was like being deprived of a much loved brother. We had a final night out in Plymouth—a film, I believe it was a musical, 'Nob Hill', and the best meal money could buy. We promised to keep in touch for ever.

Slowly the realisation came upon me that I was not going to be drafted. I was the only one of the old team left in the office and was worked to a standstill preparing the documentation for those who had left. New staff joined—Ted

Maggs and Freddie Lethbridge. The former, a Bristolian, quiet, courteous, friendly, the latter a devout Devonian, always smiling, ready wit, generous nature. I could not have asked for better colleagues. They were both pre-war, regular Naval men and had served in a peace-time environment. Neither had been to sea during the war. Their refreshing, almost casual approach was something I had not experienced. At least it made my enforced stay tolerable.

Victorious became a huge transport ship, and when we left Devonport for Sydney after a dry-dock refit we carried passengers, stores, medical supplies, uniforms, equipment and spares of many kinds.

The voyage became a cruise, the régime almost pleasurable. No Action Stations, very little cypher traffic, in fact days were strictly 0830—1700. Time to sunbathe once we had entered the Red Sea with warm weather from then on as we reached Australia in the high summer.

Those of us who had not been drafted were armed with shopping lists. My own contained requirements for pounds of knitting wools and lengths of materials for dresses and suits plus mundane items such as currants, raisins and sultanas. Sydney was almost completely back to a peace-time footing, a shopper's delight.

A few days after our arrival Frank Milton from the Captain's Office, friend and colleague, popped into my office, drew up a chair and said, 'You had better take a look at this,' handing me a letter posted locally. I did not recognise the handwriting. I took out the single page of careful, closely formed writing. As I read it I must have registered some surprise.

'Not what you expected,' said Frank.

'No, far from it!' I read it to the end before folding it, placing it in the envelope and handing it back.

'How does the Captain propose to deal with it?' I was not concerned but interested.

'He will write to Mrs. Horner and say that he has no authority to confirm or deny that you are married and that such a subject is a matter between her daughter and you.'

'That's fair enough.'

'You been leading this girl on then Ray?'

'Not at all. I have been out with her several times, stayed at her home. Her mother didn't ask me then if I was married. I have held her daughter's hand and had an enjoyable, purely platonic friendship. I wrote her a farewell letter when we left Fremantle in early October. Mind you, I had no idea I would be back here.'

'So what now?'

'I will steer well clear until we sail.'

'Right, I'll get the letter off today, that should be the end of it.'

But it wasn't. Two days later Mrs. Horner was prevented from boarding the ship by the gangway sentry who summoned the Officer of the Watch. He kindly, gently, yet firmly advised the lady she could not board without authorisation. I was already regretting the glove purchase in David Jones and literally prayed for *Victorious* to set sail for England.

When we did I heaved a sigh of relief. The ship called in Singapore on the return journey to pick up some ex prisoners-of-war who had been too ill to be moved earlier.

They came onboard, feeble and unsteady. Their eyes were still dulled and their faces aged and lined. On the dockside a party of Japanese prisoners had been carrying bags and parcels for their former victims. I watched from the flight deck. The Japanese NCO walked along the line of his men. Something annoyed him. Without a word he swung the heavy stick he was carrying, hitting one man brutally hard on the side of the head. The man collapsed without a sound, the others in the line stared unmoving. I thought as I watched, if they treat their own men like that how much worse must they have behaved towards their prisoners? He shouted a command, two of his men stepped forward, picked up their still unconscious comrade and, as they all marched off, dragged him behind, feet trailing along the ground. No-one else on the dockside took any notice.

Naturally our journey back to Plymouth was uneventful but there was one pleasing aspect. The bodies and minds of the ex POW's improved daily. They spent as much time as practicable on the flight deck, no doubt savouring the fresh sea air, sunshine and freedom. Deck Hockey games were played for their entertainment as well as Tug-of-War contests, Boxing matches and amateur singing shows. Perhaps the greatest single factor to improve their health was the knowledge that each day brought *Victorious* some 500 miles nearer to England, families and home.

When we reached Plymouth and then docked in Devonport I went ashore to visit the Drafting Office. It was now a series of temporary wooden huts, awash with both staff and documents, under the tremendous pressure of coping with the release of tens of thousands of men. Few knew what was really happening. Men were being billeted outside because the Barracks was at saturation point. They would come into the depot each day, walk around with a piece of paper, better still a file of some description, for seven or eight hours before 'going ashore' again. Somehow, amidst this chaos, I had to discover when I was to be discharged from *Victorious*. In the event no-one seemed to know and I doubted if anyone cared.

It was back to Australia yet again, and whilst life onboard was pleasurable enough most of my friends had long gone, many were now in 'civvy street', complete with 'de-mob' suit and hat, two shirts, vests, pants and shoes.

All was routine until we began our journey back to the UK. The ship had not been long in the notorious Bight when a monstrous storm developed. *Victorious* had been in many a violent sea but this one was at least the equal of the worst we had previously encountered. Most of the hundreds taking passage, and accommodated in the hangar area, were physically ill. It was impossible to go out on deck, except the sheltered and exclusive quarter deck. In consequence the atmosphere between decks was foul with the stench of vomit and stale air—this, in turn, made others sick. The ship was undergoing a tremendous battering and sometimes she shuddered, seemed to be stopped in her tracks, and then plunged on again. For those unaccustomed to the groaning of a hull under intense strains the noise was alarming.

For 48 hours the storm raged. Those who were not ill were suffering from headaches from the problem of keeping balance around the ship. One minute it was like climbing a mountain-side, the next a pell mell run forward, so difficult to control.

When we entered Fremantle I went up to the ADP to experience the joy of seeing land again. Looking forward and towards the bows it was obvious that the bow wave was irregular. A motor boat ran alongside with two naval officers peering intently at the ship's bow. On the jetty a team of divers was already waiting to go down and check the forward end of the ship. They wasted no time and it was not long before we heard that part of the *Victorious'* bow had dropped, hull plates had been torn back to reveal a hole almost large enough to drive a bus through. The steel had buckled, then become ripped like a can opening and tons of water had entered the ship. This had been confined to a small area by the water-tight doors.

Engineer Captain Craggs arrived from Sydney and a high level conference was held ashore. It was decided the *Victorious* could not proceed to Plymouth, temporary repairs would be effected in Fremantle and she would then return to Sydney and proceed into the brand new Captain Cook dry dock for a full survey and permanent repair.

Indomitable had just arrived from the UK and lay at the North Wharf across the harbour from us at Fremantle. Among her passengers, en route to Sydney, were the English Rugby League Test side.

The obvious solution was effected. All our pasengers, UK bound, were transferred to *Indomitable* and some of hers brought aboard *Victorious*. those whose presence in Sydney was urgently required, were sent by train. They included the Rugby League players.

Naturally the crew of *Indom.* were not elated at the prospect of being denied their week in Sydney, on the other hand, some onboard *Victorious* were dreading the thought of being returned to the arms of those to whom they had so recently, and so untruthfully, declared undying love.

Work to complete the repairs was undertaken efficiently and quickly at Sydney and, with only weeks remaining before our sailing date for England came the news that our passengers would include some 720 'War Brides'. It was to be my task to handle their documentation, make 'on account' payments, and prepare full records for the Admiralty at Bath. Meanwhile the hangar was totally transformed, being sub-divided into three sections. The forward part was converted into sleeping quarters, the centre section the mess and the after part a lounge area with coir-matting, occasional tables, chairs etc. The sleeping quarters were divided into cubicles, each of which contained eight three decker bunks. Wardrobe/cupboards were built down the centre of each cubicle. Ironing facilities were also provided. Washrooms and shower-rooms were installed as well as buffet pantries to serve meals. The deck-head of the hangar was studded with giant rotating fans to keep the air as cool as possible.

The ship was buzzing with excitement when about 680 came onboard in Sydney. Another 40 were to join in Fremantle. These women had married British, Dutch and even French sailors and were now to be taken to their new homelands. It would be a traumatic experience for some.

Our departure from Sydney was delayed slightly by the remarkable farewell scenes at the dockside. The ship was so festooned with streamers that it was a problem to see if the lines had been cast off. There was hysteria, joy, sadness, sorrow, relief and not a little trepidation.

The first leg of the long voyage to Plymouth was again beset by a battle with mountainous seas. The Bight was so rough that the heaving and rolling of the ship was enough to confine nearly all of the ladies to their bunks. Wind speeds of 80 mph were regularly measured over the flight deck. Guard rails were destroyed and huge waves were shipped over the bows as far back to where a new soda-fountain had been built just forward of the Bridge. It was severely damaged. Our speed was reduced to eight knots, instead of 20. On arrival in Fremantle we again sent down a diver to examine the bows—but they had remained intact.

As we sailed north from Fremantle, into the tropics, a more carefree, convivial atmosphere developed. Skimpy summer frocks with revealing necklines, swim-suited bodies lying on the decks soaking up the sun. These new features of life on a warship seemed to distract 'Jack' from his normal sparetime of playing crib, or walking the flight deck. Small mixed groups gathered, there was laughter and giggling, open-eyed wonder as some voluble sailor, with well-honed hyperbole, spun yarns of derring-do.

One morning there was a knock at the office door. I slid back the hatch by my desk to be confronted by a 'war bride'. She asked if she could come in and talk to me for a moment. I nodded, fetched a chair and placed it by my desk.

'I wonder if I could help in the office. I can type, write short-hand—not too well—and am bored with sitting around.'

I explained that there was hardly any room in the office and besides the work was such that the majority of it could not be undertaken without training. There would be some typing, manifests of the female passengers, to be done. Possibly she might help with that. If she called again after we had left Colombo I could re-assess the situation. She expressed her thanks.

By the time we reached Ceylon it had been necessary for Captain Annesley to address all onboard about the level and manner of fraternisation. The bronzed and lissom bodies of some of our passengers were magnets to some young, unattached sailors who had only joined the ship some few months earlier. It also has to be recorded that a number of the 'brides' seemed anxious to enter into liaisons, however temporary, of a nature other than platonic. The Captain warned that he had the authority to discharge from the ship any sailor or female guilty of overt sexual behaviour and evening and night patrols would be instituted to ensure there was none.

Not long after leaving Colombo the young lady returned to the office. I had by now drawn up comprehensive details of all our female passengers, full names, date of birth, date of marriage, previous address, address to which proceeding, name and rank of husband, railway ticket required from Plymouth, allotment being paid by the husband, etc. etc. It would be helpful if she could assist.

It transpired her name was Veronica, she hailed from Perth and was married to a sailor from the Midlands. Hers had been a whirlwind courtship, impetuous marriage, she hadn't seen him for well over a year. I think her story was typical, yet sadly she was now afraid of meeting her husband.

As we approached Port Said there was a deep discussion on whether the female passengers should be allowed ashore. It was finally decided that they could only do so if each was escorted by two men. Despite this safeguard one woman gave her escorts the slip and, after delaying our departure for a couple of hours, we were obliged to sail without her. Perhaps she waited for a vessel back to Australia.

Signals had been sent to all husbands, mothers-in-law, to ensure that each of our War Brides was met at Plymouth. The day before arrival I assembled all the appropriate information, as well as details of cash advance, to take personally to Bath.

There were mixed scenes at Plymouth. Some of the brides did not want to go ashore, pleading to be sent back home. Others found that no-one had come to meet them, they must now make their own way, alone, to an unfamiliar town in a strange country. Amidst the great joy of passionate reunions was sadness and disillusionment, insecurity and doubt.

The following morning I caught an early train to Bath, delivered my briefcase full of files and manifests to the office of the Director of Naval Accounts and then, on a warm, sunny day, sat in the park near the Bandstand, and listened to the Royal Air Force Orchestra. It was late summer, some of the leaves were changing colour, the grass still a brilliant emerald green. Flower beds, ablaze with many hues, but just beginning to give way to their seasonal end, reminded me that England was special, unique. I had been away too long, it was time to come ashore.

It was late October when I received orders to leave *Victorious*. The ship was about to leave for Australia, yet again, a prospect which filled me with dismay—but I was reprieved.

After five weeks short of five years I walked slowly down the gangway, green suitcase in hand, stood on the dock-side and gazed at that great ship. She was looking her age, rusty plates, paint peeling, guard rails shabby. There was a great sense of loss, a feeling of sudden homelessness. This enormous steel, flat-topped oblong had been my shelter, refuge and life for almost five of my most formative adult years. It had carried me all over the world and I had sailed more than 280,000 miles on her. She was the only warship in World War II to steam round the world, from Coral Sea to Coral Sea.

I had experienced comradeship, deep, caring friendship, bitterness and anger, devastating sadness, unimaginable fear, horror. I had also laughed a lot and found great joy. Every emotion I had taken with me to that ship had been stretched to its finite limit, it was the crucible of my manhood. Tears ran down my face, I suddenly felt insecure and lonely.

As I stared at the ship, the Officer of the Watch at the top of the gangway waved. I knew it was the final goodbye. I returned the farewell gesture, turned my back on *Victorious,* and never saw her again.

What Happened To:

Michael Maynard Denny

When Captain Denny left *Victorious* in 1945 he was promoted to Rear Admiral. From then on his considerable abilities and single-mindedness took him to one of the highest positions in the Royal Navy, Admiral of the Fleet and Fourth Sea Lord. He was also knighted.

On retirement from the Navy, in 1959, at the age of 63, he became Chairman of Cammel Laird. At that time prominent and influential ex-service officers were expected to use their knowledge and contacts to the benefit of their commercial environment. He retired in 1966, at the age of 70, and lived until April, 1972.

I never knew whether he was happy in industry, after 44 years in the Royal Navy, but I can opine on his two years on *Victorious*. He stamped his mark on the ship by his authoritarian command and bravery, allied to undoubted seamanship and tactical skills. He was a remarkable sailor and although somewhat remote, a natural wartime leader.

Lachlan Donald Mackintosh

Lachlan Donald Mackintosh, the Mackintosh of Mackintosh, 29th Chief of the Clan, retired in 1950 at the age of 54, with the rank of Vice Admiral. He died in 1957.

As *Victorious'* second Captain he was delegated the delicate task of commanding the ship when it was seconded to the US Navy in 1943. His warm, outgoing personality, relaxed friendliness combined with outright professional airmanship and seamanship, made our integration into the USN an agreeable experience for all.

I recall, in particular, his care for any bird that landed on *Victorious*. Many arrived on the flight deck exhausted, hungry and afraid. He arranged a small reception area where such birds were fed, watered and rested before being encouraged to resume their journey. It was an example of his humanity and innate goodness.

Henry Cecil Bovell

Henry Cecil Bovell, our first Captain, who enjoyed manoeuvring *Victorious* as if it were a destroyer, rose to become a Vice-Admiral, retiring from the Navy in 1947. He then lived at Warminster, Wiltshire, until his death in 1963, aged

70. Captain Bovell was dapper, neat and liked a tidy ship. His 'Captain's Rounds' were the occasion to spruce up the ship to peace-time standards. To him a clean ship was an efficient ship. He created the initial pride in *Victorious*, by the original ship's company, and this remained until decommissioning at the end of 1945.

James Hobson Jobling

'Jimmy' Jobling, one of our team of talented amateur entertainers onboard, a gifted comic actor went on to pursue a brilliant career in the Royal Navy and subsequently in civilian life. He rose to the rank of Captain (S), became Judge Advocate of the Fleet, was admitted to the Bar, Inner Temple, in 1955, and became a Magistrate and Recorder. When I asked him for his most lasting memory of *Victorious* he replied, 'The ghastly food. I left the ship weighing barely nine stones.' I reminded him that he played the Wicked Baron in our Pantomime—did he recall that event? He wrote and quoted me the first four lines of his part on stage! *Victorious* was indeed the ship to make a lasting impression. James lives in happy retirement, his favourite hobby gardening and occasionally giving advice—when asked—to his two children, both involved in the legal profession.

Leslie Vancura

Left the Navy in 1946, as Petty Officer (Stores) and returned to civilian life in Swansea. He is still there today, now retired after running his own supply business—he was indeed a stores man to the core.

What's more he has lived in the same house for 45 years, blessed with a wonderful wife and talented children. When I met him again it was the 'Ghost of Pacific Past'. The same dynamic, stocky figure, bursting with energy. He talked, as he always did, non-stop, for almost four hours.

He still maintains a daily diary, which he started 55 years ago. Les now spends his spare time fund raising for his village church and helping elderly people—he is 77.

His wartime experiences are recalled with a blend of pleasure and sadness; happy to have enjoyed the comradeship peculiar to a warship, sad to remember the splendid men who died so young.

He regards that episode of his life as one of character building and spiritual enrichment; a true Christian.

I am so grateful to him for the use of his written material in the preparation of this book about the ship we both loved. Indeed his daily jottings throughout the war enabled me to focus clearly on the events he recorded and acted as a catalyst and stimulant to my writing VICTORIOUS THE WORLD OVER.

James Anthony Sagar

After leaving *Victorious*, James Anthony Sagar was demobilised in 1946 and resumed his acting career. I lost touch with him for a while but traced him again after his appearance on a television programme.

We met, several times, and I recall our going to the threatre to see Brendan Behan's 'Quare Fellow'. We slowly drifted apart again, possibly due to my frequent and sustained travels abroad.

One evening, at a London theatre, my wife and I were watching 'There's a Girl in My Soup'. Carol was just as interested in Cary Grant who was in the audience. Then Tony appeared as the Butler to Donald Sinden. His playing of the role was tremendous and earned him a great ovation at the curtain calls. I sent a business card to his dressing room, we met, and our friendship prospered again. It was like finding a lost brother.

We met regularly and Tony and his second wife Laurel and daughter visited our home in Old Windsor. He appeared in a Richard Burton film 'Villain', as a petty crook, as well as in Dad's Army, Harry Worth, and other television series. In 1973, without warning, he died in his sleep, aged 56.

Russell Thorndike read the Oration and referred to Tony's days onboard *Victorious* and his friendship with me and others. I was very touched.

Tony was a gentleman possessed of immense charm and wit. He was imbued with a boundless love of the theatre and cricket, poetry and people. His friendship and kindness to me lightened many a dark day and I will never forget his contstant call:

'Raymond, motley is the only wear, don it and make them laugh.'

We did our best.

The Author

After being discharged from the Royal Navy the author joined Thomas Cook, at their Headquarters, Berkeley Street, London. He worked as a management trainee and then in varying junior and middle management capacities until 1957. At that time he joined Sir Henry Lunn Ltd as Sales Manager, was appointed to the Board and, in 1966, because Managing Director of Lunn-Poly, the company formed by the amalgamation of the Polytechnical Touring Assocition and Lunn. In 1971 he resigned and became a Consultant to Tour Operators, travel companies and hotel development groups, also acquiring his own travel interests in London, Middlesex and the West Country.

Ray Barker served the travel industry as the first Chairman of the Tour Operators Council and was a member of the National Council of ABTA representing the industry on radio and television.

In 1988 he sold his travel interests, and in 1989 retired to Herefordshire.

HMS *VICTORIOUS*

Victorious completed her Far East and Australian trooping in January, 1947 and later that year became a floating school and training ship. For two years she remained at Portland until, in March 1950, it was decided she should be modernised. The refit and rebuild became longer and longer as new ideas and technical improvements were incorporated during the modernisation.

It was in 1958, after eight years of work costing almost £20 million (three times her original cost) that the new *Victorious* emerged from her dockyard cocoon, as the carrier darling of the Royal Navy. She was unrecognisable, certainly to any sailor from the 1941—45 commission.

During the next few years the ship visited America, Germany, Middle East, Far East, Australia and Japan.

In March 1968 the ship's company was paid off and *Victorious* ended her great saga as a manned Royal Navy warship, almost 27 years since first commissioning.

It was more than a year later that she was sold for scrap and in July, 1969, she was towed to Faslane, Gareloch in Scotland to be broken up, a process which was to take some 12 months.

There are those who thought she should have been made into a Ship Museum, like HMS *Belfast* on the Thames. This would not have revealed to the public the real heart of the wartime ship. That had stopped beating in 1947, from then on she lived on a pacemaker with several transplants as well.

Sadly we do not have a wartime carrier in museum form; it would have been a reminder of a phase of naval warfare which relieved beleaguered Malta, protected convoys and military landings, and destroyed the second most powerful maritime force in World War II, the Imperial Japanese Navy.

The Character of *Victorious*

Victorious was a happy ship, a view expressed not only by all who served on her, but also by those who took passage or experienced a brief visit.

Why was she a happy vessel when many warships generated a depressing, sullen atmosphere, some even appearing to be downright miserable? I recall visiting a famous battleship and one could sense the unease, a brooding unpleasantness.

After all these years it is not easy to analyse the complex reasons which combined to give our ship her character; it would not have been simple at the time I served on her.

A ship begins it's life in the mind of a naval architect who must design a vessel within the parameters laid down by the Admiralty: function, size, capability and cost. He compresses all these factors onto a drawing board and an outline of a ship emerges. The architect has then made the first contribution in determining one element in the basic philosophy of its ship's company — the ship's appearance. Vessels can, and do, look ugly, unprepossessing, characterless, bland, clumsy, futuristic, even comical — yet can be happy ships despite their appearance, but *Victorious* was endowed with looks evoking power, style, security, strength, grace, pace with a hint of beauty and aggression. She had a head start.

To approach her in open water, from her starboard beam, was to witness a symbol of naval might which changed from impressive to awesome as one drew closer to her vast hulk.

All who sailed in her had, at some time, seen *Victorious* in this manner and so the impact of her physical appearance created both respect and admiration for the ship.

There are those who opine that a ship is an inanimate steel structure, characterless and soulless without the crew. This is invariably untrue and was certainly so in the case of *Victorious*. She had personality and spirit inbuilt. This communicated itself readily to her men.

But does this not suggest that her sister-ships, of precisely the same shape and dimensions, would also possess similar attributes? Not necessarily, for it seemed to me that part of the character of the men who built her was also ingrained in every rivet and plate. The lively personality of the 'Geordies', their independence, even frivolousness, was part of the ship — witness her skittish behaviour with the rudder, her ability to escape trouble, her 'luck' — all true 'Geordie' attributes.

And what of her crew? The great cavalcade of officers and men who served between 1941 and 1946, numbering in excess of 4000. Three war-time Captains, the same number of Commanders, all so different. Yet no matter how they conducted themselves the fundamental under-lying attitude of the men was invariably one of happiness (in its most simplistic form), tolerance and goodwill. Rivalries that traditionally existed ashore, or on other ships, between the differing arms of the Navy, did not manifest themselves on *Victorious* — except on the deck-hockey pitch!

216

How was this? A critical reason was that the ship's company — the men who operated the ship and not it's squadrons of aircraft — remained together, in the main, for four or even five years. This was very unusual, two years being regarded as an adequate 'commission' (period of service): but *Victorious'* good fortune in avoiding serious structural damage and, in consequence, her almost constant active service, gave little opportunity for wholesale crew changes. Thus was maintained a core of cameraderie that influenced, even conditioned, the men who came and went. There was a sense of togetherness, necessary enough in a severely crowded ship, which quickly enveloped new crewmen. They were absorbed into the sense of pride and certainty of success possessed by those they came to serve alongside.

Even the ship's crest, no emblem of force, might or invincibility, but a characterisation of an angel, wings outstretched, with a benign countenance as she held aloft a wreath of laurel, seemed to signify security and contentment.

Hard times, intolerable conditions, strict regimes, danger from the elements as well as the enemy, failed to crack or fracture the steely resolve of the crew to remain a band of men with the twin purposes of fighting hard and maintaining a true sense of comradeship.

I believe *Victorious* was unique and so do men who served on as many as half a dozen other ships of differing types. She invited, indeed instilled, a feeling of safety and well-being. This translated into acceptance of the rigours and hardships, creating a cohesive force of men happy to be together.

This still exists today, over 45 years after the end of the ship's war-time deeds and adventures. Due to the remarkable endeavours of ex-Petty Officer 'Buck' Rogers, the *Victorious* (1941-1945) *Reunion Association* was formed some nine years ago. He embarked on the daunting task of finding his old ship-mates after almost 40 years. Now, well over 200 strong, the Association, a testament to his single-mindedness, has an annual get-together at the Royal Naval Air Station, Yeovilton. It also spawns mini-reunions in provincial centres throughout the country. Seeing these men, together again after so many years, is to witness the manifestation of the profound comradeship which bound them during the war. The unashamed joy of now old men, none under 65, holding each other with unfettered affection, the buzz of animation, the relief to find 'old so and so', ostensibly unchanged, still sparkling with earthy wit and cynicism, or happily grumbling unrelentingly as of old.

These men have lived another complete life since 1945. Some have prospered, others not, they have grown-up children, grand and great-grand children, some are widowers, others infirm. There have been prominent businessmen, also the failures. There are the practical, the artistic, the creative and the mis-named 'ordinary' men. None of these men is ordinary. When they are together there is a brio, a zest for life in their behaviour; even those by nature reserved, shed their defensive demeanor when confronted by a recognised ship-mate and old friend. There exists in these meetings the warmth of flames fanned from embers by the sheer force of joyous reunion.

The happiness of 1941—1945 is re-kindled, so much so that, impatient to wait for the next annual get-together, they can be found organising mini-reunions to savour again, quickly, the precious nostalgia that evokes memories of unforgettable days.

At the 1991 Reunion at Yeovilton, Ray Kennedy said to me "Look at them Ray, listen to them. It is as if nothing has changed in 45 years. What is it that made those men, and their ship, so happy then and again now?"

I believe the ship made the men that made the ship. They reacted on each other to an equal extent to create a meld of infectious harmony. We will not see its, or their, like again.

Images

It is 45 years since I left *Victorious*. Much of the memory of the ship remains undimmed . . . Writing this book has been like slowly unravelling a tangled dream, each thread having to be teazed out to create the story. Many recollections are vivid to this day . . .

* The imperious urging of the bugled 'Alarm to Arms' and the sickening, dry mouthed apprehension as you ran to meet the unexpected.
* The sweaty bedlam and heat hell of the flight deck, a hazy, steamy mirage of ghostly machines and men shimmering in the petrol vapour. The torrid turbulence of noise as a plane lurched into take-off.
* Thump of an aircraft landing, the whine of hydraulic arrester wires, the shattering roar of a fully throttled engine on wave-off.
* Freezing pergutory as aircraft handlers tried vainly to keep the blood circulating in the bitter, biting, slashing, icy sleet of the Arctic.
* The Captain, a solitary, lonely man. Thinking by himself, exercising in isolation on the Quarterdeck, pacing his plans across the well scrubbed planks.
* *Victorious*, a huge metal claustrophobic box, an enormous labyrinth in which you could meet some-one one day and rarely see them again.
* Men moving everywhere below decks, like a theatre continously emptying into narrow streets and alleyways.
* The hangar, a gigantic floating garage with machines being pushed, pulled, shoved, knocked, banged, screwed, bolted, fixed, tested and rested.
* Gritty eyed midnight cypher watches, the endless subtraction of numbers for one-time pad cyphers. An urgent dash to the Captain with 'Hush Most Secret', to call him awake but never shake him.
* The stomach churning, spine-tingling, hypnotic, fearful excitement as a bomb or kamikaze fell, apparently with you as the single target.
* Sweat soaked pilots, clambering slowly from their humid tubes, wearily aware that once again they had survived a test of stamina, guts and skill.
* American hospitality, unboundingly generous, graciously unconditional.